MINDS ON TRIAL

MINDS

ON TRIAL

GREAT CASES
IN LAW AND
PSYCHOLOGY

Charles Patrick Ewing
and Joseph T. McCann

OXFORD
UNIVERSITY PRESS

2006

OXFORD
UNIVERSITY PRESS

Oxford University Press, Inc., publishes works that further
Oxford University's objective of excellence
in research, scholarship, and education.

Oxford   New York
Auckland   Cape Town   Dar es Salaam   Hong Kong   Karachi
Kuala Lumpur   Madrid   Melbourne   Mexico City   Nairobi
New Delhi   Shanghai   Taipei   Toronto

With offices in
Argentina   Austria   Brazil   Chile   Czech Republic   France   Greece
Guatemala   Hungary   Italy   Japan   Poland   Portugal   Singapore
South Korea   Switzerland   Thailand   Turkey   Ukraine   Vietnam

Copyright © 2006 by Oxford University Press, Inc.

Published by Oxford University Press, Inc.
198 Madison Avenue, New York, New York 10016

www.oup.com

Oxford is a registered trademark of Oxford University Press

Library of Congress Cataloging-in-Publication Data
Ewing, Charles Patrick, 1949–
Minds on trial : great cases in law and psychology /
Charles Patrick Ewing and Joseph T. McCann.
    p. cm.
Includes bibliographical references.
ISBN-13 978-0-19-518176-0
ISBN 0-19-518176-X
1. Forensic psychology—United States—Cases. 2. Forensic
psychiatry—United States—Cases. 3. Insanity—Jurisprudence—
United States—Cases. I. McCann, Joseph T. II. Title.
KF8965.A7E95 2006
614'.15—dc22   2005020568

To Angelica:

"... happily I pass the while,

thinking of your lovely smile."

(J. T. M.)

To Sharon:

With love and gratitude

from the rock.

(C. P. E.)

PREFACE

As forensic psychologists with combined careers in law and psychology spanning nearly half a century, we have been involved in several thousand cases in which we have been asked, in one form or another, to "get inside the head of" a person who was (or might soon become) a litigant. In virtually all of these cases, the determining legal issue was the individual's state of mind at the time of—or as a result of—the event(s) that led the case to court. In many of these cases, our assessments have played a major role in shaping the legal outcome.

Of course we are far from alone in the influence our forensic work has had upon the legal system. Our cases have been little more than the proverbial grain of sand on the vast beach of law and psychology. Every day, in courtrooms everywhere, people's lives are touched and shaped by judgments and verdicts influenced if not dictated by the findings of psychologists and other mental health experts. Our assessments, whether conveyed to the courts through reports or testimony, help determine who is competent, guilty, blameworthy, dangerous, entitled to compensation, fit to be a parent, and so forth. Outside the courtroom, our judgments about the mental functioning of others have assisted the police, the military, and other governmental agencies charged with maintaining public safety and security.

In our own professional work we have been blessed and burdened with unparalleled access to the minds of some of life's most fascinating and tragic figures. Having learned so much from the intensive study of these individuals and their predicaments, we hoped to produce a book that would give others a similar, albeit much more limited, "inside" look at "minds on trial."

While many of our own cases have been both fascinating and high profile, for a variety of reasons we chose not to discuss our own work in this volume. In many of our cases our role and opinions are a matter of public knowledge because we have testified in open court, but in most the details remain confidential and privileged. Moreover, it is often difficult to be objective and dispassionate in discussing one's own work. Thus, instead of focusing on some of the more interesting and notorious cases in which we have played a prominent role, we decided to take a more objective look at the work of some of our colleagues over the past fifty years. Beginning with a collection of one hundred cases, we narrowed our focus to a list of what we consider to be "twenty great cases in law and psychology," cases in which we are able to take readers "behind the scenes" and explain what led these people to the attention of the legal system and how psychological professionals, the courts, and the law have dealt with them.

The protagonists in these cases range from household names such as Lee Harvey Oswald, Woody Allen, Mike Tyson, Jeffrey Dahmer, Patty Hearst, and John W. Hinckley, Jr., to others whose brief brushes with celebrity have long been forgotten. But, regardless of notoriety or celebrity status, each of these carefully selected cases teaches important lessons about the role that psychology and the other behavioral sciences plays in our legal system.

Charles Patrick Ewing, J.D., Ph.D.
Joseph T. McCann, Psy.D., J.D.

CONTENTS

MINDS ON TRIAL

INTRODUCTION

Over the past fifty years American society has been blessed (or burdened, depending on your point of view) with a steady stream of high-profile legal cases that offer both intrigue and entertainment. Looking back over the last several years, for example, the O. J. Simpson, Scott Peterson, and D.C. sniper murder trials and the Michael Jackson child molestation case have dominated the media from television and radio talk shows to newspapers from the *New York Times* to the *National Enquirer*. Much of the coverage and commentary is pure entertainment, with the public viewing the investigations and trials as ongoing soap operas. Still, some of these high-profile trials have been not only informative but also educational. Whether viewers follow the proceedings gavel-to-gavel or simply tune in to learn the latest developments, they often come away with a deeper appreciation of how our legal system works and how justice or injustice is done.

Not surprisingly, what often captures the public interest in many of these famous cases are the profound psychological questions they pose. Cases that grab the most media attention and public fascination often deal with the insanity defense, brainwashing or mind-control, the death penalty, confessions, criminal profiling, allegations of sexual abuse, and competence to stand trial. Another factor that seems to draw attention to some of these cases is the horrific nature of the crime, whether it be a family homicide, mass shooting, serial murder, school shooting, or political assassination.

In this book, we chronicle twenty of the greatest cases of the last fifty years involving issues at the interface between law and psychology. Our goal is not to entertain but rather to inform and educate readers about the vital role psychology plays in so many aspects of the American system of justice. But if readers find the cases we have chosen to present exciting and compelling, so much the better.

Many criteria could be used to distinguish cases that are great from those that are not. Some readers may take exception to the cases we have chosen to include and our decision to leave certain cases out. Our original plan was to cover a range of cases that would encompass most, if not virtually all, great cases in the history of law and psychology. The original list we developed consisted of nearly a hundred cases, but the task of detailing such a large number posed several problems. Many features of the more interesting cases could not be covered because of space limitations. Had we covered a hundred cases in sufficient detail, as we once thought we might, the result would have been a multivolume encyclopedia that would be daunting to read and of limited interest to the general public.

Instead, we chose to narrow our list to twenty cases we consider great for a variety of reasons. Some of the cases in this book are great because they deal with a famous person or group—like comedian Woody Allen, prize-fighter Mike Tyson, or heavy metal rock band Judas Priest—involved in a highly publicized case dealing with an interesting psychological issue like child custody or the prediction and causation of violent behavior. What makes these cases great is not the mere fact that they involve a famous person, but rather that their status of being in the public eye often distorts—for better or worse—how the case is handled and viewed by the public. For example, the legal system often treats a famous person more delicately or the public harbors stronger opinions about the guilt or culpability of a famous person, leading to an interesting array of psychological issues. Various factors often make it difficult for the public, and even attorneys involved in the case, to predict the outcome.

We consider other cases to be great because they deal with extraordinary if not bizarre circumstances that seem to defy human understanding—like the cases of serial murderer Jeffrey Dahmer, kidnapper and sexual abuser Cameron Hooker, "Mad Bomber" George Metesky, and family killer Andrea Yates.

A few of the cases—like alleged Nazi John Demjanjuk, the Guildford Four who confessed to crimes they did not commit, and Patricia Hearst who went from kidnap victim to bank robber in a matter of weeks—are considered great because they deal with fascinating psychological issues that go to the heart of the search for truth, like the reliability of eyewitness testimony, the validity of confession evidence, or the likelihood that a person could be "brainwashed" into committing a violent crime.

Still other cases—like those of Ralph Tortorici, Daryl Atkins, and Colin Ferguson, all hardly household names—are great because they show how issues of mental health and mental retardation are often central to the entire process of administering justice fairly.

We have also presented a few cases we consider great because of the ways in which they have altered the course of political history—such as the cases of Lee Harvey Oswald, John Hinckley, Jr., and Dan White, all political assassins.

Finally, we selected and have presented a handful of other cases dealing with rather ordinary people because they demonstrate some of the best and worst that psychology has to offer the courts and our system of justice: for example, Gary Ramona, who fought charges that he sexually abused his daughter; Posenjit Poddar, whose rather unremarkable killing of a young woman spurred a major change in the law governing the practice of psychotherapy; and Clayton Hartwig, who was blamed by a U.S. Navy "psychological autopsy" for killing forty-seven sailors aboard the USS *Iowa*.

Some readers may quibble with a few of the selections we have made, but we believe there is no denying that all of these cases are interesting and involve important psychological questions, controversies, and unusual circumstances that make them fascinating to study. We believe the case selection reflects a broad range of mental health and psychological issues, not just those like the insanity defense or criminal profiling that often receive the most attention. The cases in this book reflect such issues as the veracity of child sexual abuse allegations, the reliability of eyewitness testimony, the validity of confession evidence, competence to stand trial, prediction of violent behavior, child custody, juvenile delinquency, coercion and mind control, competence to be sentenced to death, and the workings of the criminal mind.

In our discussions, we also strive to give professional and lay readers alike an appreciation for the complexity of the issues in great cases. A few of our discussions seek to dispel lingering myths that have been repeated over the years. Many of the cases also provide insights into what it is like to serve as an expert witness in high-profile trials. The outcome in some cases often hinges on expert testimony. In a few of the cases we examine, experts endured stinging criticism from judges or lawyers, while in other cases the involvement of mental health experts was embraced and appreciated because it helped juries or judges understand complex issues that went to the heart of the conflict.

The famous American jurist Judge David L. Bazelon, a former U.S. Court of Appeals judge known for his expertise in the area of mental health law, once said that "challenging an expert and questioning his expertise is the lifeblood of our legal system. . . . It is the only way a judge or jury can decide whom to trust."[1] Many expert witnesses in the field of psychology enter the treacherous territory of the legal arena to inform judges and juries about issues that are important in legal decision making and to help in the administration of justice. Although some experts are "hired guns" or "whores of the court" and sell their testimony to the side most willing to pay, these experts are often easily spotted on cross-examination and have short careers as witnesses.[2] The cases in this book contain examples of various kinds of experts (ranging from those who are very experienced and testify regularly in high-profile cases to those whose involvement in a case came about by chance), as well as various opinions about expert witnesses (ranging from experts who were held in high esteem to those who were chided or criticized).

The relationship between psychology and the law is about more than just expert witnesses and testimony, however. It is about the ways in which the workings of the human mind—like memory, thinking, perception, personal decision making, free will, and other complex psychological phenomena—impact important legal issues. Our hope is that the cases we discuss in this book will provide readers with an appreciation for the seemingly endless number of questions that can be raised in these kinds of cases and the way in which the outcome of litigation often hinges on the expertise of psychologists and other mental health professionals.

1

GEORGE

METESKY

Profiling the

"Mad Bomber"

In the fall of 2002, when residents of Virginia, Maryland, and Washington, D.C., were being terrorized by an unidentified serial sniper, law enforcement agents and media pundits alike offered purported profiles of the killer. Looking at the scant evidence then available, the "profilers" generated educated guesses regarding the gender, race, age, education, life experience, psychological makeup, and motives of the killer dubbed the "D.C. sniper."[1]

The speculations offered proved to be largely erroneous; to the surprise of virtually everyone, the sniper turned out be a team of two men, a forty-one-year-old and his seventeen-year-old accomplice. Still, the D.C. sniper profiles highlighted for the nation a common law enforcement practice that spans half a century: the use of crime scene evidence and other available information to develop profiles of unknown perpetrators.

The practice of criminal profiling in the United States dates back at least as far as 1956 to the case of George Metesky, the "Mad Bomber," and the pioneering work of criminal psychiatrist Dr. James A. Brussel.[2]

By the time he was captured, Metesky had been planting homemade bombs in New York City for over sixteen years. Metesky's first bomb was left outside the headquarters of the city's electric power company, Consolidated Edison, on November 16, 1940, wrapped in a note that read: "Con Edison crooks—this is for you."[3] The crudely made device consisted of a brass pipe packed with gunpowder, apparently removed from rifle bullets. The bomb did not detonate. Investigators found it curious that the bomber would have attached a note to his device since, had the bomb gone off, the note would most likely have been destroyed. Maybe the bomber was so disturbed that he had not thought that far ahead, or maybe the device was meant as a threat and not a genuine weapon.

Ten months later, in September of 1941, another unexploded bomb was found in the street a few blocks from Consolidated Edison's main offices. This time there was no note accompanying the crude device. The triggering mechanism was an alarm clock that had not been wound. Again police were puzzled. Had the bomber been trying to cause damage and been frightened off at the last minute or was his intent merely to send another message to the giant utility company?

After examining this second device, investigators concluded that the same person, most likely someone with a grudge against Consolidated Edison, was responsible for both bombs. That assumption was reinforced a few months later when the apparent perpetrator sent a letter to the police stating: "I will make no more bomb units for the duration of the war— My patriotic feelings have made me decide this—Later I will bring the Con Edison to justice—They will pay for their dastardly deeds. F.P." [4] The letter was postmarked in suburban Westchester County. Over the next five years, more than a dozen other letters—speaking of "dastardly deeds," demanding justice, threatening more bombings, and signed F.P.—were received by various New York City businesses. Just as suddenly as these letters had begun, so too they abruptly stopped. From 1946 until 1950, no one apparently heard anything further from the elusive F.P.

In 1950, F.P. broke his self-imposed moratorium when, on March 29, 1950, a third bomb was found, unexploded, in New York's Grand Central Station. This bomb was similar in construction to the first two attributed to F.P. but was bigger and showed somewhat greater sophistication in its design. F.P. had still not succeeded in blowing up anything or anyone, but he was getting closer.

Authorities felt that it was just a matter of time before one of F.P.'s bombs managed to go off and hurt or kill someone. Less than a month later, their expectations were proven partially correct. On April 24, 1950, a bomb similar to the first three attributed to F.P. exploded in a telephone booth at the New York City Public Library, causing property damage but injuring no one. Four months later, another similar bomb went off in a telephone booth in Grand Central Station. No one was hurt in that explosion, but F.P. kept trying. Two weeks later he mailed a bomb to Consolidated Edison. Shortly after that, he cut open an upholstered seat in a movie theater, removed the stuffing, and replaced it with a bomb. Neither of these latter two devices went off.

By then it was nearly Christmas 1950, a year in which F.P. had planted or mailed at least eight bombs in New York City. Just prior to the end-of-the-year holiday, F.P. sent an oddly punctuated, hand-printed letter to the *New York Herald Tribune*:

> To *Herald Tribune* Editor—Have you noticed the bombs in your city—if you are worried, I am sorry—and also if anyone is injured, but it cannot be helped—for justice will be served. I am not well, and for this I will make the Con Edison sorry—Yes, they will regret their dastardly deeds—I will bring them before the bar of justice—public opinion will condemn them—for beware, I will place more units under theater seats in the near future. F.P.[5]

A week later, F.P. followed up his letter with a call to another city newspaper, the *Journal-American*, complaining that the newspapers in town (in keeping with a request from the New York City police) would not print any of his letters, and threatening more bombings to "show you how important I am."[6]

For fear of encouraging copycats and hoaxes, law enforcement authorities decided not to go public with their conclusion that a serial bomber was at work. Whether that was sound policy or not, it certainly did nothing to deter F.P. Over the next two years, F.P. planted another four increasingly sophisticated and powerful bombs, all of which exploded in sites where people could easily have been killed. Two of the bombs were detonated in movie theaters, another in a subway locker, and a fourth in a telephone booth. By this point in F.P.'s bombing spree, it had become apparent to both the media and the public that the bombings were likely the work of a single deranged individual, a person the media then dubbed the "Mad Bomber."[7]

Though the hunt for the Mad Bomber was on, it proved futile, and like clockwork F.P. continued his bombings, setting off four explosive devices in 1953 and another four in 1954, including one at Radio City Music Hall that injured four people, two seriously. The following year, 1955, F.P.'s bombings went from quarterly to bi-monthly. Though two of these bombs failed to detonate, four others did, one nearly killing a porter at Grand Central Station.

Perhaps emboldened by his growing "success" and the failure of the police to stop him, F.P. not only continued the bombings but also stepped up his letter writing. In March of 1956, for example, he wrote to the *New York Herald Tribune*, making clear his frustration at the limited media attention he had received, touting the number of bombs he had already placed, and threatening more of the same:

While victims get blasted—the yellow press makes no mention of these ghoulish acts. These same ghouls call me a psychopath—any further reference to me as such—or the like—will be dealt with—where ever a wire runs—gas or steam flows—from or to the Con Edison Co.—is now a bomb target—so far 54 bombs placed—4 telephone calls made. These bombings will continue until Con Edison is brought to justice—my life is dedicated to this task—expect no calls about bombs in theaters as your actions—no longer warrant the effort or dime—all my sufferings—all my financial loss—will have to be paid in full—it must alarm—anger and annoy the N.Y. yellow press and authorities to find that any individual can be just as mean—dirty and rotten as they are. I merely seek justice. F.P.[8]

True to his word, in 1956, F.P. repeatedly set bombs in public locations around the city. One detonated in a telephone booth at Macy's, injuring six people. Another exploded and destroyed the kitchen of a security guard, who found it in a phone booth at the RCA Building and, not knowing what it was, took it home with him. Later, in December of 1956, another of "F.P's" bombs went off in the Paramount Theater in Brooklyn, injuring six people among the 1,500 gathered to watch the movie *War and Peace*.[9]

The December 1956 explosion marked the beginning of the end for the Mad Bomber. After that bombing, the New York Police Department assigned a task force of fifty detectives to the case, the city offered a $25,000 reward for information leading to the capture of bomber, and the police enlisted the aid of a Greenwich Village psychiatrist, Dr. James Brussel. Brussel, a former chief psychiatrist for the Army during World War II and the Korean War, was initially skeptical of his own ability to offer much help. After studying police records, however, he quickly developed both a profile and a plan to capture the Mad Bomber.

Brussel hypothesized, among other things, that the bomber was a stocky man in the forty to fifty age range who was paranoid, unmarried, living in Connecticut (alone or perhaps with an older female relative), and probably an immigrant from central or eastern Europe.

The psychiatrist's hunch about gender was derived from the observation that historically most bombers had been men. The diagnosis of paranoia was supported by the feelings of persecution expressed in the bomber's many letters. The guess about age was based on that diagnosis, since it was believed that paranoid disorders typically peaked in the early thirties and it was known that this perpetrator had started his reign of terror sixteen years earlier,

Brussel's speculation as to the bomber's marital status flowed from his knowledge that paranoids tend to be socially isolated loners. His assertion regarding the bomber's physique relied on a then-recent study of mental illness and body type that found that 85 percent of paranoid individuals were stocky. His theory about the bomber's home state came from the observation that many of the letters were postmarked in Westchester County, which lies between Connecticut and New York City. Brussel reasoned that the bomber was bright enough not to mail the letters from the area in which he lived. He also knew that many central and eastern European immigrants lived in Connecticut.

Finally, the psychiatrist's conjecture about the bomber's nationality was based upon the frequent use of bombs as weapons in the Slavic countries of central and eastern Europe as well as the stiff, pretentious language used in the bomber's letters.

Recognizing that paranoids are often obsessively fastidious about their appearance, Brussel also predicted that, when captured, the bomber would be wearing a double-breasted suit, an outfit then considered to be the most prim and proper mode of dress for men. Given the bomber's apparent obsessive traits, the psychiatrist told the police to also expect that the suit would be buttoned.

In addition to offering a profile of the Mad Bomber, Brussel used that profile to help the police develop a strategy to capture the serial offender. Brussel told police that they should publicize the profile in an effort to draw the bomber into communication with the authorities. The psychiatrist was convinced that once the profile was made public, the bomber would not be able to keep himself from responding. On December 25, 1956, the New York newspapers published Brussel's profile of the bomber:

> Single man, between 40 and 50. A lone wolf. Introverted. Unsocial, but not anti-social. Skilled mechanic. Immigrant, or first-generation American. Neat with tools. Cunning. Egotistical of mechanical skill. Contemptuous of other people. Disinterested in women. Resentful of criticism of his work, but probably conceals resentment. Expert in civil or military ordnance. Religious, probably a Roman Catholic. Present or former employee of Consolidated Edison. Possible motive: discharge or reprimand. Resentment kept growing. Probably a case of progressive paranoia.[10]

Once newspapers published the profile and encouraged the Mad Bomber to turn himself in, he wasted no time in communicating his displeasure. The bomber telephoned Brussel, identified himself as F.P., demanded that the psychiatrist abandon the case, and warned that he would be sorry if he failed to do so. The bomber also wrote a series of letters in response to the publicity surrounding Brussel's profile. In one letter, complaining bitterly about his mistreatment by Consolidated Edison, the bomber wrote: "I was injured on a job at a Consolidated Edison plant. . . . My medical bills and care have cost thousands—I did not get a single penny for a lifetime of misery and suffering."[11] In another letter he added the date of the incident that had triggered his resentment: September 5, 1931.

These communications spurred a renewed search of Consolidated Edison's files. Previous searches of the utility's records—though criticized by some as perfunctory—had resembled looking for the proverbial needle in the haystack. Consolidated Edison had thousands of employees and many more thousands of customers, many of whom had expressed complaints of one sort or another over the years. But once Consolidated Edison had a date and a likely cause for F.P.'s complaint, the search narrowed to the giant utility's employee compensation records for 1931.

On January 18, 1957, one of the secretaries assigned to search these files struck pay dirt: letters from George Metesky in Waterbury, Connecticut, ninety miles from New York City. Metesky, who had worked for one of nineteen smaller power companies that later merged and became Consolidated Edison, complained that he had been injured on the job on September 5, 1931, and was denied just compensation by his employer.

One letter blamed Consolidated Edison and threatened retaliation for the power company's "dastardly deeds."[12] Other records indicated Metesky claimed to have developed tuberculosis as the result of being struck by hot gasses from one of the company's boilers. According to the records, Metesky was knocked to the floor by the backfire of the boiler and had not received any aid until he was discovered hours later. Initially, the company had placed him on sick leave from his $37.50 a week job but soon fired him. His later worker's compensation claim had been denied because it lacked substantiation and had not been filed in a timely manner.

Two days after these records were uncovered, New York City police officers went to Metesky's home in Waterbury, Connecticut. There, much as Brussel had predicted, they found a stocky, unmarried, fifty-four-year-old son of Lithuanian immigrants who lived in the house with his two older sisters. Metesky was a former member of the U.S. Marine Corps who had learned bomb making while serving as an ordnance mechanic. In Metesky's basement police found an amateur bomb-making laboratory. Metesky soon admitted he was the bomber and volunteered that his moniker F.P. stood for "fair play."[13] Allowed to change from his bathrobe to street clothes before being taken into custody, Metesky opted for a double-breasted suit with the coat buttoned.

After Metesky's arrest, authorities learned more about the man who was the Mad Bomber. After his mother died when he was young, Metesky graduated from high school, entered the Marines, and became a trained electrician. After his military service, Metesky worked as a generator cleaner for about two years for United Electric, a company that later merged with Consolidated Edison. After the September 5, 1931, incident, Metesky was diagnosed with tuberculosis and spent time in two TB sanitariums. Thereafter, aside from a brief stint as a toolmaker, he was unemployed. After apparently giving up trying to convince his former employer that he contracted tuberculosis from his on-the-job accident and was thus entitled to disability compensation, Metesky put his electrical and metal-working skills to use building bombs in a small workshop in his basement. Although Metesky had earlier claimed to have planted fifty-four bombs, only thirty-two were discovered. Twenty-two of these bombs had detonated, injuring nearly two dozen people, but only three seriously.

George Metesky was charged with forty-seven separate crimes, including seven counts of attempted murder. Psychological experts found him to be mentally ill, suffering from paranoid schizophrenia, and not competent to stand trial. In April 1957, the Mad Bomber was adjudicated a "dangerous incapacitated person" and confined to Matteawan State Hospital, New York's psychiatric treatment center for the "criminally insane."[14] Under New York law, Metesky could be detained in this secure hospital until he was deemed competent, but no longer than two-thirds of the maximum sentence for the highest felony charge he faced—in other words, sixteen years and eight months of a possible twenty-five-year sentence. Metesky was never found competent to stand trial, served the maximum period of hospitalization, and was released from Matteawan in 1973. He returned to Connecticut, lived another twenty-one years in freedom, and died at the age of ninety.

Dr. Brussel's role in the Mad Bomber case is often cited as the first instance of American law enforcement's use of psychological profiling to solve a crime. Brussel's profile of the Mad Bomber may well have been the first of its kind but, for all the attention it has received over the years, like most of the profiles it helped spawn, it really did little, if anything, to assist police in identifying the unknown perpetrator. Indeed, as Brussel later acknowledged, his profile may have led the authorities down several blind alleys.[15]

It is often said today that psychological profiles do not identify or capture criminals, the police do. And when they do, it is most often the result of old-fashioned hard work and/or dumb luck.

In the case of the Mad Bomber, it was apparent from the note accompanying the first bomb that the perpetrator was someone with a grudge against Consolidated Edison—most likely, the police thought, a disgruntled employee or former employee of the utility. Although Consolidated Edison employees had much earlier begun the job of sifting through the company's records, they had very little to go on until F.P.'s letter revealing the date and nature of his gripe with the company. From that point on it was just a matter of time and dedication before Metesky's file would be found and identified as that of the Mad Bomber. The real question was whether the police and Consolidated Edison would give the matter the time and dedication needed.

Though Dr. Brussel's profile was uncannily correct, it was not the profile, but its publication, that apparently led Metesky to respond with a letter providing the date that led to his ultimate identification. Even that much is uncertain, since Metesky had already been corresponding with, and had written hundreds of letters to, the press. He may well have revealed this information regardless of the publication of Brussel's profile. Moreover, even with the date known to the staff searching Consolidated Edison's files, it was one of the phrases often used in Metesky's earlier notes and letters—"dastardly deeds"—that caught the eye of the clerical worker who pulled his file and then called the New York bomb squad.

While Brussel's amazingly accurate profile has often been viewed as a brilliant work of psychology and has been credited with leading the police to Metesky, the psychiatrist's own account of his role in the case is much more modest. He readily acknowledged what modern profilers have long known: (1) Criminal profiling is not a science but an art that relies as much on common sense and general knowledge as it does on psychological or psychiatric expertise; and (2) criminal profiles sometimes create a kind of "tunnel vision" that leads investigators to erroneous conclusions and, thus, delay rather than advance the investigation.

In his book, *Casebook of a Crime Psychiatrist*, published in 1968, Brussel explained the logic behind the deductions he made regarding the Mad Bomber as well as his own initial skepticism as to whether his thoughts would be of any help to the police: "Did I really know enough about criminals to say anything sensible . . . ? I'd seen hundreds of offenders in my career, but had I learned enough from them and about them? I'd had a few minor successes in psychiatric detective work, but how much of that success was due to my own knowledge and how much to sheer blind luck?"[16]

Clearly most of Brussel's profile was based upon knowledge more than luck, but for the most part it was knowledge that was not limited to the psychiatrist or to the community of mental health experts. Dr. Brussel did what most good profilers do today; he used his own knowledge base along with inductive reasoning to create a general portrait of the suspect. For example, he knew that in the past most bombers had been men, that historically Slavic people were among those most likely to use bombs as weapons, and that most Slavs were Catholic. Based upon that knowledge he speculated—accurately as it turned out—that the Mad Bomber was a Catholic male likely of Slavic descent.

What was not publicized at the time, but what Brussel revealed in some detail in his book, was the reasoning behind his speculations about the bomber's psychological makeup and motivation—the one area in which he relied almost exclusively upon his formal training and expertise in psychology and psychiatry. In that regard, Brussel had been most impressed by the bomber's handwriting and the way he slashed theater seats in planting some of his bombs.

As Brussel saw it, twenty-five of the twenty-six letters of the alphabet used in the Mad Bomber's carefully hand-printed notes were perfect. Only the letter "W" was flawed, the bottom edges rounded rather than sharp. As Brussel later wrote, the "W" in the notes "resembled a pair of female breasts as seen from the front [and] could also pass as a scrotum."[17] The psychiatrist concluded that "something about sex seemed to be troubling the Bomber."[18] That "something," Brussel thought, was also reflected in the bomber's slashing of theater seats: "Could the seat symbolize the pelvic region of the human body? In plunging a knife upward into it, had the Bomber been symbolically penetrating a woman? Or castrating a man? Or both?"[19]

Ultimately, Brussel concluded that the Mad Bomber was dealing with sexual problems related to an unresolved Oedipal complex:

> There was no other way to explain the misshapen W or the slashing of the seats. . . . The Bomber obviously distrusted and despised male authority: the police, his former employers at Con Ed. . . . To the Bomber any form of male authority could represent his father. . . . Why did he feel this form of antagonism . . . ? Perhaps because, somehow, he had never progressed beyond the Oedipal stage of love for his mother. . . .[20]

Such psychoanalytic abstractions may have helped Dr. Brussel formulate his ultimate profile. But these notions do not seem to have contributed in any significant way to identifying and capturing George Metesky.

In any event, whatever role Dr. Brussel's psychoanalytic musings played in the case, the psychiatrist also made it clear that his profile of the Mad Bomber probably led the police on a number of wild goose chases, and ultimately the case was solved not by the profile but by tedious investigative work.

For example, as Brussel notes, public presentation of his profile led to all sorts of hoaxes: "dummy" bombs were placed around the city, mailed to officials, and even thrown at people on the sidewalks. Bomb threats were called into, and resulted in the closing of, local schools. At the same time, NYPD's bomb squad started receiving fifty to one hundred "bomb" reports each day.[21]

Also, while the profile never resulted in a single report regarding George Metesky, it did generate many reports that made other innocent parties instant suspects. For instance, one middle-aged Polish immigrant who lived with his elderly aunt fell under suspicion when a neighbor noticed that whenever the aunt left home, the neighbor would hear "funny" metallic sounds emanating from the man's apartment, sounds that would cease as soon as the aunt returned. Careful investigation determined that the man, who fit Brussel's profile well, had a hobby of creating sculptures from various metal scraps, an avocation frowned upon and mocked by his family.[22]

Yet another suspect generated by Brussel's profile was a middle-aged German, electrical engineer from Connecticut who had been treated for paranoia, lived with his wife (who was ten years older than he) and her mother, and was in the habit of wearing double-breasted suits. This man caught a neighbor's attention by frequently making trips to New York City carrying a small suitcase in the trunk of his car, including one on December 2, 1956, the day one of the Mad Bomber's devices exploded in Brooklyn's Paramount Theater, injuring half a dozen people. When the man was finally confronted by the police, they discovered the contents of his valise: a pair of high-heeled women's boots. The suspect, it turned out, visited New York regularly to indulge a fetish: having sex with prostitutes paid to wear these boots.[23]

According to Brussel's own candid account, in the weeks after his profile was published, "scores of other people" became suspects in the Mad Bomber case as a result of tips from friends and neighbors and were needlessly embarrassed.[24]

Of course, causing needless embarrassment to many people was probably the least of the problems created by Brussel's profile. Even though the profile of the Mad Bomber was accurate, right down to the buttoned double-breasted suit, the characteristics listed in that profile were sufficiently common and fit so many people that, in the words of the author of a modern text on criminal profiling, "the requesting agency became deluged with essentially worthless tips and leads, each of which must be followed up, wasting valuable time and resources."[25]

2

LEE HARVEY OSWALD

The Formative Years

of an Assassin

The assassination of President John F. Kennedy ranks as one of the most controversial events in United States history. It is arguable that no other crime has been so closely scrutinized and analyzed. Two government investigative commissions delivered multivolume reports on the assassination—the Warren Commission in 1964[1] and the House Select Committee on Assassinations in 1979.[2] Hundreds of books, as well as several hundred thousand government documents and scholarly research articles or reports, have been generated on the case. It is nearly impossible to cover all of the relevant material in a single volume, let alone a brief overview of the assassin's life.

The Warren Commission, established by President Kennedy's successor, Lyndon B. Johnson, to investigate the assassination, concluded that Lee Harvey Oswald acted alone when he killed John F. Kennedy on November 22, 1963, in Dallas, Texas.[3] Some researchers question the Warren Commission report and believe that forensic evidence supports the theory that there was an extensive conspiracy behind the Kennedy assassination. One theory suggests that a second gunman fired at the president from the grassy knoll in front of Kennedy's limousine. In response to nagging questions and persistent controversy surrounding the Kennedy assassination, the U.S. House of Representatives appointed a Select Committee on Assassinations that issued a new report in 1979.[4] Although the Select Committee reaffirmed the finding by the Warren Commission that Oswald fired three shots at the president's motorcade from the sixth floor of the Texas School Book Depository, it also added that there was evidence of a conspiracy and that Oswald may not have acted alone.

Oswald's first shot missed Kennedy entirely. His second shot wounded both Kennedy and Texas Governor John Connally, who was riding in the president's limousine; this second shot is the subject of the "single (or pristine) bullet theory" and a focus of some controversy among researchers of the assassination.[5] The third shot hit Kennedy in the head and mortally wounded him. The House Select Committee concluded that Kennedy was "probably assassinated" as part of a conspiracy but the Committee reaffirmed that Oswald was the identified assassin.

Many scholars who have studied the Kennedy assassination remain convinced that Oswald did not act alone and that he was part of a conspiracy to assassinate the president. Some conspiracy theorists believe that Oswald was an operative of a formal government agency, such as the CIA, FBI, Russian KGB, or Cuban government, while others believe that Oswald was innocent and framed in an elaborate cover-up. A few conspiracy theorists believe that Oswald was innocent and took the blame to conceal the identity of the true assassin. Others who have studied the case endorse the formal conclusions of the Warren Commission that Oswald acted alone in killing Kennedy.

All official versions of the Kennedy assassination have concluded that Oswald assassinated Kennedy and that if Oswald had survived and been brought to trial he would have been convicted. When Texas nightclub owner Jack Ruby—a man with a shady background and connections to organized crime—shot and killed Oswald on live television two days after Kennedy's assassination while Oswald was being transferred to the county jail, all hope was lost of ever learning from Oswald his true motives.

In fact, Oswald's premature death prevented a trial from being held that would have provided an opportunity for his culpability in the assassination to be scrutinized in front of a jury. The Warren Commission also concluded that it was "not able to reach any definite conclusions as to whether or not [Oswald] was 'sane' under prevailing legal standards"[6] because he could not be evaluated by forensic mental health experts. If Oswald's guilt was never formally adjudicated in a trial and his competence and sanity were never officially examined by qualified experts, why would this case be considered a great case in the field of forensic psychology?

Once Oswald was identified as Kennedy's assassin, an intensive investigation into his background was undertaken that consumed a substantial portion of the voluminous literature produced on the assassination. Several details of Oswald's life provide a complex portrait of an emotionally unstable man with a history of contradictory behaviors and activities. During his teenage years, Oswald was adjudicated as a juvenile delinquent and underwent an extensive mental health evaluation and treatment that provides a classic example of how the mental health and juvenile justice systems work with one another.

Throughout the nineteenth century, *parens patriae* became an increasingly influential principle that guided the way the legal system dealt with juvenile delinquents and young offenders.[7] The concept of *parens patriae* basically means that when the natural parents of children are unwilling or unable to provide the necessary emotional, moral, and economic support to their children, the state can become the common guardian for the child. In this way, he or she can continue to grow and develop during the formative childhood years into a productive and law-abiding adult. The legal system soon came to focus less on punishment and more on rehabilitating young offenders. In 1899, the nation's first specialized court devoted to juveniles was created in Chicago, Illinois, by social worker Jane Addams and her colleagues at Hull House.[8] By the early part of the twentieth century, every state had special laws and a unique court system for dealing with troubled children and adolescents.[9]

Throughout the first half of the twentieth century, juvenile courts were meant to operate as benign caretakers for children and teenagers whose behavior or life circumstances brought them to the attention of the legal system. A variety of new terms were created to describe legal issues unique to young people, including the term "status offense" that continues to be applied in juvenile court proceedings. Individuals under a specific age can be brought under the jurisdiction of a juvenile court as status offenders if they fail to conform their behavior to certain standards, such as attending school, adhering to a curfew, or avoiding certain places or people. If the child or teenager fails to abide by rules imposed by a judge, he or she can be ruled a person or child in need of supervision and the judge can then decide whether to keep the youngster in the community or place him or her in a facility for young offenders. The concept of status offense is central to the role of juvenile courts acting as *parens patriae* to make sure young offenders get the services and supports they need.

During the early part of the twentieth century, the juvenile justice system operated under the theory that young offenders should be rehabilitated, and juvenile courts had wide latitude in how they dealt with young offenders. In some cases, this latitude meant that young people who found their way into the juvenile justice system had limited rights, did not necessarily have access to legal counsel, and were often at the mercy of the presiding judge or magistrate. However, the juvenile justice system underwent a major change in the late 1960s, beginning with the U.S. Supreme Court decisions of *Kent v. United States* in 1966 and *In re Gault* in 1967.[10] These two cases introduced the notion of due process to juvenile court proceedings in which the Supreme Court recognized that even children and adolescents must be given notice of the charges they face, access to legal counsel, and an opportunity to confront witnesses who accuse them of wrongdoing.

In 1953, before the *Kent* and *Gault* Supreme Court cases, the juvenile justice system was primarily focused on rehabilitation and treatment of young offenders. It is in this context that Lee Harvey Oswald came to the attention of the juvenile court system. Born on October 18, 1939, in New Orleans, Louisiana, Oswald was the youngest of three children. His father died two months before he was born, and Oswald was raised by his mother. He had an older half-brother, who was from his mother's first marriage, and an older brother who had the same biological father as Oswald. Because she had to work after the death of her second husband, Oswald's mother tried to place her three children in an orphanage. The two older boys were accepted, but Oswald could not be placed until he reached the age of three. Once he was old enough, Oswald lived for thirteen months in the orphanage and then returned to live with his mother, who soon married her third husband. Oswald lived with his mother and stepfather while his two brothers remained for a time in the orphanage.

As a child, Oswald was said to be quite active and would often gain attention from other children by telling them what to do. Among the earliest written documents from his childhood that were saved for the historical record were postcards he wrote to his older half-brother who was in the Coast Guard. These documents provide subtle hints of the selfishness and demanding nature that characterized his early years: "Dear John, All I have to say is get me some ($1.50) money. P.S. I want ($1.50). Lee."[11]

His mother later divorced her third husband and was forced to raise Oswald by herself. The loss of his stepfather, a man whom Oswald had increasingly come to view as a father figure, was very difficult. During the divorce proceedings, Oswald was asked to testify but he refused because he stated that he was unable to differentiate the truth from a lie. In the wake of the divorce, his mother would often complain openly about how difficult it was for her to raise three children on her own; family members noticed that Oswald appeared to be more withdrawn and kept to himself.

Oswald was very demanding and would often skip school when his mother had to work. As a single parent, Oswald's mother had to support the family, and she trained him to fend for himself. Oswald was left to get himself to school, return home to an empty house for lunch, and stay alone after school until she came home from work. Oswald's mother trained him to do this instead of play with other children,[12] which undoubtedly contributed to his withdrawal and isolation from his peers. Another matter complicating his academic adjustment was the fact that his mother moved frequently and he was never able to settle in a single school. By the time he was ten years old, Oswald had enrolled in his sixth school.

The investigation into Oswald's life following the Kennedy assassination revealed that neighbors who knew the family saw Oswald's mother as overbearing and Oswald himself as often quick to anger. In order to get some help in controlling Oswald's increasingly defiant behavior, his mother moved with him to New York City to live with Oswald's older half-brother and family. Soon after arriving, thirteen-year-old Oswald began arguing with his sister-in-law over the television. During one argument, he pulled out a pocketknife and threatened to harm her if she got in his way again. This confrontation resulted in Oswald and his mother being asked to leave the half-brother's home; they subsequently found an apartment of their own. His mother minimized the seriousness of this incident and even when testifying before the Warren Commission following the assassination she continued to downplay its significance.

Oswald and his mother moved three times within a five-month period after they left the home of his half-brother. It was during this period, the spring of 1953, that a series of court hearings were set to address the problem of Oswald's truancy. The court sent him to Youth House, a residential facility, for a psychiatric evaluation. While Oswald was at the facility, he pleaded with his mother to get him out. On one occasion he broke down during one of her visits and cried, saying that there were youths being housed there who had killed people and that he wanted to get out. On the other hand, Oswald would tell his probation officer that he did not mind Youth House, although he missed the freedom of being able to do whatever he wanted.[13]

Because Oswald often skipped school and was put on probation for truancy, the court had requested a psychiatric evaluation requiring him to stay at Youth House in New York City from April 16 until May 7, 1953.[14] During that time, a team of mental health professionals evaluated his mental state and made a set of recommendations that had the potential to alter the course of Oswald's life.

Dr. Renatus Hartogs, who was both a clinical psychologist and psychiatrist, conducted an extensive examination of Oswald, who was thirteen years old at the time. Hartogs later testified before the Warren Commission that he found Oswald to be an adolescent who was withdrawn and tense. During the course of the psychiatric evaluation, Oswald did not appear to like talking about himself or his feelings and gave the psychiatrist the impression that he was indifferent to what other people thought of him. Hartogs concluded that Oswald demonstrated a personality disorder with schizoid and passive-aggressive features. Individuals with this disturbance are extremely introverted and shy but are prone to intense outbursts of anger and rage. Oswald stated during his examination with Hartogs that he did not like people, preferred to be alone, and would occasionally hit his mother when angry. Furthermore, Dr. Hartogs concluded that Oswald was potentially dangerous to other people and had a propensity to act out explosively and aggressively. Oswald was not found to be psychotic, and he was not diagnosed with a major psychiatric disturbance such as schizophrenia. Hartogs concluded his written report with the following:

> This 13 year old well built boy has superior mental resources and functions only slightly below his capacity level in spite of chronic truancy from school which brought him into Youth House. No finding of neurological impairment or Psychotic mental changes could be made. Lee has to be diagnosed as "personality pattern disturbance with schizoid features and passive-aggressive tendencies." Lee has to be seen as an emotionally, quite disturbed youngster who suffers under the impact of really existing emotional isolation and deprivation, lack of affection, absence of family life and rejection by a self involved and conflicted mother.[15]

Hartogs concluded that although Oswald did not need to be institutionalized at the time, the troubled young man needed intensive treatment nonetheless and a recommendation was made to the court that Oswald be assigned a probation officer and placed under the outpatient care of a psychiatrist.

The psychiatric evaluation of Oswald was supported by psychological testing conducted by a psychologist at Youth House, Irving Sokolow. Among the tests administered to Oswald was the Wechsler Intelligence Scale for Children that revealed a Full Scale IQ of 118, placing him in the high average range of measured intelligence.[16] Interestingly, Oswald had been tested four years earlier while he was at Ridglea West Elementary in Fort Worth, Texas.[17] His IQ at that time was 103, revealing average intelligence. Although the discrepancy between these two measurements of Oswald's intelligence would seem to be noteworthy, the finding is not uncommon and could be explained by any number of factors, including the use of different intelligence tests or the fact that Oswald may have had different levels of motivation at the time he was tested. Nevertheless, the intelligence testing reveals that Oswald functioned in the average to above average range of intelligence and serves to dispel any myths about him being someone of limited intellect who was incapable of formulating and executing a plan to assassinate the president.

Another psychological test administered to Oswald during his evaluation at Youth House was the human figure drawing. The test requires an individual to draw a picture of a person; features of the drawing are then evaluated and the examiner draws conclusions about the individual's personality. In the 1950s, when Oswald underwent his evaluation, the human figure drawing was widely used as a personality assessment technique that operated under the projection hypothesis. According to this hypothesis, individuals who are given a rather ambiguous task to perform where wide latitude is permitted in the nature of the response allowed, will introduce—or project—into the test aspects of their personality to help them complete the task. In recent years, the human figure drawing has been surrounded in controversy, particularly with respect to its use in legal and forensic settings, because questions have been raised about the reliability and validity of scoring methods used to rate features of the drawings and inferences that psychologists make about the person.[18] While current forensic psychological practice calls for greater caution in the use of human figure drawings to evaluate individuals in legal settings, Sokolow's use of the classic projective technique was typical of practicing psychologists at the time.

The conclusions Sokolow drew about Oswald's functioning based on his human figure drawing seem valid on their face. According to the psychological evaluation report written by Sokolow, Oswald's drawings were

> empty, poor characterizations of persons approximately the same age as [Oswald]. They reflect a considerable amount of impoverishment in the social and emotional areas. [Oswald] appears to be a somewhat insecure youngster exhibiting much inclination for warm and satisfying relationships to others. There is some indication that [Oswald] may relate to men more easily than to women in view of the more mature conceptualization. [Oswald] appears slightly withdrawn and in view of the lack of detail within the drawings this may assume a more significant characteristic. [Oswald] exhibits some difficulty in relationship to the maternal figure suggesting more anxiety in this area than in any other.[19]

Of course, some of these interpretations of Oswald's drawings have intuitive appeal, such as the notion that the lack of detail in his drawings suggested he was socially impoverished and withdrawn. However, another equally compelling conclusion is that Oswald simply was unmotivated to draw many details and did not want to disclose much about himself because he was in the difficult situation of having to undergo a court-ordered evaluation in an institutional setting.

On the other hand, many of the conclusions rendered by Hartogs in his report were supported by the observations of others who knew Oswald and his family. Reports from his teachers indicated that he had very few friends in school, and his mother often impressed those who interviewed her as someone who was self-involved and had difficulty relating to other people effectively.

Although the details of Oswald's life were investigated extensively in the wake of the Kennedy assassination, the psychiatric examination of Oswald during adolescence stands as a portrait of his mental state during a critical period of his development. Gerald Posner, a Kennedy assassination researcher who supports the findings of the Warren Commission that Oswald acted alone when he assassinated Kennedy, has stated that the findings of Hartogs's examination have either been ignored or misrepresented by conspiracy theorists or critics of the Warren Commission.[20] Posner has noted that many conspiracy theorists who assert that Oswald did not act alone in the Kennedy assassination have either failed to cite Hartogs's testimony before the Warren Commission or have erroneously concluded that the psychiatric evaluation failed to uncover any mental abnormality.

In fact, Hartogs concluded in his report that Oswald was quite disturbed emotionally but the psychiatrist fell short of recommending that Oswald be treated in an institutional setting. During his testimony before the Warren Commission, Hartogs stated that he had once presented Oswald's case at a seminar for other professionals because of the unusual nature of the presentation:

> He came to us on a charge of truancy from school, and yet when I
> examined him, I found him to have definite traits of dangerousness.
> In other words, this child had a potential for explosive, aggressive,
> assaultive acting out which was rather unusual to find in a child
> who was sent to the Youth House on such a mild charge as truancy
> from school.[21]

Although Oswald's potential for violence was not analyzed in detail in Hartogs's report, he later stated that he believed the risk for violence was clear from his diagnosis of passive-aggressive personality tendencies. Whether this later testimony is prone to hindsight bias—given that the psychiatric evaluation was being evaluated with knowledge that Oswald was Kennedy's accused assassin—is an issue that must be considered when evaluating Hartogs's testimony before the Warren Commission.

Nevertheless, any propensity for violence that Oswald may have demonstrated as an adolescent does not provide conclusive evidence to support his guilt as Kennedy's assassin. Many attempts have been made by mental health professionals to identify common psychological features of assassins, yet most of these efforts have met with failure. For example, one psychiatrist who provided a retrospective review of Oswald's history concluded that Kennedy's assassin suffered from schizophrenia. In 1965, Dr. Donald W. Hastings, who was a professor and department chair in the Department of Psychiatry and Neurology at the University of Minnesota, wrote: "On the basis of newspaper and magazine accounts of Oswald's life, there is not, in my opinion, any reasonable doubt that the assassin had paranoid schizophrenia."[22] Hastings made his diagnosis without any direct examination of Oswald and relied on unspecified journalistic accounts that cannot be evaluated for their accuracy. Furthermore, Hastings appears to have made an erroneous conclusion about the evaluation conducted on Oswald by Hartogs when Hastings wrote: "a tentative diagnosis of incipient schizophrenia had been made years before by a New York psychiatrist."[23] In fact, Hartogs's own evaluation found no evidence of psychosis, and the psychiatrist did not diagnosis Oswald with schizophrenia. In the past, the schizoid personality traits that Oswald presumably demonstrated were viewed by some psychiatrists as a precursor to schizophrenia but many individuals with schizoid personality do not develop schizophrenia. Hastings's conclusion that Oswald had schizophrenia is based on a questionable method and an erroneous reading of Hartogs's evaluation of the Kennedy assassin.

Other researchers have attempted to identify a "presidential assassination syndrome" that suggests those who target U.S. presidents are inadequate, isolated loners who use assassination to compensate for their own inadequacies. Dr. David A. Rothstein, who was a staff psychiatrist at the U.S. Medical Center for Federal Prisoners, originally proposed the notion of a presidential assassination syndrome after he studied the similarities between Oswald and a number of presidential threateners referred for psychiatric evaluation.[24] Although Rothstein recognized that his conclusions were based on a limited sample of individuals, he concluded that presidential assassins may have schizophrenia, severe rage toward women, confusion about their identities, and strong identifications with other assassins.

However, the presidential assassination syndrome has not held up well to empirical testing. The most comprehensive study of assassins that has yet been conducted dispels the notion that there is a common psychological profile or syndrome that describes presidential assassins. In the U.S. Secret Service Exceptional Case Study project on assassins, attackers, and people who have approached public figures with lethal intent, no common profile or psychological pattern emerged.[25] Rather, individuals who engaged in assassination behaviors appeared to do so for a variety of reasons, but their actions were not the product of mental illness. Instead, assassination appeared to be due to an identifiable pattern of thinking and behavior that led up to the attack. Results of the Secret Service's Exceptional Case Study suggest that even though the psychiatric evaluation of Oswald during adolescence might have shed important information about his personality during the formative years of his adolescence, there is no specific variable or pattern of behavior back in 1953 that could have predicted Oswald's subsequent actions in the fateful month of November 1963.

Oswald first tried to join the U.S. Marine Corps when he was sixteen years old. He got his mother to make a false statement that he was older, but he was unable to convince authorities that he was old enough to join the military. Oswald was ultimately successful in getting into the Marines but he also began to exhibit unusual tendencies like becoming enamored with communism. During his enlistment with the Marine Corps, Oswald became a self-proclaimed communist who initially professed devotion to the U.S.S.R. during a time of intense concern in the United States that communism posed a serious threat to national security. Oswald later moved to the Soviet Union and attempted to become a Soviet citizen by renouncing his U.S. citizenship. He even made a superficial suicidal gesture by slashing his wrists when he was told after a two-year wait that his application for Soviet citizenship was denied. Although he was ultimately permitted to remain in the Soviet Union, Oswald soon became disillusioned with his life in the communist country. During this period of time, he was experiencing many personal difficulties, including conflicts with his wife. His disillusionment with the Soviet Union ultimately led him to return to the United States. Nevertheless, Oswald's thinking and behavior were inconsistent and ambivalent. While remaining in the United States, he continued to proclaim himself a communist, made an inquiry into the possibility of returning to the Soviet Union, and expressed an interest in traveling to Cuba.

His mother had an interesting observation about her son's attempt to renounce his U.S. citizenship back in November 1959. While speaking to a newspaper reporter from Fort Worth, Texas, about her son's desire to defect to the Soviet Union, Marguerite Oswald said, "He is capable of making his own decisions. . . . It's his privilege to make his own decisions. That's what we preach in the United States, isn't it?—that people have a right to make decisions. . . . I would much rather read the sort of headlines that are appearing now than headlines that Lee had killed somebody or become a dope fiend or something like that."[26]

Oswald was a troubled and unstable individual throughout his life and not the carefree, untroubled person some conspiracy theorists believe was framed for the assassination. More important, however, is the fact that the recommendations of the mental health professionals who evaluated Oswald during his adolescence went unheeded. After the psychiatric report was submitted to the court, Oswald was placed on probation and the court attempted to secure the recommended treatment for him. However, his mother frequently found ways to avoid bringing her son back to court, often refusing and claiming that he was doing better. In reality, Oswald was continuing his behavioral decline; he did poorly in school and was belligerent and defiant with his teachers.

In November 1953, the judge finally ordered that Oswald be placed in a residential facility so that he could receive mandatory psychiatric care. Oswald's mother was apparently convinced that the court was against her son, and she was set on making sure that he would not be placed in an institution like Youth House ever again. She left New York to avoid the jurisdiction of the court's order and returned to New Orleans.

Of course, it would be unfair to blame Oswald's fate solely on the decisions that his mother made with respect to the judge's recommendations for institutionalization during the accused assassin's teenage years. In fact, one psychiatrist later suggested that Oswald's mother may have rejected the court's recommendations and left New York State out of frustration over the fact that no clinic or facility in the New York City area appeared willing to offer the services he needed.[27] For nine months, Oswald's probation officer at Youth House, John Carro, made a number of referrals to various agencies and clinics to see if Oswald could get the treatment he required. Oswald's mother might have viewed this "as a rejection of herself and her son, and her typical reaction might well have been something in the nature of, 'I can handle this myself and I don't need any help,' so that she would appear to be the rejecting person rather than the rejected one."[28]

Carro admitted to the Warren Commission that "there was nothing that would lead me to believe when I saw [Oswald] at the age of 12 that there would be seeds of destruction for somebody."[29] Still, his social worker Evelyn Siegel believed that Oswald might respond to treatment if given the chance. Her report stated that:

Despite his withdrawal, [Oswald] gives the impression that he is not so difficult to reach as he appears and patient, prolonged effort in a sustained relationship with one therapist might bring results. There are indications that he has suffered serious personality damage but if he can receive help quickly this might be repaired to some extent.[30]

Therefore, when Oswald did not receive the intensive therapy that was recommended by professionals at Youth House and his mother took him back to New Orleans, an opportunity to change the direction of his life was missed.

The fateful decision to keep Oswald out of a psychiatric institution may very well have been one of the key events during his early years that maintained his life on a tragic course. One can only wonder. If Oswald had received the psychiatric care he needed as ordered by the court, then the course of history might have been altered and his mother might have avoided reading the headlines she did not want to read—that her son had indeed killed someone, namely the president of the United States.

3

PATRICIA
HEARST

Uncommon Victim

or Common Criminal?

On February 4, 1974, a nineteen-year-old Berkeley sophomore was kidnapped at gunpoint from the off-campus home she shared with her fiancé, a graduate student. That evening around nine o'clock, three armed individuals (two men and a woman) shoved their way into the couple's apartment and dragged the young woman, clothed in only a bathrobe, into a nearby car and drove away.

Had the kidnap victim been any one of the other thousands of Berkeley students, the case might not have generated much interest outside the Bay area of California. But the woman snatched by the three intruders was Patricia Hearst. Though she kept a low profile and few knew of her background, Patty Hearst was the daughter of Randolph Hearst, one of the wealthiest men in America who was heir to the Hearst publishing dynasty and owner of a national chain of newspapers and radio and television stations. As events would soon demonstrate, she had been kidnapped for that very reason.

Three days after the kidnapping, the kidnappers, a self-styled militant revolutionary group (who today would be regarded as domestic terrorists) contacted the Hearst family in what they called a "communiqué."[1] Their message to the Hearsts, accompanied by one of Patty's credit cards, was that the group, the Symbionese Liberation Army (SLA), was holding their daughter as a "prisoner of war" and that she would be executed if she resisted or if anyone else tried to interfere with the group's activities.[2] The "communiqué" added that this and all future communications from the SLA "MUST [*sic*] be published in full in all newspapers, and all other forms of media."[3]

Five days after this initial "communiqué," the SLA contacted the Hearsts again, this time delivering to a local radio station a recorded message from Patty demanding a ransom of sorts. To ensure Patty's safety, the tape said, her parents were to immediately donate seventy dollars worth of food to every poor person in California. The Hearsts wasted no time responding; within ten days they had established a program called "People in Need" and begun handing out free food.[4] In all, over 90,000 bags and boxes of food, valued at about two million dollars, were given away to needy Californians.

Meanwhile, however, Patty's kidnappers, a loosely organized band of ex-convicts and political misfits, had no intention of releasing the heiress. Their plan was to exploit her and the Hearst name and fortune in a way that America would never forget.

On April 3 the SLA issued another "communiqué," this one including a tape-recorded message from Hearst:

> I would like to begin this statement by informing the public that
> I wrote what I am about to say. It's what I feel. I have never been
> forced to say anything on any tape. Nor have I been brainwashed,
> drugged, tortured, hypnotized or in any way confused. . . . I have
> been given the choice of (1) being released in a safe area, or (2) join-
> ing the forces of the Symbionese Liberation Army and fighting for
> my freedom and the freedom of all oppressed people. I have chosen
> to stay and fight. . . . I have been given the name Tania after a com-
> rade who fought alongside Che in Bolivia. I embrace the name with
> the determination to continue fighting with her spirit.[5]

The next "message" the public would receive about Patty Hearst came in the form of a security film taken in the course of an armed robbery at a branch of the Hibernia Bank in San Francisco on April 15, 1974. The film showed Hearst and two members of the SLA, all brandishing guns. One of the robbers shouted: "This is a holdup! The first motherfucker who don't lay down on the floor gets shot in the head."[6] Another yelled, "SLA! SLA! Get down on the floor over there and you won't get hurt."[7] For her part, Hearst muttered "This is Tania . . . Patricia Hearst."[8] One person was shot and the robbers escaped with about $10,000. The SLA took credit for the robbery in another taped "communiqué" in which Hearst stated: "Greetings to the people, this is Tania. On April 15 my comrades and I expropriated $10,660.02 from the Sunset Branch of the Hibernia Bank."[9] In response, the nation's highest-ranking law enforcement official, U.S. Attorney General William Saxbe, told a Washington press conference that, from what he could see, Hearst "was not a reluctant participant" in the robbery but had become a "common criminal."[10]

A month later, on May 16, 1974, Hearst surfaced again, this time in Los Angeles where, from a car parked outside a sporting goods retail outlet, she sprayed the storefront with automatic gunfire, thereby enabling the escape of two SLA members who were being arrested by store security for shoplifting. Thus alerted to the presence of SLA members in Los Angeles, a day later police surrounded the SLA's hideout. After an exchange of gunfire between police and members of the SLA, the house exploded and burned, killing six occupants. Though police initially expected to find Hearst's body among the charred remains, she had not been in the house. She and the others involved in the sporting goods store shooting had never returned. When Hearst and her surviving SLA companions learned of the fatal fire, they fled across the country, eventually settling for awhile in Pennsylvania before returning to California in the fall of 1974.

Once back in California, Hearst and the others joined forces with several new members of the SLA to rob at least two other banks. During one of these robberies in April 1975, Hearst was the get-away driver; a woman was killed in the bank and several other customers were stomped by Hearst's accomplices. Later that year, Hearst also helped SLA members plant four bombs in the Bay area: two destroyed police cars and one exploded at the Marin County Civic Center.

On September 18, 1975, another group stormed the San Francisco house where Patricia Hearst and four other SLA members were living. Hearst would again be removed forcefully from her "home," but this time those taking her were FBI agents. "Freeze or I'll blow your head off," one of the agents yelled.[11] Hearst raised her hands in surrender. "Are you Patty Hearst?" one agent asked.[12] "Yes," Hearst replied before being handcuffed and arrested.[13] So ended the most extensive manhunt in the history of U.S. law enforcement.

Before being booked on multiple criminal charges, Hearst offered those around her a clenched-fist revolutionary salute. And when asked by the booking officer for her usual occupation, Hearst said, "Urban guerrilla."[14]

How, in a matter of months, did Patricia Hearst, who had previously led a sheltered and affluent life, go from an apolitical college student and upstanding citizen to an "urban guerrilla" and one of America's most wanted criminal fugitives?

The FBI and other law enforcers had a simple answer to that question. Though no one ever denied that Hearst had initially been kidnapped and held hostage by the SLA, those who chased her for a year and a half and ultimately prosecuted her believed that prior to the kidnapping Hearst was already a "rebel in search for a cause"[15] who, at some point early in her captivity, willingly became a member of the SLA. For example, as U.S. Attorney James Browning later explained: "When she was in that bank, she acted with verve and great purpose, and she avoided apprehension for a year and a half, when she had plenty of opportunities to walk away and come home. The fact is she had joined them."[16]

Hearst, of course, had a different explanation. From the time she was kidnapped until fifty-seven days later, she was confined to a small dark closet, where she was bound, blindfolded, gagged, sexually abused, raped, deprived of sleep and proper nutrition, and threatened with death if she tried to escape or failed to cooperate. "As a sort of tradeoff" for having her blindfold removed and being given easier access to the toilet, Hearst later said, "I agreed to read and study their recommended literature in the closet with the aid of a flashlight. They provided me with a steady supply of selected reading, books by Eldridge Cleaver, George Jackson, Marx, Engels, and others."[17] The group's leader regularly quizzed Hearst on her reading assignments and delighted in answering her questions in great detail. As Hearst feigned interest and "racked [her] brain to think up questions that would indicate [her] keen interest,"[18] she got closer to the group that was holding her. So close, in fact, that one day, the leader told her:

> You're kind of like the pet chicken people have on a farm—when it comes time to kill it for Sunday dinner, no one really wants to do it. . . . You can join us and fight with us, and that'll mean you can never go home again or ever see your folks or your old friends—or you can die. . . . You know, we've kind of gotten to like you, so we really don't want to kill you, if we don't have to. Think about it.[19]

Not long after that not-so-veiled threat, the same man presented Hearst with another "choice." "The War Council has decided that you can join us, if you want to," the leader told her. "Or you can be released, and go home again."[20] Believing that she would never be released, and that "the *real* choice was . . . to join them or be executed," Hearst replied, trying to mask her hesitation: "I want to join you . . . I want to fight for the people."[21]

Though Hearst felt no greater freedom or autonomy after having pledged her allegiance to her captors, she did feel calmer and more at peace. As she would later write, "My own course was still to live from day to day, to do whatever they said, to play my part, and to pray that I would survive. Once I came to accept in my own mind the stark reality of my new life—that I was now part of the SLA—the racking turmoil within me subsided."[22]

Charged first with robbing the Hibernia Bank, Hearst was initially represented by a team of lawyers whose court pleadings portended some kind of psychiatric defense and thereby triggered an extensive psychological evaluation by four court-appointed doctors, resulting in a confidential 162-page report. The ostensible purpose of these evaluations was to determine Hearst's competence to stand trial, but the lawyer's pleadings seemed to be aimed at establishing some sort of temporary insanity. In one affidavit filed by Hearst's first defense team, the attorneys described the awful conditions of their client's early captivity and then argued that:

> Under the pressure of these threats, deprivation of liberty, isolation and terror, she felt her mind clouding, and everything appeared so distorted and terrible that she believed and feared that she was losing her sanity, and unless soon freed, would become insane. . . .
> A short while before her arrest, she began to experience lucid intervals in which her sanity briefly reappeared. . . . When the FBI agents appeared, she thought that she would instantly be killed. When this did not happen, her mind began to clear up again, but the first full realization that she had been living in a fantasy world whose terrors could be resolved by merely returning to her family or even consulting the law officers, occurred when her mother, her father and her sisters hugged and kissed her.[23]

The court-appointed team of psychologists and psychiatrists found Patricia Hearst sane but "emotionally impaired to a significant degree" as a result of the emotional stress of the preceding year and a half.[24] Her IQ had fallen from 130 (prior to the kidnapping) to 109. Personality testing revealed a young woman who was "sad, hopeless, withdrawn, emotionally distressed and expressing a cry for help."[25] The team of evaluators further concluded that Hearst suffered from "traumatic neurosis with dissociative features"[26] (a rough equivalent of today's posttraumatic stress disorder), had been "subjected to powerfully effective coercive manipulation by her captors," and would need several months of individual psychotherapy to enable her to be fully competent to stand trial. In response, the judge scheduled trial for three months later, sealed the report, and allowed Hearst to undergo psychotherapy while jailed pending trial.

When Hearst went to trial in February 1976, she had new defense counsel and a new defense strategy. F. Lee Bailey, Hearst's new lead attorney—who had earlier defended Albert DiSalvo (thought to be the Boston Strangler) and Dr. Sam Shepard (the inspiration for the television series and movie *The Fugi-*

tive) and would later help defend O. J. Simpson—rejected any traditional psychiatric defense such as insanity or diminished capacity. Instead the veteran attorney opted for a defense of duress or coercion. Under the law governing Hearst's trial, the fact that she was kidnapped by the SLA would, by itself, be insufficient to exonerate her. However, if the jurors found that Hearst had been coerced into committing the robbery at the Hibernia Bank under a well-founded fear of death or serious bodily injury from which there was no reasonable opportunity to escape without committing the crime, they would have no choice but to acquit her.

Though duress is rarely raised as a defense, when lawyers raise it they rarely rely on expert psychological or psychiatric testimony. In most such cases, the facts speak for themselves. Though Hearst had an arguable defense of duress, given that she was kidnapped, abused, and threatened with death by members of the SLA, there were clearly holes in the argument that would need to be filled before a jury could be persuaded to acquit her. She had, after all, acknowledged joining the SLA despite being told that she would be released if she chose to be, and she carried a weapon at the robbery, protected her "comrades" at the sporting goods store, and willingly participated in numerous other crimes long after being given many opportunities to escape from her captors.

In an effort to fill those holes in the chain of reasoning needed for an acquittal based on duress, Bailey decided to bank on the testimony of four mental health experts, two of whom had been part of the court-appointed team that examined Hearst regarding her competence to stand trial. As part of Bailey's strategy, these doctors would essentially testify that Patricia Hearst had been brainwashed by the SLA and that this form of coercive persuasion explained why the young kidnap victim had, in effect, joined the SLA and become an accomplice to their crimes. Faced with what might best be called a quasi-psychiatric defense, prosecutors hired their own team of psychiatrists to examine Hearst and in all likelihood testify against her claim of brainwashing or coercive persuasion.

The decision to forego a traditional psychiatric defense in favor of a non-psychiatric defense supported in large measure by psychiatric testimony was well calculated but risky. It was a strategic move that appeared to backfire in the end, perhaps because it was not well executed and because it opened doors for highly damaging testimony by the prosecution experts that otherwise probably would not have been allowed.

The first expert to testify for the defense was Dr. Louis Joloyn West, Professor and Chairman of Psychiatry at UCLA and a national authority on coercive persuasion. For decades West had studied the behavior and adjustment of repatriated prisoners of war. At Bailey's suggestion, he had been one of the four doctors initially appointed by the court to examine Hearst. After describing in great detail the psychological and psychiatric literature on coercive persuasion, often referred to in the vernacular as brainwashing, West detailed the clinical results of his examinations of Hearst as well as the results of the psychological tests administered by Dr. Margaret Singer, a renowned clinical psychologist and member of the court-appointed team of examiners.

West then likened Hearst to the many prisoners of war he had studied and concluded that hers was a "pretty classical example actually of what we would call coercive persuasion."[27] As West then explained:

> She was persuaded to take on a certain role and she complied with everything they told her to do. If they wanted her to clean a shotgun, she cleaned a shotgun. And if she took part with the group, she just tried to blend in with the others and behave in a fashion that she understood was expected if she was to be accepted. For her, it was to be accepted or to be killed. . . . Cinque [the SLA's leader] had told her at one point, you know, you're free to leave. You don't have to stay with us. But at this point she was already convinced from things he had told her previously that he didn't intend to let her leave and that if she elected to leave, it would mean that she hadn't truly joined and therefore they'd kill her. So, she passed this test by saying I'll stay. For her it wasn't a decision between staying and leaving. For her it was a decision between living and dying. . . . Now she still wasn't sure that they really accepted her and so she thought that in the bank, that one way or another she was going to get killed. She thought that they were going to kill her in the bank unless she did exactly what they wanted and she was so paralyzed with fear that she didn't even do everything they wanted. But she did enough to suit them.[28]

Not surprisingly, at this point the prosecutor raised an understated, accurate and compelling objection:

> Excuse me, your honor. I am going to object at this point. . . .
> It's unclear whether the doctor is arguing the case to the jury or whether or not he is making a psychiatric evaluation. The larger portion of his testimony is that he believes the defendant and he is arguing the facts in the case. I don't believe we have had any psychiatric testimony yet, and I object on those grounds.[29]

Even under the liberal standards of expert testimony then governing the federal courts, the prosecutor was clearly correct. West was not giving an expert opinion but a closing argument for the defense.

While the judge allowed the testimony to stand, he admonished Bailey and West that testimony was to be given in the form of questions and answers rather than lengthy narratives of the sort West was providing. Perhaps the most significant impeachment of West, however, came when, on cross-examination, the prosecutor got him to acknowledge that, prior to being selected as an examiner and potential expert witness in the case—indeed weeks prior to Hearst's arrest—West had written a letter to Hearst's father, Randolph Hearst. The letter suggested that Patricia Hearst might have been brainwashed by her captors and that this might provide "powerful medical and legal arguments . . . for her defense."[30] As one observer of the trial noted, the letter had a "self-serving" and "almost ambulance-chasing" quality about it.[31] At the very least, exposure of this letter certainly further called into question the expert witness's objectivity. The value of West's testimony was also undoubtedly undermined when the prosecutor asked the psychiatrist if he knew who had once said "Perhaps the most insidious domestic threat posed by 'brainwashing' is the tendency of Americans to believe in its power."[32] West immediately acknowledged that those words were his and came from an article he had published in 1963.

The next expert to testify for Hearst was Dr. Martin Orne, a psychologist and psychiatrist at the University of Pennsylvania. Like West, Orne was a practitioner-academic, but unlike his colleague his direct involvement with prisoners of war and the study of brainwashing was limited to being an occasional consultant to the military and guest speaker for an organization of families of POWs and MIAs. Orne's main area of expertise was hypnosis, but he had also testified in the past regarding lie detection and polygraph testing.

Like West, Orne likened Hearst to a prisoner of war. He also went so far as to say that Hearst had been forced to commit the Hibernia Bank robbery. It was, however, in regard to Hearst's truthfulness that Orne's testimony may have been damaging rather than helpful to the young defendant.

On direct examination, Orne was asked by Bailey whether he had made "efforts to determine for yourself whether anybody had been assisting her in concocting a story that would be helpful."[33] Orne replied, "I was concerned about that, but I didn't ask her. Instead, I tried to use the kind of procedures which we found effective in some of our laboratory studies and that is to try to, in an interview, imply subtly what might be good answers which, typically, somebody trying to play a role would pick up on because they would make sense."[34] Based upon his use of these procedures, Orne testified, he had concluded that "Miss Hearst really simply didn't lie."[35]

Orne's pronouncement regarding Hearst's veracity brought an immediate objection from the prosecutor, which led the judge to give the jury a special instruction:

> The witness has made an assertion that the defendant was telling the truth. Now, the objection is that that invades your province of determining the facts, and I am now instructing you, ladies and gentlemen, that it is your duty to determine the facts, not from what this witness says, but from what you know about the facts. You may take into consideration this witness' reasons that she may or may not be telling the truth, but you are not bound by them . . . you and you alone have to make this ultimate decision and no psychiatrist, no judge, no lawyer or no one else should invade that province. [36]

On cross-examination, Orne ran into further trouble when the prosecutor asked about his testimony in another case three years earlier. The prosecutor asked Orne whether he recalled testifying that "Psychiatrists are not very good at telling the truth . . . recognizing the truth."[37] Orne acknowledged that he did recall so testifying. Confronted further, Orne did his best to put a favorable gloss on the quote, at least as regarded his evaluation of Hearst:

> What I'm trying to explain is in terms of specific lies, specific truths, that is not what a psychiatrist is trained to examine. And I would not choose to testify as a psychiatrist on someone's truthfulness on an item, or two, or three specific items. The issue here, which I am concerned with, is whether somebody was simulating a whole role, whether there was a consistent personality, or whether somebody didn't have this personality. Now, to do that, psychiatrists have some skills.[38]

Finally, Orne probably further undermined his own credibility when he acknowledged on cross-examination that while the government may have had information regarding Hearst's case that might have assisted him in his analysis, he failed to seek such information because "I was really quite outraged by what had happened with the [prosecution experts'] examination of Miss Hearst and I did not feel I wanted to contact the Government."[39]

The final expert to testify on Hearst's behalf was Dr. Robert Jay Lifton, a professor of psychiatry at Yale and a renowned authority on communist thought reform, psychohistory, and the psychological impact of mass disasters. Lifton testified that Hearst had been coerced, not converted, by the SLA but he admitted on cross-examination that he reached this conclusion prior to examining the evidence and documents in the case, including the bank robbery films and the lengthy "communiqué" in which Heart identified herself as Tania.[40]

Having given notice that he would be presenting a defense of duress based in part upon the expert testimony of mental health experts, F. Lee Bailey opened the door to having Hearst examined by experts hired by the prosecution. Had these experts agreed that Hearst had acted under duress or coercion when she helped rob the Hibernia Bank, her acquittal would have been all but assured because the prosecutors would have been legally obligated to make such exculpatory findings known to the defense.

Not surprisingly, the prosecution had no such problem. Both of the experts selected by the government—neither of whom was an expert on brainwashing or coercive persuasion—concluded that Hearst had not been acting under duress or coercion at the time of the robbery.

Dr. Joel Fort, the prosecution's first expert called to rebut the testimony of Drs. West, Orne, and Lifton, was a physician, lecturer, and consultant but not a psychiatrist, although he had given expert psychiatric testimony in over two hundred criminal cases (including the cases of Timothy Leary and Lenny Bruce) in twenty-two states. Fort held himself out as an expert in a number of fields, including public health, criminology, drug abuse, and the legal system.

Fort painted Hearst as a willing convert to the SLA, even going so far as to intimate that her sexual relations with two SLA members were consensual. Describing her pre-kidnapping personality, Fort explained in a rambling and disjointed sentence why he felt Hearst had been drawn into the terrorist group:

> She was a strong, willful, independent person, bored, dissatisfied, in poor contact with her family, disliking them to some extent, dissatisfied with Steven Weed [her fiancé] with whom she had been about three years at the time of the kidnapping, and the interaction of that, that kind of vacuum, of something missing, a missing excitement, a missing sense of meaning or purpose in life with what seemed on the surface to be offered by the SLAers as she got to know them and as she became impressed, as she describes in the Tania interview, with her commitment, and as she described to me being impressed with their willingness to die for their beliefs, I think that action was very important to her.[41]

In the guise of explaining why he felt Hearst suffered no mental illness, Fort also managed to tell the jury his views of Hearst's actions at the Los Angeles sporting goods store, a month after the bank robbery for which she was then standing trial:

> I gather a picture of the defendant sitting alone in a van outside the sporting goods store for some period of time, while the Harrises are inside, reading a newspaper. And upon finding that the Harrises are in the process of being arrested outside the sporting goods store, putting down the newspaper, and picking up a gun, and shooting in order to rescue them, and then driving away with them after they joined her in the car. To carry out those complex acts [and] not having taken any opportunity—the obvious opportunity to walk away from the van or drive away with it to be free. . . . Putting all that together, I would say it points in the opposite direction of having any kind of mental illness, and also in the opposite direction of being under any kind of duress.[42]

Though Fort's testimony was rambling and at times probably difficult for jurors to follow, it clearly dealt a serious blow to Hearst's defense. Bailey's cross-examination of the physician was merciless and scored too many points to mention. Among the highlights, he got Fort to admit that he had never published anything dealing with brainwashing, coercive persuasion, attitude change, or kidnapping; that he had approached Hearst's parents before the trial and asked them to settle the case and not go forward with the proceeding; and that as a supposedly impartial expert he had billed the prosecution for consulting on strategy.

In his closing statement, Bailey even went so far as to brand Fort a "liar" and to tell the jury that he felt it was his duty "as a service to human decency . . . to cut his legs off so that he never disgraced an American courtroom again."[43] In the final analysis, however, it can hardly be denied that Fort's testimony, flawed though it may have been, was devastating to Hearst's defense.

But the prosecution did not stop with Fort. The government also presented the testimony of Dr. Harry Kozol, a psychiatrist who had dropped out of Harvard Law School before graduating from the university's school of medicine. Kozol, then director of the Massachusetts state hospital for dangerous sex offenders, described himself as a "general practitioner in psychiatry."[44] By way of establishing his bona fides as an expert in the Hearst prosecution, he mentioned in passing that over the course of his lengthy career he had interviewed a number of prisoners of war and concentration camp survivors who had immigrated to the United States.

Kozol gave perhaps the clearest and most concise testimony of any of the experts in the Hearst case. In response to questioning from the prosecutor as to whether Hearst voluntarily helped rob the bank, the psychiatrist told the jury flat out that "I think she entered that bank voluntarily in order to participate in the robbing of that bank. This was an act of her own free will."[45] Kozol added that, in his view, Hearst had voluntarily joined the SLA "some weeks before" the robbery. For what it was worth, given his limited experience in the field, Kozol also testified that he had never known, heard, or read of any prisoners of war who had "committed any violent acts against his or her former comrades at the behest of the captors."[46]

Bailey vigorously cross-examined Kozol but the Massachusetts psychiatrist provided nowhere near the kind of inviting target Dr. Fort had. To the extent that Bailey succeeded in impeaching the credibility of Kozol, he did so by reference to statements Bailey claimed Kozol had made about the Hearst family after Patricia Hearst was kidnapped but before Kozol became involved in the case. During cross-examination, Kozol denied Bailey's charge that the psychiatrist had once stated to a psychologist that "The Hearsts are disgusting and venal" and that "Mrs. Hearst [Patricia's mother] is a whore."[47]

In rebuttal, Bailey produced the psychologist in question, Dr. Nicholas Groth, who had no other involvement in the Hearst case. Groth, whom Kozol had once attempted to fire, testified that Kozol had not only branded the Hearsts "venal and disgusting people" and referred to Catherine Hearst as "a whore" but had told Groth that "if you had grown up in a family like Patricia, you would understand what she is rebelling against. They are pigs."[48]

After deliberating less than a day, the jury convicted Patricia Hearst and she was sentenced to seven years in prison. The Los Angeles charges against Hearst were dropped in exchange for her cooperation with prosecutors against other SLA members, and her prison sentence was commuted by President Jimmy Carter after she had served just twenty-two months. The White House press announcement of the commutation made it clear that President Carter accepted the defense that the prosecution experts and the jury had rejected:

> It is the consensus of all of those most familiar with this case that
> but for the extraordinary criminal and degrading experiences that
> [Hearst] suffered as a victim of the SLA she would not have become
> a participant in the criminal acts for which she stands convicted and
> sentenced and would not have suffered the punishment and other
> consequences she has endured.[49]

Finally, twenty-two years later, Hearst received a full pardon from President Bill Clinton as he was about to leave office in 2001.

Although the trial testimony of Drs. West, Orne, and Lifton may have helped make Hearst's case for commutation and eventual pardon, her ultimate assessment of the trial, especially the role played by the mental health experts, was harsh:

> Each time any of the expert witnesses gave their opinion, the judge would remind the jury that it was only an opinion and it was for the jury alone to decide the key issue of my intent. It would be up to the jury to believe Drs. West, Orne and Lifton . . . who concluded that I was a victim, not a criminal, or to believe Drs. Fort and Kozol, who interviewed the same defendant, read the same psychological reports, and reached exactly the opposite conclusion.
>
> In my estimation, the whole trial was a farce.[50]

While the Hearst trial was without question a spectacle and certainly not one of the prouder moments for psychology and psychiatry in the courtroom, the expert testimony in the case, though flawed and inconsistent, may have helped the legal system ultimately achieve at least a roughly just outcome for society and Patricia Hearst. Taken as whole, the expert testimony could be seen, and probably was seen by the jury, as indicating that Patricia Hearst was both a victim and a criminal and that her acts, though perhaps understandable and attributable to her victimization, were nevertheless not entirely excusable.

4

THE

GUILDFORD

FOUR

"You Did It, So Why

Not Confess?"

◢

One of the most controversial issues raised in the wake of the terrorist attacks of September 11, 2001, was whether terrorists should ever
be tortured to obtain information about future attacks. The "ticking time
bomb scenario" is characterized as a hypothetical problem involving a terrorist possessing direct knowledge about the location and detonation time of a
bomb that could kill thousands of individuals. This ethical and moral problem
is often used in discussions about how to deal with terrorism. The "ticking
time bomb" question is meant to challenge people to think how far measures
should go in order to save innocent lives.[1] Scholars continue to debate the
moral, ethical, and legal implications of difficult problems that we now face in
our efforts to defeat terrorism.[2] If the loss of innocent lives could be prevented
by obtaining information through physical torture, could the practice ever be
legally, ethically, and morally justified?

The legal issues involved in the interrogation of criminal suspects have
long been of concern to counterterrorism experts. Although the prospect of
torturing terrorist suspects is extreme, an equally challenging question, and
more common concern, is: "Would a terrorist suspect confess to committing
an act of violence that he or she did not commit?" Most people assume that a
person would never confess to a crime that he or she did not commit. But real-
life experiences indicate that this belief is wrong, since there are several legal
cases where individuals have, in fact, confessed to a crime they did not com-

mit. Several high-profile cases, such as the Central Park Jogger case, involved suspects who were convicted on the basis of a confession but later exonerated when new evidence was uncovered of actual innocence.

The criminal justice system in Great Britain is one that bears many similarities to the United States system and provides us with one of the most infamous cases of wrongful conviction and a gross miscarriage of justice based on false confessions in an investigation into terrorist violence. Throughout the twentieth century, Great Britain had waged its own "war on terrorism" against the Irish Republican Army (IRA). Since the signing of the Anglo-Irish treaty in 1921 that partitioned Ireland into the twenty-six independent southern counties and the six counties of Northern Ireland under British control, the IRA has been responsible for numerous bombings and other acts of terror aimed at trying to unify the country into a single, thirty-two-county Republic of Ireland.[3] For decades, the terrorist violence waxed and waned. However, in the 1970s the IRA began a bombing campaign that saw the violence move from concentrated attacks in the northern counties of Ireland to England in an effort to force the British to confront the problem of Irish independence.

On October 5, 1974, the IRA bombed two pubs in Guildford, England. Both of the pubs were popular with members of the British military and therefore the IRA viewed them as prime targets. The first of these attacks occurred at 8:30 P.M. when an explosion ripped through the Horse and Groom pub without any warning.[4] Five people died in the attack, including four members of the British armed forces, and several others were injured. The explosion caused widespread panic. Thus, when the second IRA bomb went off at the Seven Stars pub in Guildford about an hour later, no one was injured because evacuations were initiated immediately after the Horse and Groom bombing.

At 10:00 on the evening of November 7, 1974, another IRA bomb exploded at the King's Arms house in South London. Two people died and another 27 people were injured when nuts and bolts packed around two pounds of plastic explosive ripped through the public gathering spot. A week after the King's Arms attack, an IRA operative by the name of James McDade was killed on November 14, when the bomb he was trying to place in a telephone booth in Coventry, England, accidentally detonated.[5] The IRA was so angered by the failure of their mission that they perpetrated their most serious attack. On November 21, two bombs exploded at a pair of pubs in the city of Birmingham, England. One at the Tavern in the Town pub killed eleven people and the other at the Mulberry Bush pub killed ten. Another 161 people were injured, many seriously, in these two attacks.[6]

As commonly occurs in the wake of terrorist attacks, the widespread fear among citizens of England quickly turned to outrage. There were acts of retaliation against the Irish community, including attacks on a Catholic school and pub, and fights broke out between British and Irish workers at an automobile plant. However, the anti-Irish sentiments in Great Britain soon prompted a formal legal response. In a rapid legislative effort, similar to passage of the U.S. Patriot Act that followed in the wake of the September 11 attacks, a bill known as the Prevention of Terrorism Act passed through both houses of British Parliament in less than twenty-four hours. By November 29, just eight days after the Birmingham bombings, the Prevention of Terrorism Act was in full effect. Provisions of the law granted sweeping powers to law enforcement officers:

> The [Prevention of Terrorism Act] made membership of and support for the IRA an offense. It also introduced exclusion orders which gave the British government powers to restrict the movements of designated citizens within its own borders. Additionally, the police were empowered to arrest without warrant anyone they reasonably suspected of being concerned in terrorism, but against whom they had not assembled sufficient evidence in regard to a specific offense. Police could detain someone arrested under this provision for forty-eight hours; but the Home Secretary could permit an extension of the detention for a further five days. [7]

With such broad powers being granted to law enforcement officials, concerns about possible abuses of civil liberties and the targeting of innocent individuals were raised. And, in fact, the investigation into the bombings soon led to arrests and a legal case that would span decades and result in what is often viewed as one of the greatest miscarriages of justice in recent history.

An Irishman named Paul Hill became the first person arrested under the provisions of the newly enacted Prevention of Terrorism Act. Given that the legislation granted law enforcement officials a large measure of secrecy in their efforts to combat terrorism, police officers were only required to admit vaguely that their interest in Hill was based on information they had received. However, the reason police focused their attention on Hill was the fact that he had apparently been present at a Belfast, North Ireland pub on July 20, 1974, when a former British soldier named Brian Shaw had been abducted by the IRA and executed. [8]

Hill would later claim that police officers used a number of tactics to intimidate and brutalize him during their questioning. While being transferred from one police station to another, for example, officers drove Hill past the Horse and Groom pub and told him they knew he had blown it up. Hill also claimed that he was physically beaten, had a gun held to his head during the interrogation, and was told that his girlfriend—who was pregnant with Hill's child at the time—would be harmed.

After being interrogated for nearly twenty-four hours, Hill provided a full written confession to the Guildford bombings. In his statement to police, he also implicated one of his friends named Gerry Conlon. Two days after Hill's arrest and interrogation, Conlon was arrested and questioned by police. He was also subjected to the same kind of interrogation as Hill over a period of two days. Conlon was threatened, intimidated, and warned that his father would be arrested if he did not cooperate.

The information police obtained from the interrogation of Hill and Conlon provided them with a lengthy roster of friends and relatives who were purportedly involved in the IRA and terrorist activities. Hill and Conlon each gave police officers an address where bomb-making activities were supposed to have occurred. However, the subsequent investigation revealed that neither location contained any evidence of illicit activity. The address Conlon provided was where his aunt, Annie Maguire, lived and even though no evidence of bomb-related materials were found at the address, several of Conlon's family members were detained and questioned.

Conlon's interrogation yielded the names of two people who were supposed to have been involved in the Guildford bombings: Paddy Armstrong and his seventeen-year-old girlfriend Carole Richardson.[9] Approximately three days after Conlon confessed, Richardson and Armstrong were arrested and within forty-eight hours they also admitted to being involved in the bombings. All four suspects—Hill, Conlon, Armstrong, and Richardson—came to be known as the Guildford Four after the name of the town where the first bombing occurred.

Several other individuals were arrested in connection with the case, including four who were implicated in the Guildford bombings as a result of Conlon's coercive interrogation. Conlon's aunt, Annie Maguire, John McGuiness, Brian Anderson, and Paul Colman were charged with possessing explosives but none of these individuals admitted any involvement with either the Guildford bombings or IRA activities. In fact, Maguire had an airtight alibi for the evening of October 5: she had attended a birthday party for one of her neighbor's children. Moreover, despite the fact that police had charged Maguire, McGuiness, Anderson, and Colman with possession of bombing materials, there was no physical evidence uncovered in any of their homes. Macguire was subjected to intensive and coercive questioning by police but never provided any incriminating statements. She was held for several months before all criminal charges against her, McGuiness, Anderson, and Colman were dismissed due to a lack of evidence.

On the other hand, Hill, Conlon, Armstrong, and Richardson were tried in September 1975 for their admitted involvement. At their trial, the prosecution alleged that all four were members of the IRA, yet no evidence was ever introduced that proved they were members of the terrorist group. The primary evidence against each of them was their confessions and, as research has shown, confession evidence is given the greatest weight by juries. Although other forms of evidence are weighed heavily by juries as proof of a person's guilt—including eyewitness testimony and physical evidence linking a defendant to the scene of the crime—it is confession evidence that juries view as the greatest indication of a person's guilt. After all, who would confess to a crime that he or she did not commit?

The Guildford Four challenged the admissibility and reliability of their confessions. They had each been denied access to an attorney during their questioning by police, a practice that was permissible under the recently acted Prevention of Terrorism Act. Moreover, each of the defendants provided strong alibi witnesses who testified that they were nowhere near the bombings at the time they occurred.

Richardson had one of the strongest alibis; there was photographic evidence showing she had been at a concert nearly forty miles away on the evening of the first two bombings. Several eyewitnesses to the bombing at the Horse and Groom, which Richardson was alleged to have helped commit, failed to identify her from a police line-up.[10] To make matters worse, a witness for the defense attested to the fact that Richardson was nowhere near the Guildford pub on the evening of the bombing. Frank Johnson, a friend of Richardson, went to police before trial and told them they had the wrong person because Richardson had been with him. Instead of creating doubt in the minds of police officers investigating Richardson, Johnson found himself intimidated and threatened with possible prosecution. He later claimed that police officers had detained him on a couple of different occasions for questioning, had hinted that he had bomb residue on his hands, and had threatened to push him out of a window, shoot him, and set his handicapped mother on fire. He was ultimately coerced into providing a statement that Richardson's alibi had been something they concocted together. Finally, Johnson said that when he was eventually released by the police they threatened to charge him with obstructing justice if he ended up testifying at Richardson's trial.[11] Nevertheless, at trial he resorted to his original claim that Richardson was with him and nowhere near Guildford at the time of the bombings. However, the prosecution argued that Richardson still had enough time to leave the concert and travel to Guildford in order to set off the first bomb.

Hill, Conlon, and Armstrong also presented evidence of an alibi at trial. Conlon said he had been at a lodge in London and provided the names of the people who could vouch for his whereabouts.[12] Even though police officers had a statement from a witness who confirmed Conlon's alibi, they never turned it over to the defense. Armstrong also provided names of witnesses who could vouch that he was elsewhere at the time of the Guildford bombings, but police could verify only some of the details. Finally, Hill claimed that he was in Southampton, England, with his girlfriend at the time of the bombings, but he withdrew his claim during questioning by police. Although there was a witness who could apparently verify Hill's alibi, the person was never called to testify.[13]

In all, there were over one hundred inconsistencies between the confessions of Hill, Conlon, Armstrong, and Richardson, and the manner in which the bombings were said by the prosecution to have taken place. For example, forensic evidence showed that the individuals responsible for the first bombing in Guildford on October 5 did not have enough time to plant the second bomb that was detonated almost a half-hour later on the same evening. Also, Richardson said in her confession that she had thrown one of the bombs, even though the prosecution argued that the bombs were planted.[14] In addition, Conlon had implicated McGuiness, Anderson, Colman, and his aunt Annie Maguire in his confession. Yet, police dropped the charges against these four alleged accomplices, suggesting that details of Conlon's confession could not be proven by physical evidence. Moreover, none of the confessions provided by the Guildford Four contained any information or details about the bombings that were unknown to the police. In short, it was quite possible that the police merely fed details of the bombings to each of the suspects as they were interrogated to make the confessions look authentic.

During the trial, Armstrong was given a sodium amytal interview at the request of his attorney under the presumption that Armstrong would be more likely to tell the truth about the circumstances surrounding his interrogation by police.[15] A psychiatrist from the London Hospital administered the interview one evening after trial proceedings had ended for the day. The results of this interview indicated that Armstrong had been coerced into confessing. The use of a drug-assisted interview was apparently intended to help Armstrong's attorney garner more faith in his client's claim that he had been coerced into making a false confession. However, the validity of drug-assisted interviews is questionable because various factors can influence the results, including increased suggestibility of the subject and the possibility that the person can make up details in their altered state of awareness.[16] Therefore, the results of Armstrong's drug-assisted interview played no significant role in his defense at trial.

Despite numerous inconsistencies in the confessions of the Guildford Four and the many alibi witnesses who testified on behalf of the defendants, Hill, Conlon, Armstrong, and Richardson were all convicted of murder and conspiracy charges after the jury deliberated for twenty-seven hours. Since there was no death penalty in Great Britain, none of the Guildford Four could be sentenced to death. Although all four received a life sentence, under British law the presiding judge recommended a minimum term that each convicted terrorist would have to serve before becoming eligible for parole. Conlon received a recommended sentence of thirty years to life and Armstrong was sentenced to thirty-five years to life. Due to her age, Richardson would have to serve at least twenty years before she would be eligible for parole. However, Judge Donaldson made it clear during his sentencing of Conlon, Armstrong, and Richardson that the minimum term was not meant to imply that the three would ever be released from prison. The lower terms were only intended as an absolute minimum term in prison. He told the three that they might never be released.[17]

Judge Donaldson saved his harshest words for Hill, who received a life sentence without the possibility of parole because he was implicated in the third bombing. The judge said at sentencing that the only hope Hill might ever have of being released from prison was if he were extremely old or sick and near death. The sentences received by the Guildford Four were purported to be the longest ever in the history of the modern British courts.[18]

Believing an injustice had been done, several groups started to fight for the release of the Guildford Four as they began serving their sentences. Meanwhile, in December of 1975, four IRA members were arrested following a high-speed car chase through the streets of London that ended with a police raid at a house on Balcombe Street in Marylebone. The four IRA suspects, who came to be known as the Balcombe Street four, were captured. Three of the suspects—Joseph O'Connell, Eddie Butler, and Harry Duggan—implicated another IRA suspect, Brendan Dowd, who was already in custody on another charge.[19] O'Connell and Dowd confessed to the Guildford bombings and informed police that Armstrong, Conlon, Hill, and Richardson had nothing to do with the IRA or the bombings.

Although this new evidence was presented at an appeal for the Guildford Four, their convictions were upheld. As part of his preparation for the appeal, Armstrong's lawyer hired Dr. Lionel Haward, a psychologist and professor at the University of Surrey in Guildford, to provide a hypnotically assisted interview in October 1977 to learn more about the terrorist bombings and Armstrong's police interrogation in 1974.[20] Once again, the interview indicated that Armstrong had confessed because of the intense anxiety and fear that he experienced in response to pressure put on him by the police during his interrogation. Nevertheless, the sparse experimental evidence supporting the validity of hypnosis as an interview aid, as well as the fact that many courts do not allow hypnotically facilitated testimony to be admitted in court, contributed to this new piece of forensic psychological evidence having limited impact on the success of Armstrong's appeal.

Ongoing efforts to free the Guildford Four continued over the next several years, but it was not until 1986 that additional forensic psychological evidence was produced. In April of that year, two well-known forensic psychologists who are experts on disputed confessions, Drs. Gisli Gudjonsson and James MacKeith, examined Carole Richardson at the request of the medical service at the prison where she was being held.[21] One of the physicians at the prison was apparently concerned that Richardson might have been wrongly convicted on the basis of a false confession. One of the crucial issues that arose during this examination was the effect that certain medications Richardson was taking had on her mental state during her interrogation in 1974.

The results of the examination by these two noted forensic psychologists revealed that Richardson was vulnerable to interrogative pressure and that she was prone to avoid conflict and please others when faced with social pressure. Richardson's mental state at the time of Dr. Gudjonsson's and Dr. MacKeith's evaluation was found to be "impressive,"[22] but one of the things that concerned the psychologists was Richardson's mental state in 1974 when she was going through drug withdrawal while being questioned by police. During their questioning of the convicted Guildford bomber, Gudjonsson and MacKeith asked difficult and challenging questions that were intended to uncover evidence of lying or inconsistencies. However, the examiners noted that Richardson was "spontaneous" and "unguarded" in her answers to their questions.[23] Both experts expressed doubts about the reliability of Richardson's confession to the Guildford bombings.

More specifically, a review of Richardson's confession revealed that she had been in the custody of police for several days and was subjected to repeated questioning. For several months leading up to her arrest, Richardson had been abusing various drugs and she claimed that just prior to being taken into police custody she had taken twenty capsules of a barbiturate that she had been using. When questioning began by the police, Richardson was almost certainly undergoing physiological and psychological withdrawal from the drug. As result, she was often confused, had difficulty remembering, and experienced heightened distress during questioning. During the first three days of her detainment, Richardson was apparently focused on securing her release but she found the police pressure difficult to resist. Although she initially denied any recollection of being involved with the bombings, over a period of several days she came to actually believe she was involved and was blocking out the details from her memory.

Gudjonsson and MacKeith defined this process as "memory distrust syndrome," where an individual comes to have little faith in his or her memory for a crime and succumbs to police pressure by internalizing, or believing, that he or she committed the crime despite having no recollection of the details.[24] This process leads to a form of false confession that occurs when a suggestible person is influenced by coercion exerted during intense police questioning. Although Richardson reported that she had been hit by a woman police officer during questioning and came to realize that her interrogators were in full control of her, she apparently realized that her only hope was to go agree with whatever the police wanted her to say. However, Gudjonsson and MacKeith also observed that the mental and physical effects of drug withdrawal, accompanied by the stress of the interrogation and the long period of time she was subjected to intense questioning, contributed to Richardson internalizing the belief that perhaps she had, indeed, committed the bombings. Once the police had their confession from Richardson and the interrogative pressures relaxed, Richardson's confidence about her innocence returned.[25]

The case of the Guildford Four was re-opened in 1988. An intensive review of the case revealed more than just the possibility that all four defendants had falsely confessed to the bombings. In October of 1989, an appeals court ruled that police had lied and fabricated evidence during the original investigation.[26] A criminal investigation was undertaken into the behavior of five police officers who had originally worked on the Guildford bombing case. Fourteen years had passed since the Guildford Four had been convicted and only two of the five police officers under question were still on active duty. Both of the officers were placed on suspension following the announcement of the appellate court.

In addition, new evidence came to light that the prosecution had failed to disclose the fact that a witness had been identified who could corroborate Conlon's alibi. As a result of the appellate court's ruling, the convictions of the Guildford Four were all overturned. Conlon, Armstrong, and Richardson were released from prison immediately following the announcement by the appellate court.[27] Hill had to remain in prison while he awaited the appeal of his conviction in the murder of Brian Shaw, the former British soldier whose murder in Northern Ireland years earlier had led police to suspect Hill of the

Guildford bombings in the first place. In 1994, Hill was cleared of any involvement in Shaw's murder and he was released from prison.[28]

Since the Guildford Four were released after an appellate court reviewed their case and ordered their convictions overturned, there was no new trial at which formal evidence was presented to prove their confessions were all false. Still, the subsequent evaluation of Richardson by Gudjonsson and MacKeith, and the detailed explanation of how Richardson was affected psychologically by the intense police questioning, provides an explanation of how coercive interrogation techniques, unique psychological vulnerabilities in a criminal suspect, and police officers who are unwilling to consider any possibilities other than a given suspect's guilt can lead people to confess to a crime they did not commit. It happened not once but four times in the case of the Guildford bombings.

The case is one of the most infamous occurrences of wrongful conviction based on a false confession and was one of the worst miscarriages of justice in recent history. The 1994 film *In the Name of the Father*, starring Daniel Day-Lewis, dramatized the plight of the Guildford Four, particularly the story of Conlon who watched his father die in prison during his fifteen years of wrongful imprisonment. Furthermore, Conlon detailed the "dreadful experience" that he and the others had during their years of incarceration. After his release, Conlon said to the press: "We were sent into a prison which was totally hostile towards us, we were being attacked by prison officers and cons, people urinated in our food, people put glass in our food and then when we came out onto the street there was no care from the government."[29]

Each of the Guildford Four was later given monetary compensation for their ordeal, although it took years for some of them to reach a final settlement. Over twenty years passed before they were able to clear their names, but a formal apology was issued to them by British Prime Minister Tony Blair in June 2000. In his apology, Blair stated: "I believe that it is an indictment of our system of justice and a matter for the greatest regret when anyone suffers punishment as a result of a miscarriage of justice."[30] The Prime Minister sent his letter of apology to Hill's wife, Courtney Kennedy Hill, who is the daughter of the late Robert F. Kennedy.

In looking back on the fact that each of the Guildford Four were coerced into providing a false confession that ultimately led to their conviction, it is interesting to note that there was no other evidence tying the suspects directly to the bombings. Several inconsistencies existed between the confessions and the physical evidence and testimony of several witnesses. The case raises questions about the reliability of confession evidence and supports changes in the way criminal suspects are interrogated and questioned by police. One of the best ways to preserve evidence of confession, and to ensure that police do not use coercive tactics, is to have all interrogations videotaped so a record is preserved of the entire process. Both true and false confessions would benefit from this process. Factors contributing to false confessions could be identified and studied during subsequent court proceedings. Likewise, the validity of accurate confessions would not be undercut by false claims of police coercion or intimidation.

Finally, it is worth reflecting back on the words of Judge Donaldson as he passed sentence on the Guildford Four at the conclusion of their trial. The judge noted that if capital punishment had been available in Great Britain, all four would have received the death penalty and "you would have been executed," the judge told the four convicted bombers.[31] If the death penalty had been in effect and the Guildford Four had been sentenced to death, it is quite possible that the ultimate miscarriage of justice would have been committed: Four innocent individuals would have been executed as a result of having falsely confessed to crimes they did not commit.

5

PROSENJIT
PODDAR
AND TATIANA
TARASOFF

Where the Public

Peril Begins

W hen people go to see a mental health professional for help with personal problems, they expect that whatever is said during the course of
private conversations with a therapist will remain confidential. Privacy and
confidentiality are among the most important ethical principles of professional therapists. Of course the reason is that if people are sure that what they
say in therapy will be confidential, they will be more open and the therapist
can be more helpful.

Nevertheless, complete confidentiality is not possible in most helping
relationships. Certain situations—such as the potential abuse of a child or
when a person poses a risk of harm to themselves or others—require therapists to notify others who can prevent the potential harm. Among the most
unsettling cases for therapists are those that involve a person who is at risk
of harming another person. At one time, these cases were typically managed
by having the person hospitalized—sometimes involuntarily—until effective
treatment could be provided and the danger had passed. In 1976, the California Supreme Court issued a landmark ruling in *Tarasoff v. Regents of the
University of California*[1] that added a new wrinkle to the management of
potentially violent individuals and changed forever the boundaries of confidentiality in psychotherapy. This case also changed the balance between confidentiality in mental health treatment and society's need to protect citizens
from potentially lethal individuals.

Born in Bengal, India, as a member of the "untouchable" Harijan caste, Prosenjit Poddar came to the United States in September 1967 to study naval architecture at the University of California at Berkeley.[2] Although his first year of study apparently went well, his life took a fateful turn in the fall of 1968 when he enrolled in folk dancing classes at the university's International House. While attending the classes, Poddar met an American woman by the name of Tatiana Tarasoff. From the beginning, Poddar was smitten with Tarasoff, and throughout the fall semester they saw each other weekly. On New Year's Eve, Tarasoff kissed Poddar. Although she apparently meant the gesture as a sign of friendship, Poddar took the kiss to mean much more. He believed that Tarasoff intended the kiss to convey deep affection and commitment. When Poddar professed his love for Tarasoff, she told him that she did not feel the same way about him, was not interested in having a committed relationship, and was involved with other men.

Tarasoff's rebuff caused a severe emotional crisis for Poddar.[3] He became extremely depressed, more disheveled in his appearance, withdrawn, and neglectful of his schoolwork. At times, he would speak disjointedly. Poddar and Tarasoff saw each other occasionally through the spring of 1969, yet he was often tearful and could not understand why she did not return his affection. Unbeknownst to Tarasoff, Poddar would secretly tape record their conversations at times in order to study the possible reasons that she did not want a relationship with him.[4] His behavior showed increasing signs of obsession.

When Tarasoff went to study in Brazil for the summer, Poddar's mental status improved slightly and he was encouraged by a friend to seek help at Cowell Memorial Hospital, which was a health care facility affiliated with the University of California at Berkeley.[5] The initial evaluation was conducted by a psychiatrist, Dr. Stuart Gold, who recommended that Poddar begin psychotherapy with a psychologist, Dr. Lawrence Moore.

During a therapy session with Moore on August 18, 1969, Poddar said that he planned to kill Tarasoff when she returned from Brazil. Moore believed that Poddar was serious about his intention to kill the woman; two days later he informed Dr. Gold and the assistant director of the clinic, Dr. Yandell, of his concerns. Both physicians felt that Poddar should be admitted involuntarily to the hospital's psychiatric unit.[6] Moore then called the university police to have Poddar detained and taken to a local hospital. He told officers Atkinson and Teel that Poddar should be taken into custody and brought to the hospital for involuntary commitment.[7] Moreover, in a letter to William Beall, chief of campus police, Moore informed the officers that Poddar suffered from paranoid schizophrenia and was dangerous to others, despite the fact that he could sometimes appear rational.

When campus police approached Poddar and interviewed him, they were of the opinion that he was rational and stable; he even promised to stay away from Tarasoff. Following his encounter with the university police, Poddar no doubt came to distrust Moore and abruptly stopped his therapy. Dr. Harvey Powelson, the director of the clinic where Moore had seen Poddar, learned of the failed attempt to have Poddar committed involuntarily to the hospital. According to several reports of the case, Powelson contacted the university police and asked that they return the letter Moore had sent and also ordered Moore to destroy his therapy notes concerning his contacts with Poddar. Furthermore, Powelson ordered that no further action be taken in Poddar's case.

Harvard law professor and psychiatrist Alan Stone, who has researched the case, claims that Moore's letter to police was not destroyed.[8] Therefore, Stone doubts if Powelson ever ordered Poddar's records to be destroyed. However, one thing is sure. Poddar quit his psychotherapy with Moore and the case proceeded along a path leading to a tragic event.

When Tarasoff returned to campus in the fall of 1969, she was unaware of the threat that Poddar had made during his psychotherapy sessions with Moore. The time away from Tarasoff had apparently done little to diminish Poddar's fixation on the young woman. In fact, Poddar had managed to convince Tarasoff's brother to share an apartment that was only one block from Tatiana's home.[9] On October 27, 1969, Poddar went to Tarasoff's home to speak with her. When she refused, he shot her with a pellet gun. Tarasoff ran from the home, but Poddar chased after her and when he caught her he stabbed her repeatedly. Tarasoff died as a result of her injuries. Immediately after the stabbing, Poddar returned to Tarasoff's home, called the police, and waited for their arrival.

When Poddar was charged with the intentional murder of Tarasoff, he entered a plea of not guilty by reason of insanity.[10] At his trial, Poddar presented the testimony of three physicians and a psychologist who all testified that he suffered from paranoid schizophrenia and as a result was incapable of harboring malice aforethought at the time he killed Tarasoff. One of the experts, Dr. Wilmer Anderson, was a neurologist who testified that various tests, including an electroencephalogram (EEG), showed Poddar to suffer physiological abnormalities in his brain.[11] The prosecution offered the testimony of a court-appointed psychiatrist who was of the opinion that Poddar did not have schizophrenia. The psychiatrist believed that Poddar had a schizoid personality but was capable of forming malice against Tarasoff that would satisfy the requirements of either first or second-degree murder. After hearing all of the evidence and expert testimony, the jury found Poddar to be sane at the time he killed Tarasoff and convicted him of second-degree murder.

However, the California Supreme Court found that the judge presiding over Poddar's trial had made a critical error in the instructions given to the jury. Under California law, Poddar could have been convicted of either first-or second-degree murder if his actions toward Tarasoff were done with express or implied malice. According to the California Supreme Court:

> Malice is properly implied when a killing resulting from an act involving a high degree of probability of death is accompanied by the requisite mental element. The process properly leading to a finding of that element requires three specific determinations. First, was the act or acts done for a base, antisocial purpose? Second, was the accused aware of the duty imposed upon him not to commit acts which involve the risk of grave injury or death? Third, if so, did he act despite that awareness?[12]

The jury in Poddar's criminal case believed that each of these questions were answered in the affirmative—that the stabbing of Tarasoff was done in a mean and antisocial manner, that Poddar was aware of his duty not to shoot and stab Tarasoff, and that he acted despite his awareness of this duty.

However, the presence of diminished mental capacity can negate the express or implied malice element of first- or second-degree murder, resulting in a finding of guilt on a lesser charge of manslaughter. The judge presiding over Poddar's criminal trial gave the jury a general instruction that malice can be negated by a finding of diminished capacity, but he failed to give an explicit instruction to the jury relating the defense of diminished capacity to the implied malice instructions given at Poddar's trial. For this reason, the California Supreme Court held that the instructions given to the jury at Poddar's trial were erroneous and that the oversight was prejudicial to Poddar. As a result, the court overturned Poddar's conviction and a new trial was ordered. For reasons that are not entirely clear, Poddar was never re-tried. Nearly five years had lapsed between the time Tarasoff had been murdered and Poddar was granted a new trial. Rather than attempt to track down witnesses and reconstruct evidence, the state of California released Poddar from custody with the condition that he leave the United States immediately and return to India.[13]

Left with no other recourse to have someone held accountable for their daughter's murder, Vitaly and Lydia Tarasoff, Tatiana's parents, filed a wrongful death suit against the Regents of the University of California, the mental health professionals responsible for Poddar's care, and the university police officers who were asked by Dr. Moore to detain Poddar for involuntary civil commitment to a psychiatric hospital.

The case was groundbreaking in two major respects. First, the issue of a patient's right to confidentiality in psychotherapy was pitted against the need of society to be protected from potentially dangerous individuals. Tarasoff's parents argued that the professionals responsible for Poddar's care should have warned their daughter directly of the threat he had made against her life. Second, the California Supreme Court took the unusual step of re-deciding the case in 1976 after it was first decided in 1974. It is unclear why the court felt the need to issue a revised opinion in *Tarasoff*, but "the volume of concern and controversy stirred up by the first decision undoubtedly produced some rethinking and consideration" by the California Supreme Court that led to the second *Tarasoff* decision that has become the standard reference in the case.[14]

A comparison of the 1974 and 1976 *Tarasoff* decisions provides a useful context for understanding the far-reaching implications of the case. The second published *Tarasoff* decision makes no reference to the first decision.[15] Although the California Supreme Court held in the first *Tarasoff* decision that liability could be attributed to the campus police officers for not warning Tatiana Tarasoff of the threat against her life, the second decision freed the campus police from liability.[16] Finally, the first *Tarasoff* decision held that the doctors who took care of Poddar had a duty to warn Tarasoff of the potential harm he posed, but the second decision revised this "duty to warn" into a more general "duty to protect" that could include warning as one of many alternatives to satisfying the duty.

The key holding in the final *Tarasoff* decision was the conclusion by the California Supreme Court that Mr. and Mrs. Tarasoff could bring a civil cause of action against Drs. Moore, Gold, and Powelson for negligent failure to protect Tatiana from Poddar. The basis of this potential liability was the fact that a special relationship existed between Poddar and his treating therapists. When such a special relationship exists, like that between a patient and a therapist, the law imposes on the therapist "a duty to exercise reasonable care to protect a potential victim of another's conduct."[17] The court found that a special relationship existed between Poddar and each of the defendants; Dr. Moore was the treating therapist, Dr. Powelson supervised the therapy, Dr. Gold personally examined Poddar, and Dr. Yandell had approved Moore's decision to contact campus police and initiate commitment procedures against Poddar.

One of the most controversial aspects of the *Tarasoff* decision, however, was the manner in which the California Supreme Court arrived at the conclusion that the therapists treating Poddar could have—and perhaps should have—contacted Tatiana Tarasoff directly and informed her of the threat that Poddar had made during the course of his psychotherapy with Dr. Moore. After all, Moore had taken reasonable steps that any conscientious clinician would have taken to ensure the safety of others. He consulted with colleagues who were familiar with Poddar's case, obtained consensus agreement that commitment proceedings should be initiated, and contacted law enforcement officers to have Poddar detained and hospitalized. The defendant therapists in the case could argue that it was the campus police officers' willingness to let Poddar go, and not their actions, that resulted in harm being brought to Tarasoff.

The California Supreme Court relied heavily on a law review article written by John G. Fleming and Bruce Maximov to support the notion that "by entering into a doctor-patient relationship the therapist becomes sufficiently involved to assume some responsibility for the safety, not only of the patient himself, but also of any third person whom the doctor knows to be threatened by the patient."[18] The law review article was published while the *Tarasoff* case was on appeal, yet Justice Matthew Tobriner, who wrote both of the *Tarasoff* decisions, drew heavily from the article in supporting the groundbreaking ruling that psychotherapists may have a legal duty to warn victims directly of threats that are made within the context of a confidential therapeutic setting.

Law professor Alan Stone has argued that the Fleming and Maximov article is based on legal arguments and conclusions that "rely heavily" on the views of psychiatric critics such as Dr. Thomas Szasz and others who believe that mental illness is a mythological concept used to control people.[19] Vocal opponents of the psychiatric profession claim that such practices as involuntary hospitalization and forced medication violate basic liberties and should be abolished. Fleming and Maximov recognize that "confidentiality plays an important role in psychotherapy" and that people who enter into a therapeutic relationship may reasonably expect that what they say to a therapist will remain confidential.[20] However, Fleming and Maximov also observed that the patient's right to confidentiality may sometimes come into conflict with the therapist's duty to protect third parties. Although one way that therapists can protect others is to have a potentially dangerous individual admitted involuntarily to a hospital, which is what Moore attempted to do with Poddar, Fleming and Maximov do not appear to favor involuntary hospitalization as a means of protecting society. In fact, their disdain for restricting the liberty of psychiatric patients is evident in their law review article:

> Whereas public exposure is involved in threats to patient's privacy, certain other . . . interests may suffer whether or not there is disclosure. Most prominent is his interest in personal liberty which is at

stake in any commitment proceeding, whether it ever reaches the public ear or not.

The impact of commitment—both psychological and practical—inevitably is drastic. Persons detained in mental institutions must often endure long-term separation from their families, friends, and jobs. These effects are considerable. . . .

Emergency commitment statutes illustrate these threats to the individual's liberty.[21]

It is not surprising, then, that someone adopting Fleming and Maximov's reasoning would favor a way of protecting third parties from danger that relied on a method other than hospitalizing the potentially dangerous individual. The most obvious alternative would be to notify the victim or police.

Professor Stone finds it unfortunate that the law review article written by Fleming and Maximov was cited extensively throughout the *Tarasoff* opinions. One of the greatest concerns raised in the wake of the California Supreme Court's ruling was the chilling effect that case would have on psychotherapy. If people entering therapy are told that any threats made during the course of their treatment might be disclosed not only to police but also the victim, then there might well be a drastic reduction in the number of people with violent thoughts or fantasies who would be willing to seek help from a therapist. Stone argued that limiting the scope of confidentiality as outlined in *Tarasoff* could very well have the opposite effect of reducing public safety by keeping potentially violent individuals away from treatment:

> The primary inadequacy of the court's holding is not that it does not give serious thought to protecting the public, but rather that the duty it would impose is self-defeating, increasing, rather than reducing, the overall risk. It is highly disruptive of the patient-therapist relationship and a less appropriate way of protecting those threatened by dangerous patients than the traditional alternatives of commitment or simply informing the police.[22]

These concerns about people being deterred from seeking therapy were outlined in a dissenting opinion in the *Tarasoff* decision by Justice Clark. The guarantee of confidentiality was seen by Justice Clark as necessary for allowing patients in therapy to be open about themselves, which would lead to more effective treatment. Without this guarantee of privacy, some people who needed treatment would avoid it and pose an increased risk of harm to others.

In the final decision, Justice Tobriner outlined the generalized duty to protect:

> In our view, however, once a therapist does in fact determine, or under applicable professional standards reasonably should have determined, that a patient poses a serious danger of violence to others, he bears a duty to exercise reasonable care to protect the foreseeable victim of that danger. While the discharge of this duty of due care will necessarily vary with the facts of each case, in each instance the adequacy of the therapist's conduct must be measured against the traditional negligence standard of the rendition of reasonable care under the circumstances.[23]

Despite the flexibility that this standard of care seems to give to therapists in how they respond to threats made against third parties, the standing legacy of the *Tarasoff* case is the support it lends to permitting, if not encouraging, therapists to warn potential victims. The legacy is best summed up in what has perhaps become the most memorable statement of the *Tarasoff* opinion: "The public policy favoring protection of the confidential character of patient-psychotherapist communications must yield to the extent to which disclosure is essential to avert danger to others. The protective privilege ends where the public peril begins."[24]

Another lasting legacy of the *Tarasoff* case is the confusion and mistaken beliefs that remain about the implications of the case. By issuing two opinions in *Tarasoff* and not even mentioning the existence of the first opinion in the text of the second opinion, the California Supreme Court created confusion about whether the first opinion carries any weight as a legal precedent. As a result, the *Tarasoff* opinion is often believed to create a "duty to warn," when this narrow holding of the first *Tarasoff* opinion was effectively refined in the second *Tarasoff* opinion to create a "duty to protect" in which warning the potential victim is only one of many ways that therapists can carry out this legally imposed duty.

The *Tarasoff* case has nevertheless had a lasting effect in the field of mental health treatment. It weighed the issue of patient confidentiality against the interest society has in protecting citizens from dangerous individuals, and the interest in protection won. "Tarasoff" has become a catchphrase in the mental health field for various strategies that mental health professionals may need to undertake in cases where treatment is being provided to a potentially dangerous person. "Tarasoff warnings" often refer to the practice of giving notification to an identifiable victim or law enforcement officers when a patient makes an explicit threat of harm to another person.

Despite the fact that *Tarasoff* was a case dealing with state laws governing the resolution of a civil dispute in the state of California, it had a far-reaching and lasting impact on mental health law throughout the United States. Other state and federal courts have had to confront the duty to protect in cases where the facts were similar to those in *Tarasoff* and dealt with the conflict between patient confidentiality and the protection of third parties from danger. The result has been a lack of consistency across states and legal jurisdictions in how they have dealt with the legally imposed duty of mental health professionals to protect others. Some states have accepted the reasoning of the *Tarasoff* decision and held that mental health professionals may be viewed as negligent for failure to warn a potential victim of harm committed by patients under their care.[25] In fact, a court in Vermont even extended the *Tarasoff* duty to warn or protect property after a patient told a therapist that he intended to burn down a barn belonging to another person.[26] One of the most famous post-*Tarasoff* cases dealing with the duty to protect involved a civil case brought against the psychiatrist who had treated John Hinckley, Jr., the man who attempted to assassinate President Ronald Reagan. The suit was brought by James Brady, Reagan's press secretary who was severely injured in the assassination attempt, for failure to warn the president of Hinckley's plan to assassinate him. The court held that the threat was too vague and specific victims could not be identified and therefore negligence for failure to protect could not be attributed under such circumstances.[27] Other states have failed to extend the *Tarasoff* ruling to other kinds of cases, such as those where the potential victim has more knowledge about the potential threat than the treating therapist or where a patient left treatment several months before injuring another person.

Of course, some of the most pressing questions in the wake of the *Tarasoff* ruling are, Did the decision have the chilling effect on psychotherapy that opponents of the decision feared? Were people less likely to seek treatment because of less confidentiality?

The *Tarasoff* decision paved the way for other limits on confidentiality in therapy. Mental health professionals are now required to disclose suspected cases of child abuse or neglect to the proper authorities, and many states require the reporting of suspected abuse involving the elderly or incapacitated adults. Physicians are required to report patients to the state department of motor vehicles if patients have medical conditions like seizures, visual impairment, brain damage, or severe mental illness that would render them unsafe to operate a motor vehicle.[28] Have these erosions of confidentiality and trust in the doctor-patient and client-therapist relationship led to people avoiding helping professionals or to less effective therapy?

Although there is no definitive scientific evidence demonstrating the impact of *Tarasoff* on the effectiveness of mental health services, one thing that is clear is that the groundbreaking case generated considerable professional and academic discussion and raised anxiety among those in the helping professions. Some studies have shown that mental health professionals are confused about what their duty to protect involves and whether they should take reasonable steps, all steps possible, or only certain legally mandated steps to protect third parties.[29] In some instances, studies have shown that mental health professionals are much more cautious about accepting potentially violent individuals into therapy because of the risks they may pose and there are greater concerns about being sued. Even if it remains unclear whether certain patients are reluctant to enter into therapy because of limits to confidentiality, one effect of the *Tarasoff* decision appears to be less access to therapy since many therapists are likely to balk at accepting a potentially dangerous person into their care.

On the other hand, the *Tarasoff* case appears to have had some favorable effects on how mental health services are rendered. Surveys of mental health professionals show that they are more likely to consult with colleagues when they have a particularly difficult or challenging case that involves *Tarasoff*-related issues. Furthermore, many professional associations have offered guidance to mental health professionals on how to deal with potentially violent individuals, which has led to greater awareness of the need to evaluate patients for the risk of violence and to treat and manage these cases more effectively.

It is arguable that no other civil case in the mental health field has had as far-reaching effects on the practice of psychotherapy as the *Tarasoff* case. What makes the case all the more fascinating is that it involved an interpretation of California law as it applied to a civil dispute that arose within that state, and as such the ruling was a legal precedent only for the practice of psychiatry and psychotherapy in the state of California. Yet, the broadly defined duty to protect outlined in the *Tarasoff* opinion, and the related issue of warning third parties of harm, soon became an issue that courts across the country confronted. Mental health professionals of various kinds, including psychiatrists, social workers, psychologists, and counselors, are now trained on ways to deal with the issue of "Tarasoff warnings" in cases where they arise. Moreover, the origins of the reasoning laid out in the famous *Tarasoff* case are found, in part, in a law review article that supports an approach to dealing with the mentally ill that empowers patients and seeks to minimize the power of mental health professionals over the liberty interests of patients. Yet, the *Tarasoff* case has not eliminated the need for involuntary hospitalization but has eroded slightly the confidentiality patients can expect from their therapists.

Perhaps it is not confidentiality that is the key to effective psychotherapy, as opponents of the *Tarasoff* opinion have argued. Rather, it is conscientious, caring, and competent mental health professionals who are able to foster a trusting—if not completely confidential[30]—relationship with their patients. After all, competently trained therapists know that they may be required to notify third parties of potential danger if their patient comes to pose a risk. Standard procedures for initiating psychotherapy now require that therapists inform all of their new or prospective patients about the circumstances under which a breach of confidentiality might be required. By providing patients with this knowledge beforehand, confidentiality can be guaranteed to the extent permitted by law and patients can be reassured that their therapist will impose limits if the patient's self-control fails and an open line of communication will remain between the patient and therapist. In this way, a trusting and working relationship can be maintained.

As for the specific outcome in the *Tarasoff* case, the parents of Tatiana Tarasoff were able to shape mental health law significantly with their civil case against the Regents of the University of California. Their "win," however, was bittersweet because even though they prevailed in their civil suit, they lost their daughter forever and no one was ever held accountable in a criminal court for her death. After he succeeded in his appeal to the Supreme Court of California—the same court that issued the ruling in the civil case brought by the parents of the slain Tatiana Tarasoff—Poddar was released from custody and returned to India. According to law professor Alan Stone, who reported that he had a personal communication with Tarasoff's killer following Poddar's return to India,[31] the man who killed the object of his unrequited affections is a happily married man.

6

DAN WHITE

The Myth of the
Twinkie Defense

Whenever news of a frivolous psychological defense reaches the media, reporters and other commentators almost invariably recall Dan White and his "Twinkie defense." For example, in one recent case a criminal defendant, charged with breaking onto a neighbor's home and chasing her with a dagger, claimed that he was rendered temporarily insane by ingesting too much jasmine tea. In reporting in 2003 that the charges against the man were dropped, the Associated Press told readers across the country that:

> Prosecutors likened the tea theory to the "Twinkie defense" used by former San Francisco Supervisor Dan White, who was charged with killing the city's mayor and another supervisor in 1978. He avoided a first-degree murder charge and was convicted of involuntary manslaughter after his lawyers convinced jurors that eating junk food had diminished White's mental capacity.[1]

Even noted legal scholar, Harvard Law professor, television commentator, and author Alan Dershowitz, in the glossary of his book *The Abuse Excuse*, referenced the "Twinkie defense." Dershowitz wrote, "This excuse was made famous by the Dan White case. . . . The jury accepted Mr. White's claim that he had become mentally incapacitated at the time of the killings in part because of his consumption of junk food."[2]

This characterization of the defense that purportedly led to the verdict in the White case, while popular and widely recounted, is a myth. Though high on the list of many media pundits when it comes to debunking phony excuses for criminal behavior, the "Twinkie defense," as described by most, was never raised by Dan White or anyone else associated with his case.

In 1977, Dan White, a thirty-two-year old Vietnam veteran, was elected to the Board of Supervisors in San Francisco. So, too, was Harvey Milk, the first openly gay member of the board. Both men were elected, at least in part, as a result of a reform under which Supervisors were elected by district rather than from the city at large. White was elected to represent a conservative, largely Catholic district in the southeast section of the city, where he had grown up. Milk was elected in a district that included the hub of the city's gay community. Though initially allies on the board, the two newly elected supervisors eventually found themselves at odds politically, with White opposing a gay parade in the city and voting against a proposal to prohibit job discrimination against homosexuals.

Prior to his election to the board, White had served the city as a police officer and firefighter and been decorated for bravery in the line of duty. Within a year of his election, however, White concluded that he could not afford to support himself, his wife, and their newborn son on the salary he earned as a supervisor, which was $9,600 a year. Indeed, the family was able to make ends meet only because White's wife Mary Ann worked long hours at a fast-food stand that White leased when he learned that he could not be paid as both a supervisor and a firefighter.

On November 10, 1978, depressed and frustrated, White resigned from the Board of Supervisors. By November 13, his resignation letter had been formally filed with the board, but a day later he had a change of heart and asked the mayor to reappoint him to the board.

Because White's resignation had been formally received by the board, he could not legally rescind it. He could, however, be appointed to succeed himself. San Francisco Mayor George Moscone had the authority to appoint a successor for White. Responding in part to pleas from police officers and firefighters as well as pressure from members of the community, Moscone initially agreed to restore White to the position. The mayor shared this decision with White, gave White back his letter of resignation, and even went so far as to announce publicly that White would keep his job. While Mayor Moscone spoke to the press, White held his own press conference and announced, "People unknown to me plus my family and friends have come to me and stated that they want me to stay in office. The majority of my district doesn't want to have someone appointed that they didn't elect, and I'm going to stay in my seat."[3]

That was November 15. By the next day the political pressure on Moscone not to reappoint White was increasing. Among those who urged the mayor not to reappoint White was Supervisor Harvey Milk, who recognized that appointing a liberal in White's stead would give that political faction a majority on the board.

By November 18, the mayor's press secretary was telling the media that "the only person who has come into this office indicating that Dan White should be reappointed is Dan White himself."[4] Meanwhile the mayor was telling White that it might not be appropriate to reappoint him and that White would do well to show the mayor just how much community support he had. White and his supporters immediately began a campaign that would collect over 1,100 signatures on a petition as well as numerous letters and other expressions of support from his constituents.

While this drama played out at City Hall and in the neighborhoods of San Francisco, the city's congressman, Representative Leo Ryan, and three reporters were shot and killed in Guyana, where Ryan had gone as part of an investigation into the activities of the Reverend Jim Jones. Jones led the People's Temple, a radical cultlike congregation in Jonestown, which had earlier relocated to Guyana from San Francisco. On November 18, shortly after Ryan and his party were gunned down while boarding a private plane, over nine hundred members of the People's Temple followed Jones's instructions and committed mass suicide by drinking cyanide-laced Kool-Aid.

For a time, the Jonestown Massacre eclipsed the unfolding tale of Dan White in the Bay area media. In any event, however, the tragedy in Jonestown weighed heavily on the minds of many San Franciscans including the mayor, who would soon stand for reelection. After all, the Reverend Jones had been one of Moscone's most ardent supporters when Moscone had run for mayor. Indeed, just two years before the mass suicide, the mayor had toasted Jones at a testimonial dinner and appointed him to a seat on the city's Housing Commission. Now, following the Jonestown Massacre, rumor had it that some People's Temple members had been programmed by Jones to carry out political assassinations in the United States. These rumors led San Francisco officials to install metal detectors at City Hall in the event that Jones had somehow targeted his former political allies there.

On November 20, the day after the deaths in Jonestown were first reported in the media, Moscone wrote White a letter backing even further away from his earlier promise of reappointment. After explaining that he had received many communications urging him not to reappoint White, Moscone went on to say that while he would be taking a week to "review this situation, . . . I must reiterate that I have not made any commitment of any kind to appoint you."[5]

While Moscone was consulting with politicians and interviewing a possible successor to White, White's supporters were rallying to keep him in office and his attorneys were pressing the courts for an injunction that would keep the Board of Supervisors from accepting White's resignation. As for Dan White, himself, his life appeared to be collapsing around him. He was spending more and more time alone and growing increasingly despondent.

As White's wife would later testify:

He was just . . . very withdrawn, [he would] withdraw himself from me, and anyone else. It would be where he would get up in the morning and seem okay, and then all of a sudden he would just go in his room, close the door, never come out, and if I happened to go into the room to get something, he would never speak, and if I spoke to him he wouldn't answer.[6]

On the evening of November 26, 1978, White was called at home by a television news reporter and asked if he had been informed that Moscone had decided not to reappoint him and was planning to announce the appointment of another man the following morning at 11:30. White, who had not been made aware of the mayor's plans, told the reporter that he had no comment and then abruptly hung up.

Early the next morning, November 27, White learned from the mayor's administrative assistant, Denise Apcar, that the mayor had refused to even accept petitions signed by over 1,100 people calling for White's reappointment. After the call, White gathered up a .38 caliber revolver and supply of ammunition and asked Apcar to drive him to City Hall. White arrived there just about an hour before the mayor was scheduled to publicly announce the name of his successor. Though he was dropped off in front of the building at the main entrance, White walked to the side of the building where, to avoid having to pass through metal detectors, he entered City Hall through a basement window.

Once inside the government center, White walked up a back staircase, went directly to Moscone's office and shot the mayor four times at close range, twice in the head and twice in the chest. An autopsy would later reveal that both head wounds were inflicted at a distance of about twelve to eighteen inches as the already wounded mayor was lying on the floor of his office.

Having shot the mayor, White ran to the other side of City Hall, used his own key to open the door leading to the supervisors' offices, spoke briefly to

Supervisor (later San Francisco Mayor and U.S. Senator) Dianne Feinstein, and paused to reload his gun. Speaking in a normal tone of voice, White then asked to see Supervisor Harvey Milk. Less than a minute later, he shot Milk five times in much the same manner he had shot the mayor. White fired three shots to Milk's body and two to the back of his head. As in the killing of the mayor, White shot Milk in the head at close range only after the supervisor had been knocked to the floor by the body shots.

After shooting Milk, White ran to Apcar's office, demanded the key to her car, and left when he got it. A short while later, White telephoned his wife and asked her to meet him at St. Mary's Cathedral, a Catholic church. After the couple met and White explained what he had done, they walked to a police station and White surrendered and gave a lengthy statement. White told the police that he had been under tremendous economic, political, and familial stress, and had resigned as a supervisor to reduce that stress. He also said that his family had supported his decision to seek reappointment and that he felt Harvey Milk had been using him as a "scapegoat."[7] In the recorded interrogation just hours after the killings, White explained that:

> After I [resigned], my family and friends offered their support and said whatever it would take to allow me to go back into the office, they would be willing to make that up. So since I felt the responsibility of the people that elected me, I went to Mayor Moscone and told him, that I had, that my situation had changed and I'd like to be, retain my seat, to be appointed to my seat. He initially told me that he felt that . . . I was doing an outstanding job and that if it came to a legal ruling he would appoint me, reappoint me. . . . So, with that in mind I tried to set my personal affairs in order, preparing to take my seat. And then it came out that Supervisor Milk and some others were working against me to get my seat back. . . . I could see the game that was being played, they were going to use me as a scapegoat; whether I was a good supervisor or not was not the point.
>
> This was a political opportunity and they were gonna denigrate me and my family, and the job I was trying to do, [and] more or less hang me out to dry. And I saw more and more evidence of this when the papers reported that, ah, someone else was going to be appointed. I couldn't get through to the mayor. The mayor never called me, he told me he was gonna call me before he made the decision, he never did that. It was only on my own initiative when I went down today to speak with him. I was troubled, the pressures,

my family again . . . my son's out to a baby sitter. My wife's got to work, long hours, fifty and sixty hours, never see my family. . . .

And I went in to see him [and] he told me he wasn't gonna reappoint me and he . . . was . . . intending to tell me about it. . . . He told me he had a press conference scheduled and he was going to announce it at the press conference. Didn't even have the courtesy to call me or tell me that I wasn't going to be reappointed. Then, ah, I got kind of fuzzy and then, just my head didn't feel right, and I, then he said, let's go in the back room [and] have a drink and talk about it. . . .

Just all the time knowing he's going to go out and lie and tell them, you know, that I, I wasn't a good supervisor and that people didn't want me and then that was it. Then I, I just shot him. That was it. It was over. . . .

I left his office by one of the back doors [and] then I saw Harvey Milk's aide across the hall [and] then it struck me about what Harvey had tried to do [and] I said, well I'll go talk to him. I said, you know, maybe he'll at least be honest with me. He was all smiles and stuff . . . and then he started kind of smirking because he knew, he knew, that I wasn't going to be reappointed. . . . I started to say you know how hard I worked for it and what it meant to me and my family [and] then my reputation . . . and he just kind of smirked at me as if to say too bad and then I just got all flushed and hot and I shot him.[8]

As a result of the killings, Dan White was charged with two counts of premeditated and deliberate murder, for which he could have faced life in prison or the death penalty if convicted. At trial, months later, few facts were in dispute. What was disputed was White's state of mind before and during the killings. White's attorney relied on a defense that was, at the time, unusual if not unique to California: diminished capacity.

The defense of diminished capacity was developed by the California courts over a span of approximately thirty years from 1949 to 1978, the year Dan White killed George Moscone and Harvey Milk. Through a series of cases, mostly homicide prosecutions, the courts fashioned a doctrine under which a defendant's criminal culpability could be reduced in degree by evidence of mental disorder short of insanity.[9] For example, if an "unlawful killing of a human being with malice aforethought" was "willful, deliberate, and premeditated," the crime would be first-degree murder.[10] However, such a killing that was not "willful, deliberate, and premeditated" would be second-degree murder.[11] Under the doctrine of diminished capacity, if a jury found that as a result of a mental disorder the defendant was unable to deliberate and premeditate, they could not convict a defendant of first-degree murder. Moreover, if the jury found that as a result of mental illness the defendant lacked the capacity to act with malice ("a deliberate intention unlawfully to take away the life of a fellow creature"), they could not convict the defendant of even second-degree murder.[12]

In support of the defense of diminished capacity, White's attorneys presented the testimony of five mental health experts: four psychiatrists and one psychologist. All five doctors agreed that White was suffering from serious depression when he killed Moscone and Milk. Three opined that as a result White had lacked the capacity to premeditate, one disagreed, and the other testified only that White's capacity for premeditation had been impaired. Finally, one psychiatrist and one psychologist testified that White had lacked the capacity to act with malice in the killing of his former colleagues.

Aside from the psychiatric/psychological expert testimony, White's defense consisted of the testimony of family, friends, and acquaintances who attested that he was an honorable man given to frustration and depression. White did not testify.

The prosecution countered the diminished capacity defense with a single expert, Dr. Ronald Levy, a psychiatrist who had examined White just eight hours after the killings. He testified that he found White moderately but not clinically depressed at the time of the homicides. He told the jury that White had the capacity to deliberate and premeditate and that, after reviewing the opinions of the other five experts in the case, he had seen nothing to convince him otherwise. On cross-examination, however, Levy conceded that he had not done a full evaluation of Dan White because "I was not asked to do a complete assessment."[13]

Of all the defense experts who testified at White's trial, Dr. Martin Blinder gave perhaps the most compelling and certainly the most controversial testimony in support of the diminished-capacity defense. It was Blinder's testimony that would eventually lead commentators to coin the sobriquet, the "Twinkie defense."

Blinder, a psychiatrist, testified that White had suffered from "a manic-depressive syndrome dating back to adolescence" and that this mental illness, coupled with the life stress White was under at the time of the killings, "circumvented the mental processes necessary for premeditation, malice and intent."[14] Beyond that, however, in what would ultimately propel him to the dubious status of "Twinkie shrink,"[15] Blinder explained to the jury that, like many depressed individuals, White had altered his eating habits in response to the illness. Indeed, Blinder reported that when White experienced episodes of major depression he stopped his normal healthy diet, ceased his regimen of exercise, and binged on junk food—mainly candy bars, soft drinks, and cupcakes:

> During these spells he'd become quite withdrawn, quite lethargic. He would retreat to his room. Wouldn't come to the door. Wouldn't answer the phone. Would call in sick. Wouldn't even sleep with his wife; would sleep alone on the couch outside.
>
> And during these periods he found that he could not cope with people. He would avoid them . . . because any confrontations would cause him to kind of become argumentative. . . .
>
> Whenever he felt things were not going right, he would abandon his usual program of exercise and good nutrition and start gorging himself on junk foods: Twinkies, Coca Cola.
>
> Mr. White has always been something of an athlete priding himself of being physically fit. But when something would go wrong, he'd hit the high sugar stuff. He'd hit the chocolate, and the more he consumed, the worse he'd feel, and he'd respond to his ever going depression by consuming ever more junk food. The more junk food he consumed, the worse he'd feel. The worse he'd feel, the more he'd gorge himself, and so on, in a vicious circle.
>
> Finally, after several days, he'd pull himself together, maybe start jogging a bit, feel better, stop eating this food, feel better yet, and then get back to his old diet and his old personality, which is generally pretty congenial.[16]

Later in his testimony, Blinder told the jury that White's consumption of junk food was not only a symptom but also an exacerbating factor in his depressed moods. To substantiate that point, Blinder cited studies that he said in some cases linked the consumption of large amounts of refined sugar to mood disturbances, including depression and violence. He did not, however, testify that this was what had happened in White's case or that eating junk food caused Dan White to kill George Moscone and Harvey Milk. As one commentator later noted: "Blinder commented that too much sugar can affect the chemical balance in the brain and worsen depression, but didn't blame the crime on bad diet. Rather, he offered junk food use as proof of White's mental state—in other words, Twinkie consumption was an effect rather than the cause of White's problems."[17]

The only other expert reference to White's consumption of junk food came from the prosecution's sole expert witness, Dr. Levy, who not only denied that White suffered any mental illness at all, but debunked any notion that Twinkies or any other junk food could have caused White's homicidal actions:

> [*Prosecutor*]: Doctor . . . are you familiar with any studies and any
> prevailing scientific bodies of thought relating to the ingestion
> of sugar, foods with preservatives such as what's commonly
> known as junk foods and including, for example, chocolate
> cupcakes of Twinkie variety, Coca-Cola, candy bars and potato
> chips, for example, as those relate to being causative factors in
> influencing anti-social or sociopathic behavior?
> [*Psychiatrist*]: I am unaware of any prevailing psychiatric opinion
> that such factors are significant in relationship to any type of
> mental illness.[18]

So insignificant was the junk food aspect of White's defense that his attorney barely mentioned it in his closing argument to the jury. Douglas Schmidt, White's lead attorney, told the jury that White was "guilty" and that "the only issue for you is the degree of responsibility."[19] Schmidt emphasized that the experts had had found that White was incapable of "deliberation" and that his judgment had been "fogged by passion, anger, rage, humiliation."[20] As for the role, if any, played by junk food, Schmidt said:

> I don't know whether there is a relationship between sugar and
> violent behavior. I don't know. A lot of people think so, it's hypogly-
> cemia. If there is some possible relevance regarding that then I want
> somebody to come in and tell me what it is. And that's why I called
> Dr. Blinder. He didn't come in here and talk about eating Twinkies
> and going crazy, but he did suggest, among other things, that a
> change in diet is a symptom of depression, if nothing else. His radi-
> cal changes in diet are a symptom of depression that there's some-
> thing wrong with you.
>
> Now whether or not ingestion of foodstuff with preserva-
> tives and sugar in high content causes you to alter your personal-
> ity somehow, or causes you to act in an aggressive manner, I don't
> know. I'm not going to suggest to you for a minute that that occurs.
> But there is a minority opinion in psychiatric fields that there is
> some connection.[21]

As Schmidt would later explain, he considered the Twinkie defense a "trivialization by the media."[22] As the defense attorney saw it, White's consumption of junk food was "a minor defense argument . . . not anything that I was buying into big time . . . a symptom of depression, like mood swings and insomnia."[23]

Had Dan White been convicted of murder, Blinder's testimony would have become a mere footnote in this tragedy. But, in a verdict that surprised and outraged many, after nearly six days of sometimes-heated deliberations, the jury concluded that in killing his colleagues, White had demonstrated neither malice nor premeditation and deliberation. Thus the jury acquitted him of both first- and second-degree murder and found him guilty of two counts of the much less serious crime of voluntary manslaughter. As a result, White eluded not only the death penalty but a life sentence as well.

Even then, Blinder's testimony might well have passed beneath the radar of intense media scrutiny had it not been for the sentence White received and the public response to it. For killing Mayor Moscone, Dan White was sentenced to the maximum term allowed under California's manslaughter statute, four years plus a two-year "enhancement" for having used a firearm.[24] For killing Supervisor Milk, White was given a sentence of one year plus an eight-month "enhancement" for use of a gun.[25] Since the judge ordered that the prison terms be served consecutively as opposed to concurrently, the total sentence for the two homicides amounted to seven years and eight months behind bars. That meant that with time off for good behavior and time served prior to trial, White could be paroled in roughly five years.

Many people in San Francisco and elsewhere felt that this sentence added insult to injury; not only had White been acquitted of murdering two elected officials but he had been given a sentence that was widely regarded as a slap on the wrist for two political assassinations. Especially outraged were members of San Francisco's gay community, many of whom had worked to elect Harvey Milk and regarded him as an icon whose killing was fueled at least in part by homophobia.

That outrage led to what came to be known as the "White Night Riot."[26] As word of White's lenient sentence spread, within hours hundreds were marching through the streets, burning police cars, chanting "no justice, no peace," and attempting to storm City Hall.[27] Though only a few people were injured and fewer than two dozen rioters were arrested, the message was loud and clear: In the eyes of many, Dan White had gotten away with murder.

In the aftermath of the trial, verdict, and riot, many seemed convinced that a gross injustice had been done because one of the victims had been gay and because a gullible and perhaps homophobic jury had been unduly swayed by a trumped-up psychiatric defense. In fact, neither of these explanations for the verdict rings true. As one member of the jury later explained: "People think it was about Twinkies and gays. It wasn't. I was born and raised in San Francisco. I've never been against gay people. There may have been a couple of jurors who were but they never told us they felt that way. . . . The prosecution thought it was such a clear-cut case they didn't do their job."[28] Twinkies, the juror added, "played no part" in the jury's decision.[29]

Amazingly and inexplicably, in such an important and high-profile case, faced with a cadre of five mental health experts testifying for the defense, the prosecution chose to rely on the expert testimony of a single rebuttal expert who candidly admitted that he had not done a complete evaluation of the defendant.

While the trial of Dan White concluded with the verdict and sentence, the fallout from this case was far from over. White's attorneys appealed his sentence but a California appeals court held that "the record amply supports the sentences imposed by the trial court."[30] As the appellate court explained, both victims had been shot in the head "in the manner of a coup de grâce" while lying defenseless.[31] Finally, in affirming White's sentence, the court also cited "the planning with which the crimes were carried out, indicating premeditation, prior to the actual events."[32]

While White was serving roughly five years in Soledad State Prison, in 1981 the California Legislature amended the state's penal and evidence laws in a clear effort to preclude jurors from reaching the kind of conclusion the jury came to in White's case.[33] Not only did the legislature eliminate the diminished-capacity defense, but it amended the rules of evidence to ban expert testimony regarding whether or not a defendant had the mental state required for conviction of the crime charged. Had either of these legislative reforms been enacted prior to 1978, Dan White would almost assuredly have been convicted of murder.

In 1984, Dan White was paroled from Soledad to the Los Angeles area, where he remained for nearly a year before returning to San Francisco against the expressed wishes of many, including those of then-Mayor Dianne Feinstein. On October 21, 1985, at his San Francisco home, White attached a garden hose to the exhaust pipe of his car and sat in the running vehicle in a closed garage until he died from carbon monoxide poisoning.

In perhaps the final bizarre twist in the case of Dan White, fifteen years after his suicide, echoes of the Twinkie defense continued to haunt another of the trial's key participants. On October 6, 2002, Dr. Martin Blinder was attacked and brutally stabbed by his former wife, who then proceeded to kill herself. By then, Blinder had become a well-known author, novelist, and playwright, not to mention an accomplished jazz pianist, horticulturist, and frequent guest on TV talk shows.[34] The stabbing, which Blinder survived, was reported internationally under headlines that included "Twinkie Shrink Stabbed,"[35] "Twinkie, A Chocolate Cake That Leaves Murder and Mayhem in Its Wake,"[36] and "Ex-Wife of Twinkie Defense Doctor Found Dead; Woman Was Suspected of Stabbing Psychiatrist."[37] As Blinder complained, "If I found a cure for cancer, they'd still say I was the guy who invented 'the Twinkie defense.'"[38]

7

CAMERON
HOOKER

Judging the Experts?

The abduction of fifteen-year-old Elizabeth Smart from her Utah home on June 5, 2002, gained national attention primarily because the crime occurred while she was at home with her sister and parents.[1] Nearly nine months after her abduction, Elizabeth Smart was found alive in March 2003 and reunited with her family. Her kidnappers were identified, but the joy and relief over her safe return soon gave way to questions about her ordeal.[2] The details of her captivity were puzzling because her captors had moved her around the country and even took her out in public. How could they maintain control over her while help was so near? The answer to this perplexing question can be found, in part, in an extraordinary and horrific case of abduction, mind control, and coercion that occurred years earlier.

On Thursday, May 19, 1977, twenty-year-old Colleen Stan left Eugene, Oregon, and set out for Westwood, California, to visit a friend.[3] Her roommates dropped her off near Interstate 5, and Stan planned to hitchhike the nearly four hundred miles to her friend's home. She got two rides that took her into California, but she turned down her next two—one from a carload of men and another from a couple who said they were only going a short distance.[4]

Stan then accepted a ride from a young couple, Cameron and Janice Hooker. They seemed "safe," as the wife was holding a baby in the front seat of the car and the man driving the car appeared to be clean-cut. Upon entering the vehicle, Stan got into the back seat and noticed a strange wooden box beside her.[5] A couple of minor incidents at the start of the ride foreshadowed the fact that Stan's life was about to change dramatically. As she took a sip from a bottle of juice she was carrying, Cameron Hooker—who had been glancing repeatedly at Stan through the rearview mirror—sped up, causing the juice to spill down the front of Stan's shirt.[6] She also noticed that Hooker gave his wife a look that caused Janice Hooker to shake her head with a frown.

After about a half hour of driving, Hooker decided to stop at a gas station. Stan went to the restroom and would later recall that she felt extremely uneasy about the situation. "A voice told me to run and jump out a window and never look back," she would later say.[7] Nevertheless, she ignored her concerns about the situation and returned to the vehicle. Janice Hooker offered her a candy bar as the conversation turned to the topic of ice caves. Using the topic as a ruse, Hooker casually asked Stan if she would mind if they went to see the caves, which he claimed were nearby.

After Hooker turned down a dirt road and parked in an isolated spot, he confronted Stan with a knife. He ordered her to do as she was told and then bound, gagged, and blindfolded her. He forced her head into the strange box that had been on the back seat beside her—a "head box" that was extremely hot, completely muffled external noises, and blocked out all light.

Stan was taken to the couple's home and Hooker forced her into another box in the basement that was about three feet high and just big enough to accommodate her entire body. The head box was reattached and a variety of sadistic restraints were also attached to her. Her arms were chained over her head, a spiny contraption was placed between her legs, a constricting strap was placed around her chest making it difficult to breath, and the head box made it so she could see and hear nothing.

Hooker's domination and control over Colleen had begun:

> For the next five months, he kept her—naked, bound, blindfolded, and gagged—in the basement. The first 7 to 10 days, Colleen was kept naked, chained to the rack, and wearing the headbox. For the remainder of the first five-month period, Colleen—still naked, bound and wearing the headbox—was kept in a coffin-like box in the basement, leaving it only once a day to eat, drink, urinate, and defecate, always in Hooker's presence. During this time, Hooker regularly practiced bondage on Colleen, suspending her from the rafters, constricting her breathing, whipping her, keeping her head encased in the headbox, tying her to the rack, shocking her with electrical cords, burning her pubic area with a heat lamp, and

immersing her in the bathtub until she was unable to breathe. Colleen once estimated that Hooker hung her and whipped her 90 to 100 times in the first six months.[8]

On January 25, 1978, Hooker removed Stan from the box to present her with a document entitled "This Indenture." Hooker explained that an organization called "The Company" was a network of slave traders that took women captive and sold them for profit.[9] The indenture was essentially a slavery contract that Hooker had read about in an underground newspaper catering to sadomasochistic sexual practices that was part of his vast collection of pornography and related materials. An article in one of the newspapers included a sample contract that Hooker copied. He rented a typewriter, had his wife copy the text of the indenture on a clean sheet of paper, and then added the title "This Indenture" using calligraphy stencils he bought specifically for the purpose of giving the document an "official" appearance.[10] He even added a seal to the bottom of the page.

When Hooker presented the contract to Stan, he showed her the article from his underground newspaper and was able to convince her that members of the organization knew she was with him and she had to sign the contract or face brutal consequences. Furthermore, when Hooker presented her with the contract, it was the first time she had seen his face after being subjected to his brutal treatment for nearly eight months. The language in the indenture was official sounding, if not barbaric:

> AND Slave does hereby irrevocably declare and acknowledge her everlasting unconditional dedication to serving Master to His full satisfaction; AND she ashamedly confesses that prior indulgence of her untempered conduct by others may have permitted her to become afflicted with inferior habits that may prove unsatisfactory to Master, from which imperfections she implores Master to free her by retraining with corporal punishment or any other means which He, in His unquestionable wisdom, deems effective toward directing her to her sole ambition and life-destiny of perfectly fulfilling His every desire of her.[11]

Aside from the language of the document, even the capitalization of "His" and the lowercase "her" was intended to convey the complete domination that Hooker wanted to have over his victim. Given the extreme control and deprivation to which she had been subjected, Stan was confronted with the option of either signing the contract or risk being taken by "The Company" and sold into slavery. The indenture referred to Colleen as "Slave" and "Michael Powers" (a fictitious name Hooker used with Colleen) as "Master." The indenture specified that Stan was to refer to Hooker only as "Sir" or "Master" and to subjugate his victim further, he ordered that she be given a new name, the letter "K."

For the next several years, Colleen lived under the complete sadistic control of Hooker. Much of the time she was confined to the box under the couple's bed. However, two major issues complicated the case of Colleen's confinement. First, there was Hooker's wife, who facilitated her husband's domination of Colleen—even to the point of typing the "Indenture" for him. Janice Hooker appeared to accept the presence of another woman in their home because she could avoid being the subject of her husband's sadistic sexual rituals. Yet, she also recognized that the situation was both legally and morally wrong. In addition, the Hookers' young child grew up aware that a woman was being held captive in their home. At the age of three, the Hookers' daughter was confused about why "K" always had a chain around her neck and was sometimes chained to the toilet.

The second issue complicating the case was Stan's submissive and compliant behavior toward Hooker. She would ask for permission to eat, go to the bathroom, or perform simple tasks. Stan was gradually given greater latitude in her movements and was often allowed to go jogging while unsupervised, but only after asking for permission each time.

In March of 1981 the case took a remarkable turn: Hooker permitted Stan to visit her family. He told her that if she said anything to anyone about "The Company," he would kill whomever she told. In light of the previous years of intimidation and complete control that Hooker had over her, the threat was highly effective. Stan appeared at her father's home with a small suitcase as Hooker drove away. Her family did not know what to make of the fact that she was suddenly home after having completely disappeared for four years. As Hooker demanded, she gave vague responses to the questions asked of her and told no one about her ordeal. After a two-day visit, Hooker called and told her he would pick her up; they drove back to the Hookers' home.

Stan continued in her life of servitude for three more years. Following her "year out," she was placed back in the box and was seldom seen by anyone but Hooker. The circumstances ultimately leading to her release were triggered when Hooker's wife began to experience considerable doubts and reservations about her husband's conduct.

In 1983, Hooker began talking about abducting another woman and creating a group of "slaves." Janice Hooker was becoming increasingly more distraught over the fact that her husband was having regular sexual relations with Stan and she began to take comfort in reading the Bible and attending a local church.[12] In August 1984, Janice Hooker confided in the church's pastor, Frank Dabney, and other members of the parish about a "love triangle" without providing complete details of the kidnapping, sadistic sexual practices, and domination over Stan's life. Nevertheless, the pastor told Hooker's wife that the situation was not in keeping with the church's teaching and recommended that both she and Stan leave the home. Hooker's wife confronted Stan with the truth that there was no "Company" and the entire ordeal had been arranged by her husband.

Stan was devastated by the news, but the immediate concern became how to remove herself from the situation without provoking Hooker to kill her. Both Stan and Janice Hooker stayed in the home that evening. After Hooker went to work the next day, Stan called him from the bus station and told him she was leaving. She returned to her family and told them of the ordeal she had endured over the preceding seven years. For the next few months, Stan had some contact with the Hookers, who were concerned about whether she had gone to the police. Although Stan "was grateful to have been released and wanted to forget the entire incident," Janice Hooker remained afraid of her husband. After a family friend contacted law enforcement officials in November 1984, Hooker was arrested and charged with kidnapping, false imprisonment, and multiple sex offenses.[13]

One of the key issues raised by his defense at trial was Stan's "compliance" with Hooker's demands over the years. After all, how could a woman be held for seven years and not make some attempt to escape? Moreover, how could a kidnapping victim visit her family while she was unsupervised by her captor and never disclose that she had been kidnapped? Her case calls to mind how Elizabeth Smart, hiding out with her captors in the countryside, failed to answer back when she heard her name shouted out by those who were searching for her.

When Stan was finally liberated from Hooker's control, many people were puzzled by her apathy and indifferent response to her ordeal. When Stan testified at trial, the account she gave was delivered in a "flat and unemotional" manner whereas Janice Hooker's testimony was "punctuated by emotional outbursts."[14] Jurors expected Hooker's wife to be upset about the actions of her husband and could therefore understand her emotional turmoil, but prosecutors were concerned that Stan's flat delivery might raise questions about whether some of her actions were consensual.

There were plea negotiations that threatened to grant Hooker a limited prison sentence, making him eligible for parole in as little as four and a half years. His attorney argued that even though Hooker may have kidnapped Stan, the sexual acts were consensual and should not have been considered criminal.

To rebut this claim, the prosecution sought the testimony of Dr. Chris Hatcher, a forensic psychologist and an expert in terrorism, hostage negotiations, brainwashing, and coercion. Hatcher had consulted on a number of well-known cases involving allegations of brainwashing, including Jim Jones and members of his People's Temple, and he had consulted with a number of law enforcement and government agencies, including the U.S. Secret Service, Scotland Yard, and Los Angeles Police Department. His involvement in the case was to provide valuable insights into why Stan behaved as she did both during and after her seven-year enslavement.

Hatcher interviewed Hooker's victim at length and provided a lengthy written report that served as the basis of his testimony. At trial, he testified that "brainwashing" was a rare phenomenon and occurs in very few cases. He stated that a person's "whole adult processes, their values, their way of looking at the world is changed completely" with brainwashing and he did not feel that the circumstances of Stan's confinement by Hooker resulted in her being brainwashed.[15] He placed "coercion" along a continuum from simple persuasion on the one end, to coercion in the middle, and brainwashing at the other extreme. The judge presiding over Hooker's trial, Clarence B. Knight, ruled that Hatcher's testimony would be restricted and the prosecutor would not be permitted to ask the expert to speculate on Hooker's case specifically.

Hatcher characterized the hypothetical facts of kidnapping, hanging, whipping, confinement to a box, and sensory and food deprivation—the very things Stan endured during her captivity—as an extreme form of coercion used by sadistic individuals to control another person. Hatcher added that these forms of control "would be sufficient to coerce the majority of individuals into a desired behavior pattern and to give up any overt resistance."[16]

Finally, Hatcher broke down individual forms of coercion into their effects on a person. Eliminating daylight through sensory deprivation would disorient a person. Controlling food, excretion, and other bodily functions would destroy a person's sense of privacy. A continued pattern of physical and sexual abuse would create the belief that life had been permanently changed. Isolating the person from contact with all other people would reinforce the belief that the captor is the sole source of information and creates dependency on that person. Hatcher's testimony was offered to help the jury understand how Stan could have acted as a profoundly compliant victim in light of her horrific experiences.

Before the defense countered with expert testimony of its own, the most anticipated moment of the trial came when Hooker took the stand to testify in his own defense. Although he admitted to kidnapping Stan, several years had passed since the abduction itself and Hooker disputed some of the facts of how the abduction occurred, hoping to take advantage of the statute of limitations. Hooker attempted to lessen the severity of his actions by claiming such things as not holding a knife to Stan's throat when he kidnapped her, avoiding intercourse with his victim in order to keep a promise to his wife, talking to Stan in softer tones, and hanging her from ropes for less time than the prosecution had claimed. Members of Hooker's family were also called to testify in an effort to humanize him and create sympathy among the jurors.

The defense countered Hatcher's testimony with Dr. Donald Lunde, a forensic psychiatrist who also had experience in cases involving human captivity and coercion. Lunde was on the clinical faculty of Stanford Medical School and had consulted on such high-profile cases as the Patty Hearst kidnapping. Whereas Hatcher interviewed the victim prior to testifying, Lunde interviewed Hooker as part of his preparation for trial. During his testimony, Lunde provided a narrower definition of coercion as "a psychological phenomenon that is present when someone has threatened someone else directly with death."[17] The psychiatrist then went on the testify that "the law simply does not allow for threats to other people" as falling within the definition of coercion.[18]

Lunde's testimony about the legal definition of coercion was apparently intended to suggest that because Hooker threatened Colleen's family, he had not coerced her into withholding from her family the fact that she had been kidnapped and enslaved by someone. However, Judge Knight interrupted Lunde's testimony, pointing out that the psychiatrist's claim was not accurate. After an objection by the prosecution that argued the testimony was prejudicial, the judge concurred and ordered the jury to disregard Lunde's definition of coercion.

At another point during Lunde's testimony, Judge Knight had questions of his own about Lunde's claim that some of the techniques Hooker used on his victim were no different from "attention drills" used with Marine Corps recruits in boot camp. Judge Knight decided to question Lunde himself during the trial:

Judge Knight: Doctor, I was kind of confused by a couple of things. Was it your testimony yesterday that it's your understanding

that what the victim in the case was subjected to was basically
equivalent to Marine Corps boot camp training?

Dr. Lunde: That answer was in reference to questions about attention drills, coming to attention on command; and I said that
aspect, that type of drill, was reminiscent of Marine Corps boot
camp training. . . .

Judge Knight: You didn't intend to equate what happened here to
Marine Corps boot camp training, did you?

Dr. Lunde: No. It was a specific aspect, namely, the attention drills,
being called to attention and having to hop to a stand-up-
straight position.[19]

The judge's questioning of Lunde went on for some time and covered
other issues of the defense expert's testimony, including whether it was reasonable for a victim in Stan's position to believe in the existence of "The
Company" and the possibility that Stan failed to disclose her ordeal to her
family in order to protect them from Hooker. However, Judge Knight's questioning of Lunde would later figure prominently in Hooker's appeal.

There were other interruptions during Dr. Lunde's testimony, including
objections by the prosecution and admonishments from the judge that Hooker's defense counsel refrain from using irrelevant or improper hypothetical
questions. Lunde offered the opinion that for coercive persuasion to occur, the
captor must have continuous physical control over the victim at all time.

The jury deliberated for three days. After seeking additional clarification
from the judge about the legal meaning of "duress" and "menace,"[20] the jury
found Hooker guilty on seven of eight counts, including kidnapping (with the
aggravating factor of having used a knife) and several counts of rape. He was
sentenced to consecutive sentences for the sexual offenses and an indetermi-
nate sentence of one to twenty-five years for the kidnapping, resulting in a
total prison term of over one hundred years.

Immediately following the verdict, the presiding judge made a surprising
statement to the jury. After thanking jurors for their service, he said:

I want to particularly commend you for having the intelligence to
reject the testimony of Dr. Donald Lunde, the defense psychiatrist.
I think witnesses like that are a real menace to the criminal justice
system. They come in here posing as objective scientists, when, in
fact, they are nothing but paid advocates. . . . I'm happy that you
had the good sense to see through him, because one Dan White case
is enough.[21]

Of course, Judge Knight's comment about Dan White was a reference to the man associated with the controversial, but misunderstood, "Twinkie defense" case.

Hooker appealed his conviction and raised a number of issues about the manner in which his trial was conducted and his sentence imposed. For instance, he claimed that Judge Knight's decision to exclude evidence of Stan's prior sexual conduct was improper and that the manner in which his harsh sentence was computed erroneous. However, the most interesting issue raised in Hooker's appeal was his claim that Judge Knight had assumed the role of an advocate for the prosecution by questioning Dr. Lunde in an inappropriate manner.[22]

The appellate court noted that Hooker's attorney did not object to Judge Knight's questioning of Lunde at trial and failed to make a motion for mistrial at the conclusion of the trial. According to the court:

> A trial judge has a statutory right to question witnesses the same as if they had been produced by a party to an action. The parties may object to questions asked by the judge and the evidence adduced the same as if the witnesses were examined by an adverse party. . . . The trial court's discretion to invoke its statutory right will not be disturbed on appeal unless it appears that the manner in which the judge questioned the witness tended unduly to impress the jury with the importance of the testimony elicited, or would be likely to lead the jury to suppose that the judge was of the opinion that one party rather than the other should prevail in the case.[23]

Of course, Judge Knight's commendation to the jury that they were "intelligent" enough to reject Lunde's testimony was used by Hooker to argue that the judge was indeed an advocate for the prosecution and not neutral in his treatment of the defense expert. However, the appellate court noted that Judge Knight saved his negative appraisal of Lunde's testimony until *after* the jury had rendered its verdict and that by all appearances the judge had "conducted what could have been a highly charged proceeding in an even-handed fashion."[24] One of the appellate court judges filed a concurring opinion in which it was noted that the failure of Hooker's attorney to make an objection to Judge Knight's questioning of Dr. Lunde might raise a question about the competence of Hooker's legal representation. On the other hand, Hooker's attorney may have had a strategic reason for not objecting to Judge Knight's questions at the time because the jury might have had the impression that Dr. Lunde's comments were important and worthy of greater weight because the judge felt they deserved to be clarified, an effect that might help Hooker's defense.

Moreover, even if the judge's questioning of Lunde had been deemed improper, the appellate court found that the error would not have harmed Hooker's case since there was other substantial evidence to corroborate his guilt. The testimony of Janice Hooker and Colleen Stan, as well as the physical evidence of the head box and Hooker's sadomasochistic paraphernalia, was sufficient to support a conviction. As such, Hooker's appeal was denied and his conviction and sentence were affirmed.

In the end, Colleen Stan survived her ordeal, but experienced significant anxiety and fears that emerged after her trial. She became a volunteer counselor for a crisis hotline that helped victims of domestic violence and sexual assault.[25] Janice Hooker divorced her husband, who is serving out his sentence in California's Folsom Prison.

The criminal trial of Cameron Hooker also serves as an interesting lesson in the range of experiences that expert witnesses may encounter when they enter the courtroom. Overall, the purpose of expert testimony is to provide judges and jurors with technical or specialized knowledge that will help in the process of making legal decisions. Expert witnesses are sometimes judged by the public as "hired guns," advocates for the side that hired them, irrelevant or unnecessary to the administration of justice, or sometimes a necessity to understand complicated issues. Those expert witnesses who are familiar with courtroom procedures recognize that there are both rewards (e.g., providing objective testimony that improves the administration of justice) and costs (e.g., harsh cross-examination) to testifying. Although a common belief has been that a "battle of the experts" often comes down to which expert is able to sway a jury, the Hooker case illustrates that among the many things about which judges make judgments is the credibility of the expert witnesses themselves.

⌐8

JOHN W.
HINCKLEY, JR.

Shooting for the Stars

⌐

Guns are Fun!
See that living legend over there?
With one little squeeze of this trigger
I can put that person at my feet
moaning and groaning and pleading with God.
This gun gives me pornographic power.
If I wish, the president will fall
and the world will look at me in disbelief, all because I own an
    inexpensive gun.
Guns are lovable, Guns are fun
Are you lucky enough to own one?
—JOHN W. HINCKLEY, JR., circa 1981[1]

Born in 1955, the third and youngest child of educated, well-to-do parents, John W. Hinckley, Jr., had every reason to believe that he would be a success in life. Both of his siblings were popular and successful, his father was a prosperous and powerful executive, and his mother was a stay-at-home parent who devoted herself to her children, particularly her youngest. As early as elementary school, John appeared to be following in the Hinckley family mold. A gifted athlete and natural leader, he quarterbacked the school football team and was a standout basketball player. In junior high school, he was, for two years, elected class president.

But Hinckley's early successes were short-lived. As is the case with many individuals who develop severe mental illnesses, it was not until John reached high school that anyone might have predicted the tragic course that his life would ultimately follow. Even then, however, no one could have predicted that less than a decade later John W. Hinckley, Jr., would attempt to assassinate the president of the United States and become the catalyst for the most sweeping reform in the history of the insanity defense.

In high school, Hinckley withdrew from friends and group activities, opting for a solitary life. A devoted Beatles fan, he began playing the guitar and spent countless hours alone in his room listening to and playing music. Dateless, friendless, and reclusive, he was by no means the "ordinary person" or "all-American boy"[2] federal prosecutors would describe to a jury, but he was bright and did well enough academically to graduate from high school in 1973 and get accepted to college.

Though accepted at Texas Tech, Hinckley never finished his degree. Instead, over the next seven years he attended classes there on and off, studying first business administration and then English, succeeding at neither. Hinckley's college years were punctuated by repeated periods in which he dropped out of school and moved back and forth among Lubbock, the home of Texas Tech; Colorado, where his parents had settled; and Hollywood, where he lived for a while on two occasions, supposedly pursuing his ambition of becoming a singer-songwriter.

From the time Hinckley graduated from high school in 1973 until his arrest for shooting President Reagan in 1981, he spent most of his time drifting along in what could perhaps be best described as a world of his own. For example, while supposedly pursuing a career in Hollywood one summer, Hinckley became obsessed with the film *Taxi Driver*, which he reportedly watched at least fifteen times. *Taxi Driver* featured Robert De Niro playing a violent and socially isolated cabbie named Travis Bickle who plots to kill a presidential candidate to win the affection of a woman. Unable to carry out his plot and ultimately rebuffed by the woman, Bickle turns his obsession to rescuing a twelve-year-old prostitute, portrayed by a then fourteen-year-old Jodie Foster. In the bloodbath that follows, Bickle shoots the girl's pimp, one of her customers, and the manager of the hotel where the young prostitute does business. Drawing upon the film, Hinckley created a make-believe girlfriend for himself and for years had his family convinced that she was real— so convinced, in fact, that his mother was devastated when she learned that the young woman she had heard so much about did not exist.

Had John Hinckley's fantasy life ended there, he never would have become a household name. But, of course, Hinckley's fantasies went well beyond "Lynn Collins," his fictitious lover. Hinckley's passion for *Taxi Driver* led first to a growing obsession with guns. In August 1979, Hinckley bought his first firearm, a .38 caliber pistol, which he used for target shooting and playing solo games of Russian roulette. Later he would purchase two more handguns and two rifles.

Hinckley's pathological fascination with *Taxi Driver* also appears to have led to his obsessive fantasies about co-star Jodie Foster. In 1980, Hinckley read in a magazine that the young actress was about to enter Yale University. From that point on, he became fixated on the Hollywood star—an obsession that would lead ultimately to his attempt to kill the president.

When Foster enrolled at Yale, Hinckley talked his parents into giving him $3,600, purportedly to enable him to enroll in a writing course at the Ivy League university. If such a course existed, Hinckley never enrolled, but he did travel to New Haven, Connecticut, hoping to get close to the object of his affections. Once there, Hinckley stalked Foster, tried to contact her, wrote her letters and poems, and actually may have managed to speak to her by phone on a couple of occasions.

When Foster did not respond favorably to Hinckley's advances, Hinckley took his obsession with her to another level. He decided he could gain the actress's attention and love by assassinating the U.S. president. Thereafter Hinckley began stalking President Jimmy Carter, following the president's campaign entourage to Dayton, Ohio and Nashville, Tennessee. Indeed, President Carter could easily have become Hinckley's victim. On one occasion, Hinckley showed up at a Carter campaign rally but had left his guns in his hotel room. On a second occasion, when Hinckley went to Nashville for a Carter campaign appearance, he was arrested when airport security personnel found guns in his suitcase; the guns were seized but Hinckley was merely fined and released.

Following the election in which Ronald Reagan defeated President Carter, Hinckley, who had purchased new weapons, transferred his homicidal attention to the president-elect. Hinckley's parents had no idea what he was up to, but meanwhile they had insisted that he get psychiatric treatment. During the fall of 1980 and winter of 1980–81, Hinckley was seen perhaps a dozen times by a Colorado psychiatrist, Dr. John Hopper, during Hinckley's frequent trips to his parents' home from the east coast. Though Hinckley confided to Hopper that he was infatuated with Foster, he never shared with the psychiatrist the full extent of his fantasy life, particularly his thoughts of violence. Hopper felt that Hinckley needed to become independent of his parents, who until then had been financially supporting their son and unwittingly bankrolling his stalking trips. Hopper recommended that the Hinckleys require John to leave their home and begin supporting himself. The agreed-upon plan was that Hinckley would do so by the end of March 1981. When, by the end of February, Hinckley had found no employment, he decided to leave home.

On March 7, 1981, Hinckley's father met him at the local airport. As the elder Hinckley would later recall,

> I told him how disappointed I was in him, how he had let us down, and how he had not followed the plan that we had all agreed on. And that he just left us no choice but to not take him back to the house again, but to force him to go on his own, And so that's what I did. . . . I had a couple of hundred dollars with me that I had brought from the house. And I gave that to him and I suggested that he go to the Y.M.C.A. He said he didn't want to do that. . . . I said, "O.K., you are on your own. Do whatever you want to."[3]

Hinckley then flew to Hollywood. After spending just a day there, he took a bus to Washington, D.C. where, on March 29, 1981, he checked into the Park Central Hotel. The following day, after seeing the president's daily itinerary in the *Washington Post*, Hinckley decided to try to kill Ronald Reagan. Just before leaving his hotel room, he wrote a letter to Foster:

> 3/30/81
> 12:45 P.M.
> Dear Jodie,
> There is a definite possibility that I will be killed in my attempt to get Reagan. It is for this very reason that I am writing you this letter now.
>
> As you well know by now I love you very much. Over the past seven months I've left you dozens of poems, letters and love messages in the faint hope that you could develop an interest in me. Although we talked on the phone a couple of times I never had the nerve to simply approach you and introduce myself. Besides my shyness, I honestly did not wish to bother you with my constant presence. I know the many messages left at your door and in your mailbox were a nuisance, but I felt that it was the most painless way for me to express my love for you.
>
> I feel very good about the fact that you at least know my name and know how I feel about you. And by hanging around your dor-

mitory, I've come to realize that I'm the topic of more than a little conversation, however full of ridicule it may be. At least you know that I'll always love you.

Jodie, I would abandon this idea of getting Reagan in a second if I could only win your heart and live out the rest of my life with you, whether it be in total obscurity or whatever.

I will admit to you that the reason I'm going ahead with this attempt now is because I just cannot wait any longer to impress you. I've got to do something now to make you understand, in no uncertain terms, that I am doing all of this for your sake! By sacrificing my freedom and possibly my life, I hope to change your mind about me. This letter is being written only an hour before I leave for the Hilton Hotel. Jodie, I'm asking you to please look into your heart and at least give me the chance, with this historical deed, to gain your respect and love.

I love you forever,
John Hinckley[4]

Less than an hour later, armed with a Rohm R6-14 revolver loaded with "devastator" bullets, in front of a group of television reporters, Hinckley pulled the weapon and fired six shots. The president was struck in the chest while three others (his press secretary, a Secret Service agent, and a police officer) were also wounded. Still pulling the trigger on an empty gun, Hinckley was wrestled to the ground as the president's limousine hurried away. Initially, Secret Service agents believed that Reagan had not been shot, but as it turned out a bullet had ricocheted off the limousine, struck the president, and lodged itself close to his heart. Two hours of surgery saved Reagan's life, and Hinckley was charged with multiple counts of attempted murder.

When Hinckley was tried, more than a year later, his defense was insanity. Prior to the Hinckley trial, most jurisdictions in the United States adhered to one or the other of two longstanding insanity laws. Most states followed the so-called M'Naughten test, which was developed in nineteenth-century England and used in the United States as early as 1895. Under M'Naughten, a defendant was not guilty by reason of insanity if by reason of mental illness he was unable to appreciate either the nature and consequences or the wrongfulness of his criminal act.[5]

Under a second test, developed by the American Law Institute between 1952 and 1962 and adopted by a minority of states and the federal government, a defendant was not guilty by reason of insanity if, at the time of the offense, "as a result of mental disease or defect he lack[ed] substantial capacity either to appreciate the criminality of his conduct or to conform his conduct to the requirements of law."[6]

Charged in the U.S. federal district court for the District of Columbia, Hinckley was tried under what was essentially the American Law Institute insanity standard. In an extraordinary display of resources made possible by the high-profile nature of the case as well as the wealth of the Hinckley family, Hinckley was examined by at least eight forensic mental health experts, four retained by each side in the litigation. Unlike the typical insanity case, in which the defense and prosecution each have one or, at most, two experts who examine the defendant for a few hours, John W. Hinckley, Jr., was interviewed and examined by these teams of experts for hundreds of hours at a staggering cost rarely if ever matched. It has been estimated that "the doctors for the government charged over three hundred thousand dollars in fees and expenses, and those for the defense about half that."[7] Of the approximately $450,000 spent on experts in the case, over a quarter of that amount went to one expert for the prosecution, Dr. Park Dietz, a forensic psychiatrist.[8]

The first question to be addressed by the experts who examined Hinckley was whether the twenty-six-year-old would-be presidential assassin suffered from a mental illness. In that regard, all the experts were in general agreement: Hinckley suffered from a diagnosable mental disorder. The question was: What disorder? Two psychiatrists retained by the defense found that Hinckley suffered from schizophrenia, perhaps the most severely debilitating of all mental illnesses. A third psychiatrist on the defense team said Hinckley suffered from schizotypal personality disorder, which he linked to schizophrenia, reporting that Hinckley presented "all the negative symptoms" of schizophrenia but not "the florid positive symptoms."[9] A clinical psychologist who had administered a battery of objective psychological tests to Hinckley at the behest of defense counsel concluded that the defendant had an IQ of 113, placing him in the "bright normal" range but that his responses to the Minnesota Multiphasic Personality Inventory made it clear that he was suffering from a severe mental illness.[10]

Not surprisingly, the prosecution experts had a different take on the nature of Hinckley's mental disorder. All of these doctors concluded that Hinckley was not schizophrenic and had not been psychotic when he shot the president. They diagnosed Hinckley as suffering from dysthymic disorder (essentially depression), narcissistic personality disorder (largely characterized by a self-centered, self-absorbed nature), and schizoid personality disorder (characterized by aloofness and inability to relate meaningfully to others).

Having answered the mental illness question in the affirmative, the experts then tackled the question of whether, by virtue of his mental disorder, Hinckley met the criteria for insanity spelled out in federal law. Testifying for the defense, Dr. William Carpenter awkwardly summarized the defense experts' conclusion and reasoning that Hinckley had been insane when he shot President Reagan:

> [Hinckley] lacked substantial capacity to appreciate the wrongful-ness of his conduct. . . .
>
> The reason for this opinion is that . . . in his own mind, his own reasoning, the predominant reasoning had to do with two major things, the first of which was the termination of his own existence; the second of which was to accomplish this union with Jodie Foster through death, after life, whatever. . . . He was not able to—he was not reasoning about the legality issue itself.[11]

Similarly, Dietz testified for the prosecution why he and his colleagues on that side of the case had concluded that Hinckley was not insane as the law defined that term:

> Mr. Hinckley did not lack substantial capacity to conform his con-duct to the requirements of the law. . . .
>
> His background indicates that in the past he had conformed his behavior, that he had had the ability to do so and had, in fact, done so. . . .
>
> He was able to make other decisions on that date. He decided where to go for breakfast, what to eat. He decided to buy a news-paper, to shower. He made personal decisions of that sort. He was not a man incapable on that day of making decisions about his life, about which of these relatively minor things to do. He deliberated and made a decision to survey the scene at the Hilton Hotel. . . .
>
> We know from the facts that he chose his bullets, that he loaded his revolver. . . . He chose the exploding bullets. This reflects deci-sion making and choice. He is controlling his conduct, is taking the time to write the "Jodie letter." . . . A man driven by passion, by uncontrollable forces, is not often inclined to take the time to write a letter to explain what this is about. He did. . . .
>
> He concealed the weapon . . . until the moment he chose to draw his weapon. . . . A man driven, a man out of control, would not have the capacity to wait at that moment for the best shot. . . .

The evidence of Mr. Hinckley's ability to appreciate wrong-fulness on March 30, 1981, [also] has a background. That background includes long-standing interest in fame and assassinations. It includes study of the publicity associated with various crimes. It includes extensive study of assassinations. . . . It includes his choice of concealable handguns for his assassination plans, and his recognition that the 6.5 rifle he purchased was too powerful for him to handle. It includes his purchase of Devastator exploding ammunition on June 18, 1980. It includes multiple writings about assassination plans. . . .

In that letter to Jodie Foster, he indicated he was going to attempt to get Reagan and he indicates his knowledge that he could be killed by the Secret Service in the attempt.

That is an indication that he understood and appreciated the wrongfulness of his plans because the Secret Service might well shoot someone who attempted to kill the President.[12]

Despite what many pundits and commentators regarded as the more persuasive testimony of the prosecution experts, particularly Dietz, after three days of deliberation, a jury of seven women and five men found John W. Hinckley, Jr., not guilty by reason of insanity. As the jury foreman later said, "The prosecution evidence was not strong enough."[13] And as another juror elaborated: "The evidence being what it was, we were required to send John back insane."[14]

Almost from its announcement the Hinckley verdict was sharply criticized and denounced. Blasting psychiatry as "ideology masquerading as medicine," conservative columnist George Will wrote that "the Hinckley verdict illustrates [that] the most morally indefensible crimes are becoming the most legally defensible."[15] But such critiques came not only from the political right. U.S. House Speaker Thomas P. ("Tip") O'Neill said he was "shocked" by the verdict and observed that in many other parts of the world, having shot the nations' leader, "Hinckley would be dead and buried in eight days." Even the public at large seemed outraged that a man videotaped shooting the President could somehow be found "not guilty." Undoubtedly speaking for many, one angry anonymous citizen interviewed by a public television reporter said:

I think it's disgraceful, frankly. I think it's a miscarriage of justice. We're going to be a laughing stock around the world. It's giving license to people to simply go out and shoot whoever they wish, and then parade a bunch of so-called expert witnesses out on trial, and they testify that in one case that you're guilty and in another case that, well, you're innocent because you're supposedly insane. And you throw temper tantrums in court and get out and run out of the courtroom whenever you feel like it, and all of a sudden you're scot-free.[16]

Before long these criticisms of the Hinckley verdict made their way to the halls of Congress and various statehouses around the country. Soon federal and state legislators were busy revising or abolishing insanity laws in an effort to make sure that another Hinckley verdict would never occur.

With virtually no opposition, Congress quickly amended federal insanity laws. In addition to removing the so-called volitional prong (lacking substantial capacity to conform one's conduct to the requirements of law) from the federal insanity test, the Federal Insanity Law Reform Act of 1984 changed the requirement of a "mental disease or defect" to a "severe mental disease or effect."[17] In the same sweeping reform, Congress also shifted the burden of proof from the prosecution to the defendant (thus requiring a defendant to now prove that he was insane rather than requiring the government to prove that he was not). Finally, as of October 12, 1984, Congress altered the Federal Rules of Evidence to provide that, while expert witnesses may still give opinions as to the ultimate issue in any case, they may not do so when that issue involves the mental state or condition of a criminal defendant:

> No expert witness testifying with respect to the mental state or condition of a defendant in a criminal case may state an opinion or inference as to whether the defendant did or did not have the mental state or condition constituting an element of the crime charged or of a defense thereto. Such ultimate issues are matters for the trier of fact alone.[18]

While Congress was busy reforming federal insanity law in the wake of the Hinckley verdict, many state legislatures also followed suit. Indeed, in the several years following Hinckley's acquittal, half the states in the country enacted one or more reform measures aimed at limiting the application of existing insanity laws. To summarize these reforms: seven states placed the burden of proving insanity on the defendant; four states added laws allowing jurors to find defendants guilty but mentally ill; and one state, Utah, abolished the insanity defense altogether.

Despite the flurry of legislative reform that followed the Hinckley trial, the insanity defense remains a viable option for criminal defendants in the vast majority of states as well as in the federal jurisdiction. Also, there is little evidence to suggest that these reforms have made any significant impact on the way the defense is used or how successful it is. Recent estimates indicate that fewer than 1 percent of criminal cases involve an insanity plea, and the majority of those cases end up with a verdict of guilty.[19] But, as the Hinckley case itself illustrates, even where a criminal defendant does manage to obtain a verdict of not guilty by reason of insanity, in many cases it may be a pyrrhic victory.

Upon acquittal in 1982, John Hinckley was committed to St. Elizabeth's Hospital, a federal psychiatric center in Washington, D.C., where he was evaluated and found to be a danger to self and others, including Jodie Foster, for whom he continued to express his love. Under law, Hinckley is to remain there until such time as he is no longer deemed mentally ill and dangerous.

In 1985, Hinckley sought increased privileges at the hospital, testifying in court that "my doctors and I believe that my judgment is much better and my obsession with Jodie Foster has been over for 19 months." To that testimony, Hinckley added:

> I think I am ready, too, for limited ground privileges. . . . All I want
> is the chance to have my therapy in the sunshine for a change
> away from the walls and fences and bars and every other depress-
> ing thing.
>
> I now cherish my life and believe that everyone's life is sacred
> and precious. I will never again harm another human being. Please
> give me the opportunity to prove to you and the hospital and the
> entire world that I am getting well.[20]

Despite Hinckley's moving testimony, the court denied his request for grounds privileges and an end to restrictions on interviews. Two years later Hinckley applied for a court order allowing him periodic home visits. As part of the review of this request, the judge ordered Hinckley's hospital room searched. Carrying out that order, hospital officials found photographs and letters showing a continued obsession with Foster as well as evidence that Hinckley had exchanged letters with serial killer Ted Bundy and had sought the address of mass murderer Charles Manson. Again the court denied Hinckley's request for additional privileges.

In 1999, seventeen years after his initial commitment, Hinckley, whose psychosis had been in remission for years, was again turned down for additional privileges. This time, however, an appeals court reversed the trial court's judgment, and Hinckley began a series of supervised trips off the hospital grounds, all of which proved to be uneventful.

In 2003, the court finally held that Hinckley, then forty-eight years old, was no longer a danger to self and others and was thus capable of handling unsupervised visits with his parents. A year later, in November 2004, the court heard testimony from psychologists, psychiatrists, and other professionals at St. Elizabeth's that, after more than twenty-two years of hospitalization, Hinckley was finally ready to be released from the hospital under his parents' supervision because his psychiatric illnesses remained in remission.

Rejecting the staff's testimony as well as Hinckley's request for a four-day home visit every two weeks, the judge granted Hinckley up to six trips with his parents to last no more than thirty-two hours each and involve travel no more than fifty miles from the District of Columbia. As they have done in the past, the U.S. Secret Service planned to observe all of Hinckley's trips off hospital grounds.

9

JUDAS PRIEST

A Message

in the Music

∎

E qually disconcerting and puzzling are cases in which young people direct violence toward themselves in the form of suicidal behavior. There are many factors that contribute to self-destructive behavior, including depression, hopelessness, substance abuse, and peer influences. Identifying a specific cause for violent and suicidal behavior in young people has been extremely difficult. So when a young person commits suicide and grief-stricken family members look for a reason, the direct or proximate cause of the suicide is often difficult to identify. Furthermore, if surviving family members claim that a certain product on the market or another person contributed to their child's death, a lawsuit often quickly follows. Wrongful death suits are complex and often raise interesting questions about causation. A civil suit against the British heavy metal music group Judas Priest, brought by the family members of two teenagers who shot themselves, focused on one of the most perplexing questions ever raised about the psychological causes of self-destructive behavior. Was it possible that subliminal messages on a record album induced two young men to shoot themselves?

On December 23, 1985, eighteen-year-old Raymond Belknap and twenty-year-old James Vance had spent several hours drinking beer, smoking marijuana, and listening to Judas Priest music at Belknap's home.[1] At some point the two men entered into a suicide pact. They took a sawed-off shotgun to a children's playground located in an empty churchyard. Belknap was the first to put the gun to his throat and pull the trigger; he died instantly. Vance then took the shotgun and put it under his chin. At the last moment, the gun moved and Vance blew off the lower portion of his face. He endured thirteen separate surgeries attempting to reconstruct his face. Among the various procedures that Vance underwent were the construction of a new nose and two surgeries to implant a bone where his chin had once been. The judge who presided over the case would later describe the results of Vance's suicide attempt as "the most horrible, disfiguring injury that this court has ever observed."[2]

In recent years a number of violent crimes committed by children and teenagers have received considerable media attention. Among the most visible have been the shootings at Columbine High School and the Washington, D.C., sniper attacks. Although these cases differ in their facts, a common theme among all of them is that in their wake they always seem to evoke questions of why. Why do some young people commit such severe acts of violence, and why does it appear that juvenile violence has been on the rise? In the search for answers, the influence of violence in the media has often been a focus of concern. Social scientists, observers in the media, and legal experts have turned their attention to violence in video games, television programs, music lyrics, and movies as possible causes of violence in young people.

Despite having to endure hundreds of hours of surgery and incurring over $400,000 in medical expenses, Vance remained horribly disfigured. Because most of his face was destroyed by his suicide attempt, Vance drooled constantly, had to wear a bib most of the time, and was required to sleep with a towel under him. He also experienced recurrent nightmares as a result of witnessing Belknap's suicide. Although Vance survived the shooting and even went on to father a child, he died three years later on November 24, 1988, from a methadone overdose that was believed to be caused by complications stemming from his injuries and the use of prescription medications.[3]

Sometime after Belknap and Vance had left to carry out their suicide pact, Belknap's mother, Aunetta Roberson, went into her son's room to find the remnants of their drinking and marijuana use. In addition, she found an album on the turntable of her son's record player entitled *Stained Class* by Judas Priest. One of the songs on the album, "Heroes End and Saints in Hell," caught her eye.[4] Another song, "Better by You, Better Than Me," that would later become a major focus in the search for answers as to why Belknap and Vance shot themselves, was face down on the other side of the album. Roberson flushed the marijuana down the toilet, threw out the empty beer cans, and called the police because her son was missing.[5] At that point, she did not know what had happened.

When Vance was interviewed by police officers the next day, he told them he had attempted suicide because "life sucks," yet he made no mention of Judas Priest or their music.[6] Over the next two years, however, Vance and his family, as well as Belknap's mother, came to believe that there was another cause for the suicide pact.

Another publicized tragedy may have had an impact on how the Judas Priest case developed. On January 12, 1986, the father of a California teenager issued a public statement that he was going to sue rock star Ozzy Osbourne and CBS Records.[7] The teen's father claimed that his son killed himself in 1984 after listening to Osbourne's music. In February of 1986, following the man's announcement, Roberson contacted an attorney and asked him to file a suit against Judas Priest and CBS Records claiming that the heavy metal band's music caused her son to commit suicide. Vance's mother initially declined to join the suit when Roberson contacted her to see if she wanted to sue Judas Priest and their record company.

However, Vance informed the police in March that the music he and Belknap were listening to right before their suicide attempt may have contributed to their behavior. He wrote a letter to Belknap's mother stating, "We were mesmerized. There was no doubt, no second thought in my mind that I was going to pull that trigger, even though I didn't want to die."[8]

On May 8, 1986, Roberson's lawyer filed a civil lawsuit claiming that the music of Judas Priest was the direct cause of her son's suicide. Two months later on July 10, 1986, the Vance family filed their own lawsuit, and five months later the trial judge consolidated both cases. The families of both Belknap and Vance were claiming that the album *Stained Class*, produced in 1978, contained the song "Better by You, Better Than Me" in which the heavy metal group was alleged to have intentionally included the subliminal phrase "do it." The lawsuit sought to recover money from the band and their record company to reimburse medical expenses related to treatment that Vance received for his injuries, compensate the families for the deaths of both young men (once Vance died), and support the child Vance fathered following his suicide attempt but prior to his death in 1988.

The band members denied placing any subliminal messages on the album. Rob Halford, lead singer of Judas Priest, stated: "In my opinion, even if you do—and we didn't—put a backward message [on the record], it's protected by the First Amendment. . . . It's freedom of speech. Their allegations to us were on a different matter: They said we put in a forward message that the brain listened to backwards."[9] Furthermore, Halford believed the deaths of both Belknap and Vance were due to a combination of factors, including their substance abuse, a lack of proper care and guidance from their families, and long-standing emotional problems.[10] The general position taken by the defendants was that the lawsuit was merely an attempt to shift the responsibility for the deaths to someone other than Belknap and Vance.

The legal questions raised by the case were novel and had not been extensively addressed in prior cases. One legal issue was whether subliminal messages should be considered speech that is protected under the First Amendment of the U.S. Constitution.[11] Regular lyrics on a musical recordings are considered a form of artistic expression and have First Amendment protection. But Belknap and Vance would argue that subliminal messages are different and not protected speech. A second question raised in the case was a factual one: Did Judas Priest place the subliminal message "do it" on their recording of "Better by You, Better Than Me"? Finally, the key issue in this case, and one that would hinge on expert testimony from a number of psychologists, was whether subliminal messages could cause a person to commit an act such as suicide. In order for the families of Belknap and Vance to prevail, they would need to convince a jury that there indeed was a subliminal message (i.e., "do it") on the Judas Priest record, that this phrase was intentionally placed on the record by the band, that the phrase referred to suicide, and that it was the direct cause of Belknap's and Vance's suicidal acts.

Just before the case was to go to trial, both the plaintiffs and the defendants waived a jury trial and agreed to have the presiding judge, the Honorable Jerry Whitehead of Washoe County, Nevada, hear testimony and decide the case. In a pretrial ruling, Judge Whitehead had disagreed with a claim by Judas Priest that subliminal messages, even if they were present on the album, were protected by the First Amendment. Judge Whitehead ruled that subliminal speech is not protected by the First Amendment because it does not communicate any information and other people have the right to be free of unwanted speech. The key issue at trial was whether subliminal messages on the Judas Priest record caused the deaths of Vance and Belknap.

Subliminal messaging first gained attention in September 1957 when James Vicary, a motivational research specialist, publicized his development of a technology that would allow advertisers to insert messages within advertisements that gave suggestions to individuals without their conscious awareness as a way of influencing their behavior.[12] At his press conference, Vicary reported the results of an experiment he had conducted where he flashed phrases such as "Hungry? Eat Popcorn" and "Drink Coca-Cola" during a motion picture at 1/3,000th of a second every five seconds during the film.[13] The results showed that popcorn sales increased 57 percent and sales of Coca-Cola increased 18 percent among groups that were shown the messages. As a result of Vicary's announcement, strong public criticism arose that subliminal messaging was unethical because it attempted to influence people's behavior without their awareness. Over the years, various attempts have been made to regulate the use of subliminal messages in advertising with limited success. One of the few legal restrictions on subliminal messaging has been its prohibition from use in the advertising of alcoholic beverages. However, Vance and Belknap were attempting to prove that subliminal messages had caused their lethal behavior. A computer expert for the plaintiffs prepared a tape of the twenty-four-track recording of the song "Better by You, Better Than Me" that broke the song down into smaller components. Initially, Judge Whitehead was able to hear the phrase "do it" on the recording and believed that it was intentionally placed on the album. The judge listened carefully to the recording both in open court and privately in his chambers, using sophisticated audio equipment.[14] However, members of Judas Priest testified that the phrase was not placed on the recording and provided the judge with a studio recording that revealed the words "do it" were the result of a combination of two tracks containing singer Rob Halford exhaling on one and a guitar on the other. After hearing the new evidence, Judge Whitehead concluded that, even though the phrase could be heard in the song, it was due to a chance combination of sounds on the recording rather than intentional speech.

In his decision, Judge Whitehead held that because Judas Priest had not acted intentionally when the phrase "do it" was included on their recording, the lawsuit by Vance and Belknap would be dismissed and Judas Priest would not be held liable. However, the judge went on to discuss the issue of whether the subliminal message caused Belknap's suicide and Vance's attempted suicide. Since the issue of music lyrics causing self-destructive behavior in young people had not been litigated in any previous cases, Whitehead's decision broke new ground and therefore became a leading case in forensic psychology.

The lawyers for Belknap and Vance had called psychologist Howard Shevrin as an expert witness to support their claim that the subliminal message in the song by Judas Priest caused Belknap and Vance to shoot themselves. Dr. Shevrin was a highly respected researcher who had published over fifty articles on the subject of subliminal perception and its effect and the unconscious. Judge Whitehead had the "highest respect" for Dr. Shevrin and wrote the following about the plaintiff's expert:

> His academic credentials are excellent, his experience is very strong, his research in the field is by far the most extensive of any witness to testify, and he is not a professional witness. This is the only trial

in which he has ever testified. The Court concludes that he testified based upon sincere beliefs and not merely as an advocate for the side that called him.[15]

At trial, Dr. Shevrin testified that subliminal information is received by individuals at a "supraliminal" level, meaning that a person is unaware the information has been received. Nevertheless, his research purportedly showed that people react to subliminal messages and that these messages can affect a person's behavior, emotions, and health.

Dr. Shevrin also testified that in order for subliminal messages to be capable of influencing a person's behavior, the person must have a "personality predisposition" that makes it more likely that he or she will engage in a particular act.[16] However, situational factors also predispose a person to commit a particular act. According to Shevrin, if a person is predisposed to commit suicide as a result of any number of factors in his or her personality, and situational factors interact with predisposing factors, a person is in a "suicide zone." He testified that: "the subliminal command 'do it' created a compulsion towards doing that which James [Vance] and Raymond [Belknap] were already predisposed to do, to commit suicide."[17]

The scientific basis of Shevrin's testimony, of course, was challenged by lawyers for Judas Priest. Before trial, Shevrin was asked by Bill Peterson, a lawyer for Judas Priest, "What experiments are you referring to when you say you're referring to a body of literature, experiments on which you base your conclusion that subliminal messages may be sufficient to induce suicidal behavior?" Shevrin replied, "I'm basing my opinion, my expert judgment, on a corpus of literature, on hundreds of experiments." Peterson, however, pressed Shevrin to name one study that would support his contention that subliminal messages could cause suicidal behavior.[18] Although Shevrin pointed to a handful of studies that purportedly showed subliminal messages could cause suicidal behavior, experts for Judas Priest argued that none of the studies cited by Shevrin had anything to do with proving subliminal messages induced certain motives or behavior in people.

The entire scientific basis of subliminal influences has been a controversial area in psychological science, one that some have called "pseudoscientific."[19] A confusing aspect of the plaintiff's case came when Susan Rusk, a guidance counselor at James Vance's school, testified that she had questioned Vance about the suicide attempt. Rusk said that Vance told her he and Belknap received the message "do it" from the Judas Priest record, suggesting that the two men had been consciously aware of the message. If Vance and Belknap knew they were hearing the message, then Shevrin's claim that the messages were subliminal, or out of conscious awareness, was incorrect. As a result, Vance's suicide attempt and Belknap's suicide could be attributed to something other than the Judas Priest song, such as situational factors (e.g., substance abuse) or the personal motives of Vance and Belknap.

A number of experts testified for the defense. Dr. Anthony Pratkanis, a social psychologist and professor at the University of California at Santa Cruz, testified about research he had conducted that demonstrated subliminal self-help tapes were essentially ineffective for influencing human behavior. Like Shevrin, Pratkanis was viewed favorably by Judge Whitehead, who was of the opinion that Pratkanis "also made a sincere effort to objectively review the subject matter and testify in an impartial manner."[20]

Although Pratkanis had conducted some research on subliminal perception, it was noted that he was not a clinician trained to diagnose and treat mental disorders. Pratkanis testified that while research tended to show that subliminal stimuli can have an effect on mental processing, much of the research was limited to "semantic priming" where people can decrease the amount of time it takes them to recognize the meaning of a target word when a related word is presented subliminally right before the target word.[21] However, Pratkanis was of the opinion that there was no scientific evidence of a dynamic unconscious part of the mind that could be influenced by subliminal messages that would in turn cause a person to act in a particular way.

Another expert, Dr. Timothy Moore, testified about the flaws that existed in many of the studies on subliminal messages and the influence these messages have on human behavior. Moore also testified that he believed there was dubious scientific evidence to support many of the psychodynamic concepts about which Shevrin testified. Moore was of the opinion that no scientific evidence supported the notion that subliminal messages could induce suicidal behavior. A cognitive psychologist, Dr. Don Read from the University of Lethbridge, also testified for the defense about how people comprehend and retain reversed speech. This issue was related to the claim by plaintiffs that backward messages were contained in the *Stained Class* album. Although the practice of placing backward messages in recordings is apparently quite prevalent among rock bands, their influence on behavior is untested.

Overall, the expert witnesses for Judas Priest were of the opinion that Vance's suicide attempt and Belknap's suicide were due to depression brought about by alcohol and marijuana consumption and a host of personality, employment, and family problems that the two men experienced. In his opinion, Judge Whitehead expressed surprise that there were no controlled experiments on the issue of whether subliminal messages could influence behavior. Furthermore, the judge found there was adequate scientific evidence to support the notion that people perceive stimuli at a subliminal level and that there was credible evidence that Vance and Belknap perceived the subliminal message "do it." However, Judge Whitehead did not elaborate on an apparent contradiction: If Vance and Belknap perceived the phrase, then how could it have been "subliminal?"

More important was the fact that Judge Whitehead concluded there was simply no scientific research to support the theory that subliminal messages on the Judas Priest album caused the suicidal behavior by Vance and Belknap. Other factors were noted by the judge that could have been causal factors, although he was mindful of the fact that he did not want his discussion of these factors to appear as though Vance and Belknap were being "demeaned."[23] The factors listed in the judge's opinion were intended to illustrate that there were other factors that placed Vance and Belknap at high risk for suicide.

Among the concerns noted by Judge Whitehead was the fact that Vance and Belknap had extremely poor school adjustment. Vance had a learning disability and dropped out of school in his sophomore year and Belknap dropped out in his junior year. Both young men had been expelled for defying authority and they each had a history of violent behavior. For example, Vance had choked his mother on one occasion and Belknap had been expelled in junior high school due to a sexual assault. There was extensive substance abuse in the histories of both Vance and Belknap, as they used alcohol, marijuana, and cocaine. Heavy metal music played an important role in the lives of both Vance and Belknap; they shared an affinity for Judas Priest music because of its loudness and the aggressive nature of the lyrics. Moreover, Vance and Belknap had conflict with their families over their love for heavy metal music and there were violent outbursts when attempts were made by their parents to limit their playing of the music.[24] Overall, Judge Whitehead believed that a combination of factors precipitated the suicidal behavior of Vance and Belknap and none of the evidence pointed to a specific legal or proximate cause.

Although the case of Judas Priest and alleged subliminal messages was interesting, it was also a defining case in several respects. For one thing, Judge Whitehead's pretrial ruling that subliminal messages were not protected by the First Amendment because they serve no legitimate purpose and may constitute an unwarranted invasion of privacy[25] has been cited in other cases involving allegations of subliminal influences by heavy metal artists. A similar suit was brought against heavy metal singer Ozzy Osbourne but later dismissed. In addition, the Judas Priest case involved a claim that did not appear to be clearly resolved in the field of psychology—namely, whether subliminal messages can induce someone to act in a certain way, let alone commit suicide. In fact, some have argued that the entire notion of subliminal messages influencing human behavior to any appreciable degree is pseudoscientific, which makes it somewhat surprising that the Judas Priest case ever made it to trial.

Thomas Moore, one of the experts who testified for Judas Priest, later commented that the judge may have been "seduced by psychodynamics" but nevertheless arrived at a conclusion that was supported by scientific research.[26] Still, Moore appeared to take exception to some of the judge's treatment of the research on subliminal perception offered by Shevrin. Moore felt that the judge may have afforded the research more credibility than was warranted. In particular, Moore pointed out that there is an important difference between "subliminal stimuli," that can have some effect on mental processing, and "subliminal influences" that supposedly influence unconscious motives and behavior. Moore dismissed the notion alluded to in Judge Whitehead's opinion that subliminal messages might affect the unconscious mind.

The differing opinions of the expert witnesses in the Judas Priest trial reflect a split in the field of psychology that has important implications. More specifically, there is a rift between many clinicians and researchers about the scientific basis of certain principles, particularly psychodynamic or psychoanalytic concepts like the unconscious mind. The plaintiff's expert, Dr. Shevrin, was trained as a clinician who had experience in the diagnosis and treatment of mental disorders. His testimony indicated that he accepted not only that unconscious motivations and personality dynamics can influence human behavior but also that subliminal messages can induce certain motivations and influence behavior. Many of the experts for the defendants, including Drs. Pratkanis, Moore, and Read, were experimental psychologists trained to conduct research on social and cognitive aspects of human behavior. However, the court opinion recognized that these experts were not clinicians trained to treat mental disorders. As such, these experimental psychologists tended to view abstract concepts such as the unconscious mind with skepticism and were of the opinion that the scientific basis of many psychoanalytic principles was very weak.

Of course, not all clinicians in psychology have a psychoanalytic perspective. There are many different theoretical models that can be used to understand and treat psychological problems, including behavioral, humanistic, cognitive, and eclectic models. In the Judas Priest case, Judge Whitehead wrote a very prudent, respectful, and balanced opinion in which he gave the testimony of each expert appropriate weight and consideration. Despite the standard "battle of the experts," the judge seemed to see the psychological experts as credible and having something to contribute to the major issue in the case. Still, an implicit theme that runs through the court's opinion in the Judas Priest case is the notion that there is a marked split between clinicians who accept the validity of certain abstract theoretical positions and empiricists who view certain theories and techniques as pseudoscientific or lacking in scientific merit. There are many areas of professional practice where this split between science and practice is quite noticeable, such as whether the Rorschach inkblot method is a reliable and valid assessment technique or if repressed memories of childhood abuse are reliable. With respect to the profound differences between clinicians and researchers in their approach to problems in forensic psychology, the Judas Priest case was a harbinger of things to come.

From a legal perspective, the Judas Priest case also broke new ground. In light of the fact that the plaintiffs were unsuccessful in proving that rock lyrics were the proximate cause of their suicidal behavior, there have been no subsequent cases in which musical groups have been held liable for self-injurious or violent behavior as a result of subliminal messages being placed on a musical recording. Judge Whitehead's opinion was a trial court decision and therefore it has no authority as a legal precedent over lower courts. Nevertheless, his legal analysis involving First Amendment issues, where he held that subliminal messages are not protected speech when they are received by individuals without their knowledge or consent, remains persuasive and has served as a guide for other cases involving subliminal messages in heavy metal music.[27]

One of the main reasons that there has been no increase in litigation over subliminal messages in rock lyrics in the wake of the Judas Priest case is the fact that the trial judge was unpersuaded by the scientific evidence that subliminal messages caused behavior of the magnitude that Vance and Belknap committed. Still, some legal commentators have stated that the scientific evidence demonstrating that subliminal messaging can cause self-destructive behavior is far from settled and there is hope that "[a]s further [research] results become available, the relationship between subliminals and the ability to elicit behavior will be clarified."[28] At least one legal commentator has suggested that the result of the Judas Priest case, or one with similar facts, would be different if the scientific evidence was able to prove a causal relationship between subliminal messages and injurious behavior.[29]

However, this argument seems extremely weak. Absent clear scientific evidence, it seems very doubtful that proximate causation could be shown merely "when a harmful message is perceived and action follows from the message."[30] It seems that legal arguments such as the one advanced by Vance and Belknap are prone to an error in judgment known as "illusory correlation" wherein causal significance is wrongly attributed to one factor (in this case subliminal messages) merely because it happens to occur close in time to another factor (suicidal behavior). Expert testimony supported by sound scientific research is one of the ways in which reasoning errors of this nature can be avoided.

Despite the fact that the Judas Priest case appeared to be a "battle of the experts," during which widely differing opinions were offered as to the interpretation of scientific evidence and the application of research findings to the cause of Vance's and Belknap's suicidal behavior, the case was decided judiciously and fairly. Even as more scientific research comes forth to improve our understanding of how people process subliminal information, it is very likely that there will be competing views of how this research should be interpreted and applied to real-world cases.

The Judas Priest subliminal messages case impacted the lives of a number of people. As a musical group, Judas Priest faced the onerous task of having to defend not only their music against a claim that it had caused someone to commit suicide, but also the genre of heavy metal music, which has been seen by many people as having an adverse impact on the psychological development of young people who listen to it. Whether or not these claims are true should be based on scientific research, not emotional claims or biased arguments. As Rob Halford, the lead singer of Judas Priest, queried, "Why didn't it [suicide] happen to more? Why did it just happen to these two? Half a million people listened to it [the album]."[31]

On the other hand, Raymond Belknap, James Vance, and their families suffered the most. The lives of both young men were cut short, albeit by their own hands. Perhaps the most important and useful scientific research will come from studies that help us understand how a wide range of factors—not just a single one—interact with one another to cause young people to kill themselves. If we understand suicide better, then we can develop more effective ways of preventing tragedies before they occur.

⌐10

JOHN
DEMJANJUK

Is He "Ivan

the Terrible"?

◢

Many highly celebrated criminal trials throughout American history, such as the Lindbergh baby kidnapping and O. J. Simpson cases, have remained controversial. Debate continues over the guilt or innocence of the defendants in these cases long after the trials have finished. One of the reasons that some cases remain unresolved, at least in the minds of some, is the absence of eyewitnesses to the crimes. Therefore, many controversial cases—such as Scott Peterson who is the California man convicted and sentenced to death for the murder of his pregnant wife—must be tried on the basis of circumstantial evidence.

Eyewitness testimony is highly probative evidence, meaning that when witnesses can testify that they saw who committed a crime jurors are likely to give great weight to the testimony. However, a specialized area of study in the field of forensic psychology known as eyewitness testimony research has demonstrated that eyewitnesses are not always accurate in their ability to identify the perpetrator of a crime. Psychologists who study eyewitness testimony rely on the basic principle that if you can preserve an objective record of an event, such as a videotape, and then study how people respond to the event, it is possible to evaluate the accuracy of testimony about the event.[1] Unfortunately, objective records of criminal activity—like videotapes—rarely exist in the real world, so the accuracy of eyewitness testimony must be evaluated in light of crime-scene evidence.

Suggestive questions also shouldn't be asked in therapy?

When witnesses testify at trial, they must rely on memory of the event in order to tell a story of what they saw at a particular time and place. However, human memory is fallible because at each stage of the memory process something can occur to disrupt or impair a person's ability to accurately recall a series of events. A person must acquire information by perceiving and attending to an event; if stress or some other factor distracts the person then the acquisition of information might be impaired. Additionally, a person must retain the information by encoding it and placing it into memory; if the passage of time or information obtained after the event (e.g., a suggestion from another person) causes the information to change, then eyewitness accuracy can also be influenced. Finally, a person must be able to retrieve the information from memory; if the person is asked leading or suggestive questions, then the person's recollection may change. All of these factors can lead to questions about the accuracy of human memory and eyewitness testimony in court.

When a defendant's life hangs in the balance, the accuracy of eyewitness testimony becomes a paramount concern. In one of the most celebrated criminal cases of all time, the psychology of eyewitness testimony became the crucial issue that would help shed light on accusations of war crimes, Nazi atrocities, and lingering questions about the true identity of an unassuming elderly man.

For nearly three decades, John Demjanjuk lived in relative obscurity as an automobile plant worker raising a family near Cleveland, Ohio.[2] He immigrated to the United States shortly after obtaining a visa in 1951 and appeared to live the life of a model citizen. In 1975, however, the name Ivan (John) Demjanjuk was found on a list of suspected Nazi war criminals given to the U.S. Immigration and Naturalization Service by a native of the Soviet Ukraine living in the United States.[3] Over the next few years, government officials began to suspect that Demjanjuk may have served as a guard at Sobibor, a smaller Nazi camp near the larger Treblinka death camp in Poland.[4] Although initially no evidence was uncovered that pointed to Demjanjuk ever having killed anyone, his U.S. citizenship was nevertheless revoked in 1981 because he had lied on his 1951 visa application by failing to disclose his Nazi affiliations during World War II.[5]

The publicity surrounding Demjanjuk's case led to wide circulation of an identity card obtained from Soviet records that purported to show Demjanjuk's picture with a Nazi SS identification number.[6] Shortly after the revocation of his U.S. citizenship, Demjanjuk was identified by survivors of the Treblinka death camp as "Ivan the Terrible," a sadistic guard who ran the gas chambers and tortured prisoners at the camp.

Was Demjanjuk really "Ivan the Terrible" or was he the victim of mistaken identity? Were witnesses able to identify Ivan accurately after nearly forty-five years, or were their memories susceptible to error given the passage of time? These questions were addressed at Demjanjuk's trial after he was extradited from the United States to Israel and became the first man to be tried as a Nazi war criminal since 1961 when Adolf Eichmann was convicted for orchestrating the Holocaust.[7]

Demjanjuk's alibi was based on his claim that he never knew anything about the Treblinka or Sobibor camps until after World War II was over.[8] He claimed to be a member of the Red Army when Germany attacked the Soviet Union in 1941 and to have been captured by the German army in May 1942. Demjanjuk maintained that he was held in various German POW camps until the middle of 1944 when he was released to fight in an anti-Soviet Ukrainian army. He alleged that following the end of World War II he joined the Allied forces in Bavaria. Of course, the U.S. government did not accept Demjanjuk's claims. They believed he joined the German forces and became a Nazi prison guard who was ultimately stationed at the Treblinka camp.

The evidence against Demjanjuk included not only the identity card, but also five eyewitness survivors of the Treblinka camp who identified him from two small photographs. One of the most dramatic moments of Demjanjuk's trial came when Eiliyahu Rosenberg, a sixty-two-year-old man who had survived Treblinka, was asked to look at the accused man. Rosenberg asked the judge to have Demjanjuk remove his glasses. Despite objections by Demjanjuk's attorney, the judge ruled the request permissible and directed the defendant to remove his glasses. Demjanjuk then asked his attorney to have the witness come closer and, after removing his glasses, gestured to shake hands with his accuser and said "Shalom."[9]

Rosenberg was shocked and stumbled backwards; his wife fainted in the courtroom after the accused man gestured to her husband. As stunned observers looked on, Rosenberg shouted, "It is Ivan. I say unhesitatingly and without the slightest doubts. This is Ivan from the gas chambers. The man I am looking at now. I saw his eyes, I saw those murderous eyes. I saw that face of his. How dare you put out your hand to me!"[10] Although Demjanjuk's attorney argued that the gesture was merely an attempt to wish peace to a mistaken accuser, other courtroom observers thought it was a form of "psychological torture" by a sadistic guard from a Nazi concentration camp.

In order to prove that Demjanjuk was the victim of mistaken identity, his lawyers needed to prove that the eyewitness identification of his accusers was faulty and that their memories were mistaken. Expert testimony was needed to demonstrate that the memories of witnesses identifying Demjanjuk as Ivan the Terrible were wrong because Demjanjuk's photograph from a Nazi identification card had been repeatedly shown in the context of recent newspaper articles about Nazi atrocities. Were the memories of eyewitnesses about Demjanjuk being at Treblinka based on actual events or were they the product of recent articles suggesting Demjanjuk was Ivan the Terrible?

The police division responsible for investigating the possibility that Demjanjuk had been the sadistic Nazi prison guard was the Division for the Investigation of Nazi Crimes, a unit of the Israeli police force. Meriam Radiwker and Martin Kollar were employees of the division who took responsibility for most of the witness interviews in the Demjanjuk case. Radiwker took out an initial newspaper advertisement in which she sought information from survivors of Sobibor and Treblinka announcing, "The Nazi Crime Investigation Division is conducting an investigation against the Ukrainians Ivan Demjanjuk and Fedor Fedorenko. Survivors of the Death Camps at Sobibor and Treblinka are requested to report to the Israel Police Headquarters."[11] The problem with this initial solicitation for eyewitness identification purposes was that any witnesses coming forward who would be asked to identify Ivan the Terrible would also know that Demjanjuk's last name was the focus of inquiry. Did this initial solicitation create a potential source of bias for witnesses to identify Demjanjuk as Ivan?

One source of error in eyewitness identification involves a phenomenon known as _unconscious transference_.[12] In cases where witnesses have recognized the face of another person, the witness may sometimes be unclear about the original circumstances in which the face was first seen. This process, in which the witness may incorrectly identify a face seen in one context (e.g., an innocent bystander) as belonging in a different context (e.g., to the perpetrator of a crime), is referred to as unconscious transference. However, empirical evidence in support of the validity of this concept is inconclusive because it is difficult to create the process in psychological laboratories. Whether unconscious transference is a special psychological phenomenon that occurs among eyewitnesses with certain characteristics or is merely the result of confusion on the part of some witnesses remains unclear. Nevertheless, there have been actual criminal cases where mistaken identities were the product of unconscious transference.

In the case of John Demjanjuk, it might have been possible that some witnesses identifying him as the sadistic Nazi prison guard were mistaken because they had seen him in another context. If Demjanjuk had been at the prison camp but had worked in a benign capacity, some witnesses may have mistakenly recognized his face but placed it in the erroneous context of being

Ivan the Terrible. In fact, some survivors of the Treblinka camp were uncertain if Demjanjuk was, in fact, Ivan the Terrible. Prisoners at the camp reportedly never knew the last names of their guards (hence, "Ivan the Terrible" rather than a complete name). So questions arose over the identification of one survivor, Eugen Turowski, who claimed under questioning by Israeli police that he knew the name "Demjanjuk" and recognized it as belonging to the dreaded guard "Ivan."[13]

Further concerns arose over the possibility that some eyewitnesses who identified Demjanjuk as Ivan the Terrible were influenced by other eyewitnesses. Although Turowski could not initially identify Ivan the Terrible from a photo spread containing Demjanjuk's picture, he subsequently identified Demjanjuk after another witness, Avrajam Goldfarb, had remembered the name Ivan Demjanjuk and identified his photograph from the layout prepared for witness identification. Goldfarb's identification was shrouded in controversy as well because he had apparently written in a memoir after the end of World War II that Ivan had been killed in the 1943 uprising of prisoners at the Treblinka camp.[14] One of Demjanjuk's defense attorneys, Mark O'Connor, noted that Goldfarb and Turowski knew each other and had been questioned within hours of one another. An argument advanced by the defense, therefore, was that some witnesses spoke to each other and came to the same conclusion that Ivan the Terrible was alive and that John Demjanjuk was Ivan.

Another problem that arose in the questioning of witnesses had to do with the photo spread police used to question witnesses. The picture of Demjanjuk that was used had been taken in 1951 at the time he had immigrated to the United States. However, witnesses were basing their identification on experiences they had with Ivan the Terrible nine years earlier. Many of the survivors were believed to have had only fleeting encounters with Ivan the Terrible, yet they were being asked to identify a man they had seen nearly thirty-five years earlier by a picture of what the man might look like nine years after their encounter. The photo spread would become a focus of contention for the defense and would figure prominently in the forensic psychological testimony presented at Demjanjuk's trial.

Other survivors of the camp who were doubtful about identifying Demjanjuk as the sadistic guard had their doubts negated by other people.[15] At a 1976 reunion of survivors from the Treblinka camp held in Tel Aviv, Israel, seven individuals were originally unable to identify Ivan the Terrible from a widely distributed photograph. However, a number of other survivors who were in attendance at the reunion had already been interviewed by police officers, and the ensuing discussion among those in attendance at the reunion may have had considerable impact. One camp survivor who did not identify

Ivan the Terrible from a photo spread containing Demjanjuk's picture was Schlomo Helman. Moreover, Helman had been shown fewer photographs than the other witnesses and still he was unable to identify Demjanjuk. Helman died before Demjanjuk's trial began, and his death was considered a blow to the defense.[16]

Experimental research also demonstrates that among the factors contributing to erroneous eyewitness identification are suggestive questioning and exposure to misleading information. Each of these factors can adversely impact information retained in memory.[17] Therefore, the memories of those witnesses who may have doubted that Demjanjuk was Ivan the Terrible may have been contaminated as a result of the external influence of other witnesses who seemed more sure.

The criminal investigation that sought to determine if Demjanjuk was Ivan the Terrible was also flawed because it increased the likelihood that eyewitness survivors of the camp would be more inclined to identify the Cleveland autoworker as the dreaded Nazi guard. When officials from the United States sent Demjanjuk's 1951 immigration picture to Israeli officials, the photo was published in a number of newspaper advertisements that asked prison camp survivors to contact Israeli police if they had information about an ongoing investigation into Ukrainians who were suspected of being Nazi guards. In the advertisements, Demjanjuk was mentioned by name but he was identified as "Ivan Demjanjuk" in the same context in which his immigration picture appeared.[18] The pairing of the photograph and the name "Ivan Demjanjuk" in the same context made it almost certain that the memories of some survivors would be shaped to produce a positive identification.

As part of Demjanjuk's criminal defense, his attorney, Mark O'Connor, sought out the services of Elizabeth Loftus, a pioneering researcher in the field of human memory and eyewitness identification. Loftus has been listed as one of the one hundred most influential psychologists of the twentieth century due, in part, to her studies that show how a variety of factors can cause inaccuracies in eyewitness identification and testimony. Given her stature in the field, along with the fact that primary evidence against Demjanjuk consisted only of a handful of survivors from the Treblinka camp who claimed he was the infamous guard after decades had passed, Loftus appeared to be the ideal expert for the defense. Therefore, when O'Connor first contacted Loftus by telephone to become involved in the case and she subsequently declined because of other commitments, he decided to fly to Seattle to try and convince the noted expert that she had to take the case.[19] O'Connor was convinced of Demjanjuk's innocence and he needed testimony from Loftus about the fallibility of eyewitness testimony to avert what he believed would be a miscarriage of justice if Demjanjuk was convicted of being "Ivan the Terrible." For two days, O'Connor gave Loftus an impassioned presentation of the evidence of Demjanjuk's innocence.

Stress can impair a person's perception of an event. If someone perpetrating a crime has a gun, for example, witnesses often focus on the weapon rather than the features of the perpetrator,[20] a phenomenon known as the *weapon focus effect*. In addition, some individuals can be induced through repeated questioning to "remember" incidents that supposedly happened years ago but never actually occurred. Furthermore, research conducted by Loftus has shown that the degree of confidence witnesses have in their recollection of an event is not always related to the accuracy of the memory. Indeed, the amount of stress experienced by the Treblinka survivors was profound. The death camp was designed to efficiently exterminate Jewish prisoners. The average trainload to the camp consisted of about six thousand people, and the average time between arrival and death for each person on board was only an hour and a half.[21] Approximately one million people were killed at Treblinka, but in 1943 there was an uprising by about two hundred prisoners, and fifty to sixty of those individuals ended up surviving the war. The trauma of surviving the camp, along with the awareness of being one of the fifty individuals out of one million to survive, would certainly have a psychological impact on one's memory of the prison camp experience.[22]

Because jurors rely heavily on eyewitness testimony and find it to be very persuasive, expert witnesses such as Loftus are frequently called upon to testify in criminal trials in order to demonstrate the difficulties with this form of evidence. Rather than providing an assessment of the accuracy of a particular witness, expert testimony on eyewitness identification is often used by defense attorneys to help jurors weigh such evidence more accurately. On the other hand, prosecutors who rely on eyewitness testimony often argue that such testimony is prejudicial to their case, irrelevant, and likely to confuse the jury. The decision to admit such eyewitness testimony is left to the judge.

When experts on eyewitness identification are called upon to testify in court, the most common focus of their testimony is how police procedures can affect witness testimony and general psychological factors that can impact the accuracy of witness memory. That is, expert witnesses in the field of eyewitness identification will commonly instruct jurors on how the wording of questions by police and the characteristics of a lineup may impact eyewitness identification. In addition, eyewitness experts often testify about research that shows that the confidence of an eyewitness does not predict accuracy in the identification of a suspect. Some people mistakenly identify as the culprit a person they have seen in a different context, and high levels of stress can impair the accuracy of eyewitness identification.[23]

In the case of Demjanjuk, Loftus was sought as an expert to provide jurors with an understanding of how human memory works—that it is not like a video recorder collecting memories in clear and neat pictures or narratives. Rather, memory depends on a number of factors, including the accuracy of the initial perception, rehearsal of the material, and strategies that people use to reconstruct their memories. Demjanjuk's attorneys sought to create doubt as to the ability of survivors of the Treblinka death camp to accurately identify a guard after so many years.

Despite the fact that Loftus appeared to be the expert witness with the ideal academic, scientific, and professional credentials to testify at Demjanjuk's trial, she ultimately declined to take the case. Loftus, who is Jewish, declined the defense's offer to become involved in the case as a result, in part, of political pressures involved in the prosecution of Demjanjuk and the raw emotions surrounding the trial of the suspected Nazi war criminal. The fact that Loftus reportedly "agonized over whether to take the case" and ultimately decided against testifying[24] demonstrates how responsible and ethical expert witnesses must sometimes examine their own personal feelings about certain cases when making decisions about whether to testify.

Nevertheless, Loftus recommended a colleague who could serve as a defense expert. Moreover, she agreed to travel to Israel during Demjanjuk's trial, at the expense of the defense, in order to serve as a consultant and advisor during the testimony of the defense's memory expert.[25] Loftus recommended Dr. Willem Wagenaar, a professor of experimental psychology at the University of Leyden in the Netherlands.

The facts of the Demjanjuk case appeared to be ideally suited for raising questions about the reliability of witness memories. Although pretrial newspaper reports claimed that the memory of witnesses in Demjanjuk's case would be questioned, the focus of Wagenaar's testimony went in a very different direction. Rather than focusing on the unreliability of eyewitnesses who were basing their identification of Demjanjuk on memories that were over forty years old, Wagenaar directed his testimony to problems with facial recognition that were inherent in the procedures Israeli police used to have witnesses identify Demjanjuk as Ivan the Terrible.[26]

Wagenaar testified about two sources of bias that could create mistaken identification when questioning witnesses about the identity of a suspect using a layout of photographs. One source of bias, known as *positive response bias*, occurs when a person feels compelled to point to a suspect in the photo spread even if the suspect is not present.[27] There are various reasons that a witness might feel the need to identify a suspected criminal in an array of photographs, such as when police ask leading questions like, "Which one is he?" rather than the more appropriate question, "Is he in this group?" A second source of bias about which Wagenaar testified was "specific response bias" in which, once a witness has made a decision to choose one of the photographs in a layout, he or she will use specific information to select one photo over another. The information may or may not be accurate and could conceivably be the result of factors unrelated to the witness' memory, such as newspaper reports about the appearance of a suspect. In Demjanjuk's case, all of the Treblinka survivors noted that Ivan the Terrible was balding and had a round face and short neck.[28] Survivors would therefore be compelled to select Demjanjuk's photo from the array because his physical appearance matched the general description of Ivan the Terrible.

To demonstrate that procedures used by Israeli police were flawed when they had Treblinka survivors identify Demjanjuk from photographs, Wagenaar testified about results from an experiment he conducted with students at the university where he taught. In one condition, Wagenaar used the photo spread used by Israeli police, and 100 percent of the students selected Demjanjuk when they were asked to "pick out the criminal with the round face, short neck, and who was balding."[29] However, when students were given a different photo array in which Demjanjuk's picture was interspersed with pictures of individuals who all shared the same physical characteristics used to describe Ivan the Terrible, only 8 percent of the students chose Demjanjuk's picture. The results of this study were used to support Wagenaar's contention that the Israeli photo spread used in their investigation was not a valid measure of witness memories for identification purposes.

Another focus of Wagenaar's testimony was on memory gaps that Demjanjuk displayed when he testified about his war background. For instance, Demjanjuk could not remember the name of the POW camp where he had allegedly been kept when he was captured by the Germans. According to Wagenaar, the problems with Demjanjuk's memory may have been due to any number of factors, including the fact that he never learned the name of the camp, that he was confused about where or when certain events had occurred, or that he had never had the right cues to trigger accurate memories.[30]

Michael Shaked was the prosecutor who cross-examined Wagenaar about his expert testimony. At first, Shaked addressed a criticism of research on eyewitness testimony that is frequently made: the conditions for testing memory and eyewitness identification accuracy of college student subjects in a laboratory are very different from the real-world conditions of individuals who witness actual crimes. Prosecutors faced with testimony from defense experts often cast doubts on the ability of laboratory research to generalize to actual court cases. Therefore, Shaked got Wagenaar to concede that the circumstances of Nazi death camp survivors who actually knew Ivan the Terrible were very different from college students who were tested in a laboratory and who had never met the infamous prison guard. Moreover, Shaked challenged Wagenaar's study by making the observation that the experiment did not attempt to re-create the actual conditions of a Nazi death camp and therefore the results could not generalize to the conditions under which eyewitnesses identified Demjanjuk as Ivan the Terrible.[31]

The prosecution then turned to Wagenaar's testimony about the possible sources of error in Demjanjuk's memory about his alibi. Shaked found it suspect that Demjanjuk could be sure about many aspects of his war experiences but confused about other details such as the name of the POW camp where he was held. Shaked asked if these memory problems were "selective."[32] Wagenaar responded that Demjanjuk might have simply failed to bring up a detail, such as an experience he allegedly had shoveling peat at the POW camp, at the proper time.

The prosecution also sought to undermine the impact of Wagenaar's testimony by pointing out limits in the expert's experience in the field. For example, Shaked claimed that none of Wagenaar's eighty-seven publications addressed the specific issue of identification from photo arrays, and he also got Wagenaar to admit that only one of the forty cases in which he had testified as an expert had to do with suspect identification from photographs or lineups.

In response to these challenges, Wagenaar stated that his area of expertise was "how memory is tested in general and whether such a test provides a valid picture of the contents of memory."[33] However, Shaked challenged the body of research on which Wagenaar based his testimony by pointing out that only one study evaluated the accuracy of memories that were more than forty years old. The prosecutor asserted on cross-examination that, in fact, this one study tended to prove that a photograph could be a good cue for getting people to remember a person after forty years.

Wagenaar's testimony played an important role in the closing arguments of both the defense and prosecution and, ultimately, the decision of the three trial judges who determined Demjanjuk's fate. Of course the prosecutors attempted to cast Wagenaar's expert testimony as not being expert at all once it was placed under scrutiny. Despite the impassioned argument of defense attorneys that Demjanjuk was wrongly accused and that the eyewitness identification of him being Ivan the Terrible was erroneous, Demjanjuk was convicted by the trial judges and sentenced to death.

Wagenaar later wrote about the scientific and ethical issues expert witnesses must consider when testifying in criminal cases, and he outlined the specific challenges he faced when testifying in the trial of John Demjanjuk. For instance, Wagenaar noted that expert witnesses must make a distinction between conclusions that are permissible for an expert and conclusions that are permissible only for the court. In the Demjanjuk case, Wagenaar stated that he believed it was appropriate for an expert such as himself to use scientific evidence to testify that "the conditions under which Demjanjuk was identified as Ivan are known to have produced mistaken identifications before."[34] The scientific evidence on eyewitness testimony about which he testified supported this conclusion. On the other hand, Wagenaar noted that only the Israeli court, and not an expert witness, could properly draw the following conclusion: "Given the conditions in which the identifications were made, there is no sufficient proof that Demjanjuk is Ivan."[35]

Wagenaar also noted that expert witnesses testifying about eyewitness identification must recognize the limitations of the research upon which their testimony is based. He also made the point that most expert witnesses create problems when they begin to offer conclusions that are best left to the court, such as which witnesses are credible or whether specific eyewitness identifications are accurate.

Finally, another interesting set of observations made by Wagenaar had to do with the reactions of some people to his willingness to testify for the defense of an individual many believed to be a Nazi war criminal. The reaction by many individuals that expert witnesses have no place in the courtroom is often based on the perception that experts are merely advocates for the side calling them to testify, rather than objective and impartial advocates for science or an opinion. In Wagenaar's case, he clarified his reasons for becoming involved in the Demjanjuk case, pointing to the need to advocate not for Demjanjuk but for science when he later wrote: "After a careful study of the immense file, I chose to act as an expert witness summoned by the defense of John Demjanjuk because I felt that some matters had to be presented in court. No individual scientists could be forced to testify in this case. But what about the obligations of science as a collective?"[36] Advocacy of science and understanding, rather than advocacy for the defendant, appears to have been the guiding principle for Wagenaar's expert testimony in one of the most contentious criminal cases in recent history.

However, when the trial court had its opinion read publicly, one of the presiding judges, Judge Zvi Tal, noted that the court did not accept Wagenaar's testimony about Demjanjuk's forgetfulness over his POW camp experiences. In fairness to Wagenaar, he appeared to base his opinions on the existing literature in experimental psychology and he refrained from offering opinions about the validity of the photo spread used to identify Demjanjuk. However, when his testimony began to address the issue of Demjanjuk's memory, the opinions appeared to be based more on theory and speculation in light of Shaked's cross-examination.

The trial judges stated that they were convinced "unhesitatingly and with utter conviction" that Demjanjuk was the sadistic Nazi guard and sentenced him to death.[37] Demjanjuk began his appeal to the Israeli Supreme Court on May 14, 1990.[38] However, subsequent events in the case revealed just how contentious and volatile the Demjanjuk case was for those who were directly involved. One week before the appeal was to be heard, one of Demjanjuk's appellate attorneys, the former Israeli District Court Judge Dov Eitan, committed suicide by jumping off the fifteenth floor of a building in Jerusalem.[39] Although the death was suspect because no suicide note had been found and none of Eitan's family members or friends believed him to be depressed, the death was officially ruled to be a suicide. At Eitan's funeral, one of Demjanjuk's defense lawyers at trial, Yoram Sheftel, was assaulted by a seventy-seven-year-old man who threw hydrochloric acid in the attorney's face. Sheftel's left eye was severely injured, and he required a number of surgeries to restore vision in the eye. The man who had thrown the acid blamed Sheftel for Eitan's death and was subsequently convicted of assault, sentenced to five years in jail, and ordered to pay medical costs and restitution to Sheftel. Indeed, the Demjanjuk case was emotionally charged for expert witnesses and lawyers alike.

In 1993 the Supreme Court of Israel reversed the lower court's findings and acquitted Demjanjuk of all charges because newly discovered evidence purportedly suggested another person, not Demjanjuk, as being Ivan the Terrible.[40] Upon his release from prison, Demjanjuk returned to Cleveland and his U.S. citizenship was restored in 1998. However, his legal troubles did not end. In 1999, attorneys from the U.S. Department of Justice filed another lawsuit to have Demjanjuk's U.S. citizenship revoked because he had failed to disclose his Nazi affiliations on his original visa application in 1951. After a trial in federal court, Demjanjuk's citizenship was once again revoked and he faced deportation.

Now in his eighties, Demjanjuk continues to face legal battles over questions about his identity and citizenship. There is no country that has extended an offer of citizenship to Demjanjuk; thus he is a man without a country to call home. Yet his case remains one of the classics in forensic psychology because of the issues it raised about the accuracy of eyewitness identification in criminal prosecutions.

⌐11

THE USS IOWA

Equivocating on Death

⌐

Autopsies are conducted in cases where a person has died under suspicious circumstances and legal considerations dictate that a detailed medical examination be performed on the body to determine the exact cause of death. It has also been suggested that surviving family members have autopsies performed on their loved ones who have died—even if health insurance does not pay—because results from the procedure may be of considerable benefit to biological relatives.[1] More specifically, autopsies can provide evidence of illnesses and other medical conditions that went undetected while the person was alive. Autopsy results may point to the need for screening or other preventive measures that surviving family members might need to take against serious medical conditions that have a strong genetic component.

Medical autopsies are intended to shed light on the cause of a person's death and to be of benefit not only to family members in their search for the cause of death of a loved one, but also to the legal system in its search for truth. But what if autopsy results merely add to the confusion arising from a suspicious death? The findings can often mislead investigators, who can misconstrue what really happened.

The psychological autopsy is a specialized procedure intended to provide insight into the mental state of a deceased person at the time of his or her death. The Federal Bureau of Investigation (FBI) has developed its own process called "equivocal death analysis," which is similar to a psychological autopsy in that a determination is made as to whether a person died as a result of homicide, suicide, or accident. Determining the manner of a person's death may be particularly important in legal cases, such as settling life insurance claims, where a person's mental state at the time of death is a key factor.

Psychological autopsies—or equivocal death analyses—are considered by some to be controversial because they are based on procedures other than access to the person whose mental state is being assessed. After all, a dead person cannot be interviewed to determine what he or she was thinking at the time of death. Instead, examiners must rely on interviews with other people who knew the person, documents and records relating to the dead person's background, written materials (e.g., diaries), and other resources that can provide some insight into the person's mental state at the time of death.

One of the most infamous cases of equivocal death analysis arose from a tragic incident that occurred on April 19, 1989, aboard the battleship USS *Iowa*. During a U.S. Navy training exercise in the Caribbean Sea, one of the sixteen-inch gun turrets on the *Iowa* exploded and killed forty-seven crew members.[2] Immediately following the incident, the Navy began an intensive investigation into the cause of the explosion. This investigation ultimately led the Navy to seek out the services of agents at the FBI's Behavioral Science Unit at the National Center for the Analysis of Violent Crime in Quantico, Virginia. The Navy was looking for an equivocal death analysis on Petty Officer Clayton Hartwig, who was one of the crew members killed in the explosion.[3]

To fully appreciate the controversy that would soon emerge in the wake of the official version of the cause of the incident as set forth by the Navy, it is important to know something about the history of the *Iowa* and its service in the Navy. Originally designed in 1938, the *Iowa* was built to withstand very rough sea conditions. The battleship was equipped with three gun turrets that mounted guns with massive sixteen-inch-wide barrels. These weapons were capable of launching 2,700-pound bombs over a distance of several miles with considerable accuracy. The amount of explosive force needed to power these mammoth guns was immense.

After being used in both World War II and the Korean War, the *Iowa* was decommissioned and spent the next twenty-six years in storage.[4] In 1983, the *Iowa* and three other Navy ships were all refurbished and recommissioned during the Reagan administration in an effort to beef up the U.S. military. Although the *Iowa* was modernized with updated equipment, numerous problems plagued the ship, including escape hatches that had rusted shut, electrical circuits that would short out, outdated gunpowder that was considered dangerous, hydraulic leaks, and a bulky design that made maneuvering at sea difficult.[5]

In addition, many senior members of the *Iowa* crew felt increasing pressure to make the refurbished battleship compete effectively in modern warfare. For instance, when the *Iowa* competed in war games with naval forces from Britain, Canada, and West Germany, it was defeated soundly.[6] Therefore, the crew conducted dangerous experiments to boost the effectiveness of the ship's capabilities. One of these experiments, designed by a Master Chief aboard the *Iowa*, involved the mixing of "supercharged" propellant powder to increase the power behind the ship's explosive shells. While concerns were raised as to whether the ship's gun barrels could withstand the increased force from the volatile powder, the improvised shells were nevertheless used in test firings. In another experiment, an executive officer ordered a test involving the simultaneous firing of all six guns in the two forward turrets of the *Iowa*. The experiment placed several crew members in danger because there was a risk that the guns would turn to the side and shoot off the bow of the ship. Fortunately, the experiment did not cause any serious injuries or damage. Several crew members had expressed concern that they were sailing aboard a hazardous ship. On one occasion several senior crew members were reported to have discussed suicide because of the pressure they felt to take risks that would increase the efficiency of the ship.

In the months leading up to the explosion, several crew members expressed fear and concern to family members that the *Iowa* was unsafe. Among the issues later cited were that old gunpowder could easily ignite, experimental test firings of the sixteen-inch guns sometimes violated safety standards, and untrained personnel were often called upon to man the huge guns.[7] The gun turrets were described as extremely dangerous and some crew members felt one mishap could ignite the powder and create a fiery deathtrap.

Therefore, when the *Iowa* engaged in a routine training exercise on the morning of April 19, 1989, there were many factors that could have contributed to the tragedy that ensued. During preparations for firing the main guns aboard the *Iowa*, senior crew members who were monitoring telephone conversations with crew members inside the gun turrets heard someone yell, "Oh, my God! The powder is smoldering."[8] At 9:53 A.M., the center gun of turret number two exploded, sending a fireball of between 2,500 and 3,000 degrees Fahrenheit throughout the decks surrounding the turret. The fire triggered additional explosions when bags of explosive powder ignited and billowing clouds of deadly gases erupted. In all, forty-seven crew members were killed by the blast and several others were injured.

As the fires caused by the explosion continued to burn, many of the ship's 1,550 surviving crew worked furiously to avoid injury from secondary explosions, extinguish fires, and recover the bodies of dead and injured shipmates. A small group of crew members took advantage of the ensuing chaos by stealing money, jewelry, and other valuables from the lockers of those who had perished in the explosion and other crew members who were working to minimize damage and keep the ship afloat.[9]

The investigation into the cause of the explosion was hampered by a number of factors, not the least of which was the fact that those witnesses who directly observed the cause of the tragedy had died in the blast. Responsibility for investigating the cause of the mishap was given to Rear Admiral Richard Milligan. Although Naval regulations and the Uniform Code of Military Justice prohibited investigations such as the one undertaken by Admiral Milligan to be influenced by higher command, the USS *Iowa* investigation was "closely scrutinized" and "micromanaged" from a higher level within the Pentagon.[10] Following a five-month investigation, the Navy issued its official finding on September 7, 1989. Accidental causes of the explosion were all ruled out, including unstable gunpowder, friction, electrostatic charges, or negligence on the part of crew members.[11] The document concluded that Second Class Gunner's Mate Clayton Hartwig "'most probably' killed himself and his shipmates because he was 'a loner, a man of low self-esteem who talked of dying in an explosion in the line of duty and being buried at Arlington National Cemetary.'"[12]

The Navy relied heavily on an equivocal death analysis conducted by two experienced FBI agents—Richard Ault and Roy Hazelwood—who had extensive experience in criminal investigative analysis, behavioral and psychological profiling, and equivocal death analysis.

The initial investigation of the explosion led agents of the Naval Investigative Service (NIS) to suspect that Hartwig had intentionally caused the explosion. The NIS wanted to develop a psychological autopsy of the petty officer's state of mind. However, there were concerns that if the autopsy was performed by the Navy's own investigative service, it might not be taken seriously.[13] As a result, an outside agency was sought and the FBI was given the responsibility of piecing together Hartwig's possible motive.

Ault and Hazelwood relied on a number of documents, materials, and interview transcripts to formulate their assessment of Hartwig's state of mind at the time of the explosion. However, the focus of the evaluation appeared to be dictated by information the FBI agents were given by the Navy. Hazelwood and Ault were apparently told that the explosion was not an accident; they were only to determine if there was convincing evidence to conclude whether Hartwig committed suicide, homicide, or a combined suicide/homicide.[14]

Among the key pieces of evidence were a pair of books found among Hartwig's possessions: *Getting Even: The Complete Book of Dirty Tricks* and a military manual called *Improvised Munitions Handbook*.[15] Other evidence indicated that Hartwig had a long history of interest in explosives and weapons and was a loner who had difficulties in his relationships. In Naval records, Hartwig was described as an individual who was immature, lacked leadership skills, and was not particularly assertive. Letters that Hartwig had written to other people suggested he was egocentric and self-centered. At the time of his death, Hartwig had almost no money, very few civilian clothes, and a run-down vehicle—all signs that he was possibly withdrawn and depressed at the time of his death.

One important aspect of Hartwig's life that emerged in the equivocal death analysis was that he had formed a close friendship with Petty Officer Kendall Truitt. Long before the explosion occurred, rumors had circulated around the *Iowa* that Hartwig and Truitt were homosexual lovers, but the Navy investigated the allegations and ruled them to be unfounded;[16] still, the rumors persisted. When Truitt started dating a girl, the friendship between the two crew members cooled. In the wake of Hartwig's death, it was discovered that Truitt had been named as the beneficiary of a $100,000 life insurance policy Hartwig had taken out on his own life.[17]

The fifteen-page equivocal death analysis report produced by Ault and Hazelwood provided a psychological portrait of Hartwig as an emotionally unstable individual. Various factors were expanded upon to support the theory that Hartwig had committed suicide. The equivocal death analysis concluded that Hartwig had low self-esteem because he had been repeatedly rejected by other people and had only a handful of close friends.[18]

One piece of evidence that was considered significant in pointing to Hartwig's psychological instability was a poem entitled "Disposable Heroes," which consisted of rewritten lyrics from music by the heavy metal band Metallica. The lyrics were written on a paper posted in turret number two aboard the *Iowa* and ended with the line: "Left to die alone in a sixteen-inch gun."[19] Although the author of the poem was James White, another gunner's mate aboard the ship, investigators initially believed that Hartwig had written the poem. Although forensic investigators at the FBI crime lab compared "Disposable Heroes" with letters Hartwig had written to friends, the analysis failed to identify Hartwig as the author.[20] Still, the words in the poem figured prominently in the equivocal death analysis. Hazelwood would later testify before the House Armed Services Subcommittee on Investigations that whether or not Hartwig actually wrote the poem was "immaterial."[21]

The psychological portrait of Hartwig that Ault and Hazelwood painted was the epitome of an emotionally unstable, suicidal person. They concluded that he was a loner who was dissatisfied with his life and had a number of reasons to kill himself: Suicide would mean avoiding having a number of lies he had told to others revealed and exacting a kind of revenge for having been disciplined and having his rank reduced.[22] Hartwig was described as an immature individual who held grudges, was under significant stress, and had serious suicidal ideation. He had "the knowledge, ability and opportunity to ignite the powder in the same fashion that occurred on the USS *Iowa*" the equivocal death analysis concluded.[23]

The theory was that Hartwig may have committed suicide by deliberately detonating the explosion inside the gun turret because he was rejected by Truitt. The final conclusion that Hartwig had intentionally caused the explosion aboard the *Iowa* created a storm of controversy. Hartwig's sister mounted a campaign to clear her brother's name, Truitt hired an attorney and brought suit against the Navy and the media alleging that his life and reputation had been harmed by the investigation, and the equivocal death analysis performed by Ault and Hazelwood was targeted by Congress and the media as highly speculative and based on faulty scientific principles.

The House Armed Services Subcommittee on Investigations conducted a formal hearing into the validity of the Navy's investigation of the USS *Iowa* tragedy. House Representative Nick Mavroules, a Democrat from Massachusetts who chaired the House Subcommittee on Investigations, outlined the key focus of the Congressional inquiry into the Navy's findings: "Was Clayton Hartwig a suicidal murderer? Was he capable of such a heinous act? The FBI says he was. The NIS psychologist says he might have been and the independent psychologists contacted by this committee generally agree that he was not. Given the serious defects in the Navy investigation that we have uncovered in our previous hearings, today's testimony becomes even more crucial to the Navy's case against Hartwig."[24]

The "serious defects" uncovered by the House Subcommittee to which Mavroules was referring involved a scientific analysis of the evidence by professionals at Sandia National Laboratories who worked on the Navy's investigation into the cause of the explosion. Scientists from the laboratory had been retained by the Senate Armed Services Committee to examine the findings. Results of the analyses pointed strongly to an accidental cause of the explosion.[25] If the cause was accidental, then the House Subcommittee believed that the equivocal death analysis conducted by Ault and Hazelwood deserved careful scrutiny.

Before the two FBI agents testified at the House Subcommittee hearing on December 21, 1989, the Assistant Director of Training at the FBI Academy, Anthony Daniels, provided an overview of services provided by the National Center for the Analysis of Violent Crime (NCAVC) at the FBI's training academy. The NCAVC was developed to provide investigative support to federal, state, and local law enforcement agencies using criminal investigative analyses.[26] Among the various types of analysis offered are criminal profiling, where crime scene and other forensic evidence is used to provide a psychological analysis of an unknown offender that can be used to direct a criminal investigation. The NCAVC also offers equivocal death analysis, which Daniels described as the investigation of "a death whose manner, whether it be homicide, suicide or accident, has not been resolved through normal investigative activities."[27]

Ault testified first and described how an equivocal death analysis begins with an examination of all available evidence, including witness statements, procedures and protocols, autopsy reports, and other relevant materials to arrive at a conclusion. Hazelwood then testified about the details of their analysis by noting the various hypotheses that were considered and the evidence that supported their conclusion that Hartwig intentionally caused the blast. The two FBI agents were challenged by one of the House Subcommittee members, Representative Les Aspin, on the certainty of their opinion.

Aspin asked Hazelwood, "How definitive do you have your judgments in these cases? [sic] . . . Do you always—are you always as definitive as you are in this case?"[28] Hazelwood replied, "Yes, sir." The definitive conclusion contained in the FBI's equivocal death analysis became a point of contention raised by other experts who were asked to review the findings. In addition, Subcommittee Chair Mavroules challenged the reliability and validity of equivocal death analysis, to which Ault responded with some apparent irritation: "I certainly appreciate that wonderful academic approach to a very practical problem. It's typical of what we find when we see people who have not had the experience of investigating, either crime scenes, victims, criminals, and so forth, in active, ongoing situations. . . . I can say that we have been successful. We don't keep academic—or we don't keep research records with great internal validity because we're simply not oriented that way."[29]

The House Armed Services Subcommittee on Investigations not only cross-examined the individuals who conducted the equivocal death analysis but also solicited help from the American Psychological Association (APA). In particular, the Subcommittee asked the APA to provide assistance in assembling a panel of experts to conduct a peer review of the equivocal death analysis. Twelve psychologists were identified who were considered to be experts in fields of psychology that were relevant to the investigation, including adolescent and adult development, suicide, psychopathology, forensic psychology, risk assessment of violent behavior, and personality assessment.[30] In addition, two psychiatrists were chosen by the House Armed Services Subcommittee.

The panel of fourteen experts addressed four basic issues: (1) How valid was the Navy's conclusion that Hartwig had intentionally caused the explosion? (2) Were the materials used to develop the psychological profile of Hartwig valuable and was the investigation exhaustive? (3) What were Hartwig's motives, was he suicidal, how likely was it that he committed the act, and what alternative conclusions might be drawn from the material reviewed on Hartwig's psychological functioning? (4) What are the limitations of evaluating suicidal tendencies and behaviors after a person has died?[31] Each of the experts prepared a written report independent of the others, but only six of them ended up testifying before the House Armed Services Committee on the same day that Ault and Hazelwood testified.

Although four of the professionals who reviewed the FBI's findings felt the suicide theory about Hartwig's motives was plausible, ten of fourteen professional psychologists contradicted the equivocal death analysis, and all fourteen reviewers criticized the technique as too speculative.[32] A nationally recognized psychiatrist, Dr. Douglas Jacobs of Harvard Medical School, also concluded that the evidence did not support a conclusion that Hartwig intentionally caused the explosion. Dr. Jacobs faulted the FBI for not conducting its own set of interviews. Dr. Roger L. Greene, a psychologist and expert in personality assessment who is on the faculty of the psychology department at Texas Tech University, concluded that there were "a number of potential problems with the logical links between the evidence and the conclusions drawn by the FBI equivocal death analysis."[33]

On the other hand, a forensic psychologist who served as one of the peer reviewers for the House Armed Services Subcommittee, Dr. Elliott Silverstein, wrote that the conclusions of the FBI equivocal death analysis were "plausible" provided that the evidence was true and accurate.[34] Dr. Alan Berman, a nationally recognized expert on suicide, viewed the finding that Hartwig killed himself in the explosion as "most reasonable."[35]

Although most of the professionals reviewing the FBI's equivocal death analysis were generally critical and contradicted the findings, there was considerable diversity among the various opinions. With well over a dozen different experts weighing in with their own opinions about the cause of the explosion aboard the USS *Iowa* and the adequacy of the equivocal death analysis conducted by the FBI, the House Armed Services Subcommittee on Investigations was confronted not with a "battle of the experts" but with a "war of the experts." Could any sense be made of the various opinions as to the reliability and validity of the various conclusions about the analysis of Hartwig's motives?

A team of psychologists from the Department of Law and Mental Health at Florida Mental Health Institute at the University of South Florida analyzed each of the opinions offered by the fourteen panelists who reviewed the FBI's equivocal death analysis.[36] The experts generally agreed that psychological autopsies could be of some use, but there was considerable diversity in the experts' opinions as to the specific methods used by the FBI examiners and the conclusions they reached about Hartwig's guilt in causing the explosion. Although there was general agreement that Hartwig was emotionally unstable, the evaluation of the FBI experts tended to be more negative and critical of the gunner's mate. Despite some of these similarities between the FBI agents and the APA's panel of experts, on the whole the experts were more tentative and equivocal in their conclusion as to whether Hartwig was guilty of causing the explosion aboard the *Iowa*.

Norman Poythress, Randy Otto, Jack Darkes, and Laura Starr, researchers from the University of South Florida who summarized the findings of the APA panel of experts, concluded that equivocal death analysis should not be used in legal settings.[37] They based their conclusion primarily on the fact that very little research existed to support the reliability and validity of psychological evaluation methods that attempt to reconstruct a person's past mental state using indirect methods of assessment when the person is not available for direct examination. Poythress and his colleagues also noted that if questionable methods such as equivocal death analysis were allowed in legal and administrative proceedings, other questionable methods might soon follow, such as "equivocal burglary analysis" or "equivocal kidnapping analysis."[38] Furthermore, Poythress and his colleagues suggested that if mental health professionals offered their services in psychological autopsies and equivocal death analyses, they should refrain from offering conclusive statements about the cause of a person's death. Furthermore, experts should avoid misleading courts, administrative committees, or other decision-making bodies about the reliability or accuracy of these equivocal methods of evaluation.

In fairness to the FBI agents conducting the equivocal death analysis, they had the challenging task of reconstructing Hartwig's mental state without the benefit of speaking to him directly. Moreover, the focus of their examination was dictated by the Navy's firm conclusion that the explosion was not an accident. Much of the data used to formulate the equivocal death analysis was provided by the Navy, which had already concluded that Hartwig was the culprit. These issues, along with the generally speculative nature of psychological autopsies, created a very difficult challenge for any forensic investigator. Furthermore, Ault and Hazelwood approached their evaluation from the perspective of law enforcement officers with special training in the behavioral sciences, rather than mental health professionals who were providing assistance to the legal system. This distinction between the perspective of law enforcement officers and mental health professionals is significant because the professional demands and needs of police officers and mental health professionals are very different. Law enforcement officers approach their work with expediency; they need to solve crimes and identify suspects to prevent crimes from occurring and to make sure justice is administered quickly. Mental health professionals, on the other hand, are trained to evaluate and test hypotheses and offer only those conclusions that can be supported by scientific data. Sometimes mental health professionals can provide only tentative conclusions that do not always satisfy the needs of courts or fact-finding committees that need to render definitive rulings.

The congressional investigation into the Navy's report of the explosion aboard the USS *Iowa* found there was insufficient evidence to conclude Hartwig was the cause of the fatal blast.[39] Kendall Truitt endured the stress of having the Navy read his mail and tap his phone during the course of their investigation.[40] Truitt got married four months after the explosion, but divorced two years later because of the pressure and scrutiny he experienced. He left the Navy and is now a civilian.

As for Hartwig's family, they received vindication in October 1991 when the Navy formally repudiated its conclusion that Hartwig had intentionally caused the explosion and issued a formal apology to Hartwig's family. Moreover, a review of the investigation into the explosion revealed that critical physical evidence had been lost or mishandled. When a former U.S. Secretary of the Navy, Admiral Frank Kelso, testified during a deposition in a lawsuit brought by Hartwig's family, he admitted that the Navy found Hartwig was not a homosexual. Kelso also said he "rejected the FBI's 'equivocal death analysis'" and that "sabotage had been a theory, not a proven fact."[41] The family of Clayton Hartwig received a formal apology when Kelso stated publicly, "I extend my sincere regrets to the family of Hartwig. We're sorry Clayton Hartwig was accused of this."[42] However, Kelso also added that there were still no clear answers as to what caused the explosion aboard the battleship.

Roy Hazelwood stood by his analysis. "I'm as convinced today as I was then that we were correct," he later stated.[43] Hazelwood noted further that within days of Admiral Kelso's public apology to the Hartwig family, the

Naval Sea System Command issued a final opinion that in the absence of any evidence of an accident, the cause of the explosion was an intentional act.[44]

The explosion aboard the USS *Iowa*, and the ensuing investigation into its cause, resulted in the application of a controversial technique—psychological autopsy, or equivocal death analysis—and considerable confusion about what actually caused the tragedy. In this particular case, the result was an official report issued by the Navy that subsequently led to intensive scrutiny by the media, lawsuits, and a formal apology to the family of one of the men who was killed in the explosion. A number of military careers were adversely impacted or ruined by the investigation.[45] As for the *Iowa* itself, the World War II battleship was officially retired from Naval service in October 1990.

The case raises significant questions about the reliability and validity of psychological assessment methods like equivocal death analysis and psychological autopsy. In the years since the *Iowa* tragedy, research has still not answered all of the questions that were raised by the case. Certainly, more research will help to establish what works and what fails when mental health professionals attempt to reconstruct the past mental state of a person at the time of his or her death. The lack of research has therefore contributed to psychological autopsy and equivocal death analysis being kept outside the realm of generally accepted methods of evaluation by some members of the psychological profession, even though several courts have embraced psychological autopsies as helpful in resolving legal disputes.

◤12

JEFFREY
DAHMER

Serial Murder,

Necrophilia,

and Cannibalism

◢

On September 26, 1988, twenty-eight-year-old Jeffrey Dahmer went hunting on the streets of Milwaukee. His quarry? A teenage boy he could sexually molest and perhaps kill. After a number of street-wise youths spurned Dahmer's offer of fifty dollars for the chance to take nude photographs of them in his nearby apartment, one youngster, Anoukone Sinthasomphone, a thirteen-year-old Laotian boy, agreed to the deal.

Once in the tiny apartment, Dahmer persuaded him to remove some of his clothes and pose on the bed. Dahmer took Polaroid photos, fondled the boy's penis, kissed his stomach, and offered him an alcoholic drink laced with a powerful prescription sleep medication. Though drugged and incoherent, the boy managed to get out of Dahmer's apartment and find his way home, where his parents noticed his condition and took him for medical care.

Before long, Anoukone explained what happened and identified Dahmer as his abuser. Dahmer was arrested early the next morning and charged with second-degree sexual assault and enticement of a child for immoral purposes. After entering a plea of not guilty, Dahmer was released on $10,000 bail to await further proceedings.

Over the next several months, while Dahmer was on bail, authorities had a chance to get to know him better. His criminal record revealed that six years earlier he had been charged with lewd and lascivious behavior for masturbating publicly in front of a group of children at the Wisconsin State Fair. Though Dahmer claimed that he was simply urinating, he was convicted, fined, and sentenced to one year of probation. Authorities also learned that, earlier in 1988, an Illinois man had complained to the police that he had met Dahmer in a gay bar, gone home with him, been drugged, and awakened to find his money and jewelry missing. This time no charges were brought because the police bought Dahmer's explanation: the man had simply gotten too drunk to go home and had slept off his intoxication until Dahmer courteously walked him to a bus stop and gave him a dollar for the fare.

Though Dahmer eventually pleaded guilty to sexually assaulting and enticing Anoukone Sinthasomphone, he never really admitted to any sexual contact with the thirteen-year-old victim. He claimed he had no idea that Anoukone was a minor, denied touching his penis or kissing him, and claimed that the drugging must have occurred accidentally when the boy drank out of a cup Dahmer had earlier used to take sleep medication but failed to clean thoroughly. As Dahmer told it, he had simply paid a young man fifty dollars to pose for some photographs.

Prior to sentencing for this offense, Dahmer was evaluated by three psychologists, all of whom concluded that Dahmer was a manipulative alcohol abuser who lacked insight and motivation for treatment.[1] One concluded that Dahmer might suffer from a schizoid personality disorder, the hallmarks of which are "detachment from social relationships and a restricted range of emotional expression."[2]

Another psychologist, however, was monitoring Dahmer while on bail and felt that the accused sex offender was making some progress. According to this psychologist, Dahmer had "begun to come out of his shell" and was "more verbal, amiable, and relaxed . . . less lethargic . . . more willing to interact . . . instead of staying home constantly."[3]

In May 1989, Dahmer was finally sentenced for the September 1988 assault and enticement. The prosecution asked for a prison sentence, arguing that Dahmer preyed on children, was likely to re-offend, and suffered from "extreme emotional instability" that was not amenable to treatment outside of prison.[4] Dahmer's defense attorney argued for leniency, acknowledging that Dahmer was "sick" and needed treatment but arguing that "the kinds of things that Jeff Dahmer needs are more available through the probation department with a very strong prison sentence withheld and a very long period of probation."[5] Dahmer, himself, begged the judge to "please spare my job . . . please don't destroy my life."[6] Responding to the prosecutor's argument that he was not motivated to change and would likely re-offend if not locked up, Dahmer told the judge: "I do want help. . . . This one incident had jolted me like nothing else. . . . I desperately want to change my conduct for the rest of my life."[7]

By the time he passed sentence on Jeffrey Dahmer, Judge William Gardner knew that Dahmer was a long-time alcohol abuser with at least two sexual offenses against children, that several mental health experts had examined Dahmer and seen little if any hope that he could be turned around, and that Dahmer's own father had asked the court to lock him up at least until he could receive adequate treatment for his alcohol and sexual problems. What neither the judge nor anyone other than the defendant knew was that the charges stemming from the 1978 assault on Anoukone Sinthasomphone were only the tip of an ever-growing iceberg of sex crimes committed and to be committed by Jeffrey Dahmer.

Not knowing that Dahmer had already sexually assaulted and killed five men (ages fourteen to forty-eight) over the preceding eleven years, including one man Dahmer murdered just two months earlier while on bail awaiting this sentencing, Judge Gardner ignored the psychological findings, said he could see no reason to send Dahmer to prison, and told the budding serial killer: "You'd come out [of prison] probably worse than you are right now."[8] Dahmer faced a combined maximum sentence of ten years in prison, but on the sexual assault charge the judge imposed a sentence of only five years' probation plus one year in a work-release program. Under this order, Dahmer would sleep in a jail dormitory for twelve months but be allowed to continue working at his night-shift job in a local candy factory. For enticing a child for immoral purposes, the judge imposed a sentence of three years probation, to run concurrently with the five-year probationary term imposed for the assault.

Ten months later, Dahmer was released from all confinement and told to see a probation officer weekly, seek counseling, and stay away from minors. Within a few months of his release, Dahmer would resume his killing ways, embarking upon a yearlong string of at least a dozen more sex killings. In each of these murders, Dahmer's modus operandi was essentially the same. Meeting his male victims (who ranged in age from fourteen to thirty-three) in gay bars, bathhouses, and other homosexual gathering places, Dahmer would invite the men to his apartment, offering them money in exchange for sex or photographs. Once there, the men would be drugged (with five or six sleeping pills crushed and stirred into drinks), sexually molested, killed, further sexually abused post-mortem, and finally cut into pieces which were either stored in the apartment or cooked and eaten by the serial killer.

Amazingly, Dahmer was able to successfully carry out these killings without even becoming a suspect until he was arrested in July 1991. Only once in the course of killing a dozen men after serving his work-release sentence did Dahmer even come close to being apprehended. On May 27, 1991, Dahmer lured fourteen-year-old Konerak Sinthasomphone to his Milwaukee apartment. Ironically and tragically, Konerak was the younger brother of Anoukone Sinthasomphone, the thirteen-year-old Laotian boy Dahmer had sexually assaulted three years earlier.

With both Sinthasomphone brothers, Dahmer's modus operandi was the same. Like his brother, Konerak was lured to Dahmer's apartment with a promise of money if he would pose for photographs. Konerak, who already had a juvenile record for prostitution, followed Dahmer without question. Konerak posed for Dahmer in his bikini briefs, watched a video, and passed out after consuming a drink laced with sedatives. Satisfied that his young victim would be unconscious for awhile, Dahmer left the apartment to buy beer. While Dahmer was gone, however, the Laotian boy revived and fled the apartment. Neighbors who spotted Konerak on the run immediately contacted the Milwaukee police.

Officers responded with a patrol car and an ambulance to find the boy bruised, naked, drugged, and incoherent. By the time they arrived, however, Dahmer was back and standing at Konerak's side. Dahmer explained that Konerak was staying with him, had too much to drink, and had started to act irrationally. As Dahmer put it, "He's nineteen. We live together, right here at 924. We're boyfriends, if you know what I mean."[9] Dahmer showed legitimate identification to the officers, who concluded that this was a "domestic situation" requiring no further police action.[10]

Over the protests of neighbors who complained that Konerak was "just a boy" and "badly hurt,"[11] the officers escorted Dahmer and his victim back to Dahmer's apartment, where they found Konerak's clothing neatly folded. Apparently to prove that he actually had a sexual relationship with Konerak, Dahmer boldly showed the police the photos he had just taken, Polaroid pictures of the fourteen-year-old posed in his bikini underwear. The police officers never bothered to check to see if Dahmer had any criminal record. Nor did they follow up on the foul odor emanating from the bedroom of Dahmer's two-room apartment, where the three-day-old corpse of his latest victim lay decomposing.

Once the police left, Dahmer strangled Konerak Sinthasomphone, sodomized his corpse, took additional photos, and then dismembered the boy's body. Sadly, when Dahmer's neighbors called the police again about an hour later to inquire about the child's safety and whereabouts, an officer told them that Konerak "wasn't a child" but "an adult" and that he had been returned to his "boyfriend."[12] When the caller persisted, the officer added, "I can't do anything about somebody's sexual preferences in life."[13] Days later, after learning of the disappearance of Konerak Sinthasomphone and seeing his photograph in the newspaper, the same neighbor would call the police and even the FBI to report her belief that Konerak was the boy both she and the police had seen with Dahmer. Neither agency took any action.

Two months and four murders later, in July 1991, Jeffrey Dahmer's killing spree came to an abrupt end, not through any investigative prowess on the part of the police but quite by chance. On July 22, Dahmer made his usual money-for-modeling pitch to Tracy Edwards, a thirty-two-year-old man who agreed and readily accompanied Dahmer to his apartment. Departing from his usual successful routine of sedating his victims with concealed drugs, Dahmer suddenly handcuffed one of Edwards's wrists, pulled a knife on him, showed him a human skull, and told him that he, too, would be staying with Dahmer. After about four hours of being held at knifepoint, Edwards responded with a punch and a kick that enabled him to flee Dahmer's apartment and flag down a passing police car.

Two officers listened to the strange tale told by the man with the dangling handcuff and then accompanied him back to Dahmer's apartment to see for themselves whether he was exaggerating. After asking Dahmer's permission to look around, the officers almost immediately entered a literal chamber of horrors: drawers full of photos of mutilated bodies and graphic homosexual pornography featuring these victims while they were alive; a refrigerator containing a severed human head and a freezer filled with two others; boxes, drawers, closets, and coolers jammed with decaying torsos, hands, male genitals, and other body parts; and a shelf lined with two human skulls.

Charged with multiple counts of murder, Dahmer cooperated with investigators. Dahmer admitted killing seventeen men, beginning with an eighteen-year-old man he killed, dismembered, and buried when Dahmer was seventeen years old and living at his parents' home in Ohio. A thorough search of Dahmer's Milwaukee apartment turned up body parts of eleven of his victims—some boiled, stripped of flesh, and painted, and others preserved in formaldehyde like lab specimens. At least some of the victims' body parts had been cooked and eaten by Dahmer. As he later explained to the FBI, he would cut thighs, biceps, and various internal organs into pieces small enough to eat, and then cook them in a stovetop skillet before consuming them. They tasted, he told one agent, like filet mignon.

Authorities suspected that Dahmer had killed others as well, including Adam Walsh, the son of John Walsh, creator of the television program "America's Most Wanted." Adam was just six years old when he was kidnapped in 1981 from a Hollywood, Florida mall and later found decapitated. Dahmer was known to have been in the area at the time of this killing. In fact, one witness claimed to have seen Dahmer at the mall the very day Adam was kidnapped. Questioned at length, Dahmer denied this killing or any others, except the seventeen to which he had already confessed.

Even taking Dahmer at his word, why would he have committed such a gruesome series of crimes—homicides in which he not only drugged and killed his victims, but also had sex with, dismembered, and even ate portions of their dead bodies? That question was, of course, immediately on the minds of the police investigating Dahmer's crimes, but it also became a national puzzle when media across the country began reporting on the exploits of the "Milwaukee Cannibal." The need to answer that question took on even greater urgency for Gerald Boyle, who had been Dahmer's defense attorney in the Anoukone Sinthasomphone case and would now represent the accused serial killer.

As the police, defense counsel, media, and the public at large would soon learn, Jeffrey Dahmer's background had given perhaps some clues that he might one day become a violent sex criminal but, for the most part, there was little in his development to suggest that he was destined to become one of America's worst serial murderers.

Dahmer grew up the older of two boys in an apparently normal middle-class family in a suburban home set on a couple of acres near Akron, Ohio. His father was an engineer with a doctorate who earned a good living. His mother may have suffered some emotional problems but, if so, they were minor in nature. A probation report would later say that Dahmer had been sexually abused by a neighbor at the age of eight, but both he and his father vehemently denied that claim. Most who knew him growing up regarded Dahmer as a normal youngster, though in retrospect some recalled him as a bit "weird."[14] For instance, as a boy he reportedly collected insects and preserved them in jars of formaldehyde, may have demonstrated cruelty to small animals, possibly started several fires, and was regarded as the class clown. But the single definitive youthful predictor of future trouble emerged only once Dahmer had reached high school. By then, though he never posed any disciplinary problems, it was clear to many that Dahmer already had a serious alcohol abuse problem, a growing obsession exacerbated by his parents' divorce when he was a senior.

What observers of Dahmer's youth did not know, however, was that from about the age of thirteen on he struggled with the growing realization that he was gay and that, by the time he left home for college, he was already a murderer. At age seventeen, Dahmer had picked up a hitchhiker of roughly the same age, lured the young man to his home, beaten and strangled him, and then dismembered and buried his remains in the back yard.

Not long after his first killing, Dahmer began attending Ohio State University. Failing as a college student, his drinking getting beyond his control, Dahmer dropped out of school and joined the Army. Less then two years later, after a series of alcohol-related incidents, Dahmer was discharged from the Army as an untreatable alcoholic.

Dahmer started his post-military career as a phlebotomist, drawing (and on one occasion drinking) blood at a plasma center in Milwaukee. Within a year he was laid off and began his career as a criminal defendant after exposing himself at the State Fair in 1982. After several years of unemployment, Dahmer found work as a mixer at a Milwaukee chocolate factory, a job he would maintain steadily for years, even while becoming a serial killer. Not long after beginning this job, Dahmer found himself in trouble again, once more exposing himself and masturbating in public. Though his 1986 conviction and probation carried with it an order that he undergo psychotherapy, he merely went through the motions and few if anyone could have foreseen what was to come.

Steadily employed and with little else to occupy his time, Dahmer began frequenting gay bars in Milwaukee and Chicago. In November 1987, he committed his second known homicide. Though Dahmer later admitted killing this man, whom he met in a gay bar and accompanied to a nearby hotel room for sex, Dahmer always claimed he could not recall how the man died. Dahmer did, however, remember carrying the man's body from the hotel room to his grandmother's house in a large suitcase. There, he told authorities, he masturbated over the body, skinned and dismembered it, and deposited the remains in the trash.

Two months later, Dahmer began his longstanding modus operandi of luring men to his apartment by offering them money to pose nude for him. In what would be the first of another fifteen similar slayings, Dahmer strangled and dismembered a Native American teenager he had met earlier outside the Milwaukee bus station.

And so it went for the next three and a half years. Dahmer's killing spree, which began slowly, escalated rapidly, especially toward the end. In the last six months before he was arrested, Dahmer took the lives of eight men—the last four of whom he killed within a span of about twenty days.

Faced with trying to understand the unfathomable (how any sane human being could possibly murder seventeen men and boys, then sodomize, dismember, and, in some cases, eat parts of their dead bodies), the attorneys charged with prosecuting and defending Jeffrey Dahmer looked to mental health professionals for answers and assistance. What they got from a team of three psychologists and four psychiatrists was a classic "battle of the experts": some opining that Dahmer had clearly been insane (unable to appreciate the wrongfulness of his conduct or unable to conform his conduct to the requirements of law) when he killed his victims while others concluded that he did not even suffer from a major mental illness, much less legal insanity.

Dr. Kenneth Smail, a Milwaukee court psychologist who spent more time than any other expert examining Dahmer, concluded that Dahmer was competent to stand trial but did not offer an opinion at trial regarding Dahmer's sanity or lack thereof. Smail reportedly saw Dahmer as a man whose "sensory functioning was not impaired . . . [who] could think logically . . . [showed] no gross impairment in his emotional functioning [and] could delay gratification, set goals and problem solve with relative effectiveness."[15] While such a finding would not be consistent with a conclusion that Dahmer had been insane, according to one expert who did testify at trial, Smail had written that his testing of Dahmer revealed "the possibility of a major mental illness, either of the quality of a schizophrenic disorder or a major affective disorder."[16]

The expert who quoted Dr. Smail's report was a Chicago psychiatrist, Dr. Carl Wahlstrom, who was retained by and testified for the defense. Wahlstrom found Dahmer to be a man "with a long history of serious mental illness which was essentially untreated."[17] He testified that Dahmer had performed a primitive sort of brain surgery on a number of his victims in an effort to "create a zombie to keep him company" and "remain his personal friend and possession."[18] One of his victims, Dahmer had said, actually survived for two days after this "operation." As Dahmer explained to the psychiatrist: "I wanted to induce a permanent zombie-like state to make them pliable, obey my wishes, so they would be permanent, always with me, never leave my apartment. If they had their own thought processes they might remember that they had to leave, or (that they) lived somewhere else."[19]

According to Wahlstrom, Dahmer believed that eating parts of his victim's' bodies would keep "them closer to him for a longer period of time" and kept their bones because he felt they "could endow him with magical powers."[20] Dahmer, he testified, also had explained that he wanted to build a temple to his victims in order to help him "get financial gain, perhaps success in the real estate market."[21] Such thinking Wahlstrom characterized as "psychotic," part of a "bizarre delusional" system, and symptomatic of a borderline personality disorder, an illness sometimes characterized by transient psychotic episodes.[22]

Two other mental professionals, both experts on sexual disorder, testified for the defense. Dr. Fred Berlin, a psychiatrist who directed the sexual disorders clinic at Johns Hopkins University, diagnosed Dahmer as suffering from necrophilia, a paraphilia or fetish that involves sexual attraction to corpses. Other paraphilias include, for example, pedophilia (sexual attraction to prepubescent children), exhibitionism (deriving sexual satisfaction from exposing one's genitals to others), transvestism (deriving pleasure from cross-dressing), and voyeurism (sexual arousal from the surreptitious observation of others nude, disrobing, or engaging in an act of sex).

As Berlin testified, paraphilias are recognized as mental illnesses in the American Psychiatric Association's Diagnostic and Statistical Manual of Mental Disorders. Calling necrophilia a "cancer of the mind," Berlin testified that Dahmer had "overpowering urges to kill to have sex with dead bodies" and tried "very hard not to give in to these urges" but was "beaten by the disease."[23] "This is a love sickness," Berlin added. "[Dahmer] wanted to sustain a relationship with these people."[24]

Also testifying for Dahmer was Dr. Judith Becker, a clinical and research psychologist from the University of Arizona and a former member of the U.S. Attorney General's Commission on Pornography. Becker agreed that Dahmer had killed as a result of a mental illness he was unable to control: "I believe that Jeffrey Dahmer killed his victims because he is interested in engaging in sexual acts with either a total corpse or body parts of someone who is not living."[25]

While not unique, Becker told the jury, Dahmer's case was extremely unusual. Citing 122 documented cases of necrophilia, she noted that only fifteen of them, including Dahmer's, involved actually killing sex partners. Becker added that Dahmer's penchant for having sex with comatose individuals was a unique paraphilia that might be described as "kumaphilia" based upon the Greek word for coma.[26] In any event, the psychologist testified that Dahmer was insane and that, while necrophilia does not appear to be successfully treatable, it would be a "miscarriage of justice" to send him to prison rather than a mental hospital where he would, in her view, spend the rest of his life.[27]

The testimony of Wahlstrom, Berlin, and Becker was countered in whole or part by four other experts, two testifying for the prosecution and two appointed by the court.

Dr. Frederick Fosdal, a psychiatrist in private practice in Madison and a frequent expert witness in the courts of Wisconsin, testified that Dahmer had "a mental disease" but that this illness did not interfere with his ability to conform his conduct to the requirements of law or to appreciate the wrongfulness of his conduct. Thus, Fosdal concluded that Dahmer had not been insane at the time of the murders.

On cross-examination by Dahmer's attorney, Fosdal acknowledged that Dahmer said he drilled holes into the skulls of some of his victims and poured a chemical into the holes in a failed effort to "keep them around longer by making them zombie-like."[28] But the psychiatrist defended his opinion by stating that neither Dahmer's proposed altar nor his eating of various body parts reflected delusional thinking. Indeed, amazingly, Fosdal did not even regard Dahmer's effort to create a "zombie" as delusional:

> [*Defense counsel:*] What about his desire to create a zombie? Do
>   you consider that to be delusional thinking?
> [*Dr. Fosdal:*] No, it was a very practical and reasonable attempt to
>   achieve his aim.[29]

Also testifying for the prosecution was Dr. Park Dietz, a forensic psychiatrist from California who had years earlier made his reputation by testifying in the trial of John W. Hinckley, Jr. (who had been charged with attempting to assassinate President Ronald Reagan). Dietz, a well-known and frequent witness for prosecutors across the country, testified that Dahmer suffered from several paraphilias, including necrophilia, but refused to say whether Dahmer suffered from an "abnormal condition of the mind."[30]

Dietz downplayed the significance of Dahmer's necrophilia, telling the jury that neither necrophilia nor any other paraphilia would have rendered Dahmer unable to appreciate the wrongfulness of his acts or stop himself from committing them: "What the paraphilias do affect are sexual interests. But mental processes, the ability to think clearly and use logic, are untouched by the paraphilias."[31]

As the psychiatrist further explained his view of the matter, "Most paraphiles never act on their paraphilia in a criminal way. The paraphile is as free as any other human being to choose whether to commit a crime to gratify his wishes."[32]

Dietz also argued that Dahmer's paraphilias, including necrophilia, had not driven him to commit his crimes. "There was no force pushing him to kill," Dietz testified. "There was merely a desire to spend more time with the victim."[33] Moreover, Dietz expressed the opinion that, in any event, "The intensity of his sexual urges at that point was less than many teenagers experience in back seats with their girlfriends."[34]

Finally Dietz said that his opinion regarding Dahmer's sanity rested upon Dahmer's apparently calculated behavior. For example, Dietz observed, Dahmer committed all of the killings in private; used condoms when having sex with the corpses; gave up on the idea of freeze-drying the corpses due to the cost of the necessary equipment; crushed the sleeping pills used to debilitate his victims before luring them back to his apartment; and had made plans ultimately to destroy the evidence of his crimes by using acid to completely obliterate the various body parts he had collected.

Dr. George Palermo, a psychiatrist at the Milwaukee County Mental Health Center appointed by the court to examine Dahmer, concluded that the serial killer was "a sick person" but "not psychotic."[35] In Palermo's view, Dahmer was suffering from "a very serious" antisocial personality disorder but was "not legally insane."[36] Palermo described Dahmer as a sexual sadist and liar who may well have embellished certain details of the murders, such as the mutilation and cannibalism, describing his fantasies rather than what actually occurred.

Still, Palermo was not without a modicum of sympathy for Dahmer. The psychiatrist testified that "Jeffrey Dahmer killed these people . . . because he wanted to kill the source of his homosexual attraction. . . . He was not really gratified from the killing. He was afraid they might abandon him. . . . He's not such a bad person, even though he did what he did. . . . Wherever he goes, I think he should receive treatment."[37]

The other court-appointed expert, Dr. Samuel Friedman, a Milwaukee psychologist, agreed that Dahmer suffered from a severe personality disorder, which he characterized as a mental disease. He also testified that Dahmer's killings were part of an effort to maintain a relationship with his victims. Like his court-appointed colleague, Dr. Palermo, Friedman seemed sympathetic to Dahmer's plight, telling the jury that Dahmer was "amiable and pleasant to be with, courteous, with a sense of humor, conventionally handsome and charming in a manner" and that "he was, and still is, a bright young man."[38] Also, like Palermo, Friedman saw a glimmer of hope for Dahmer: "I hope that something can be done to reconstruct this individual, who certainly has the assets of youth and intelligence."[39] In the final analysis, however, the psychologist also concluded that Dahmer had been sane at the time of the killings.

Just as the experts split on Dahmer's sanity, so did the jury. After only a day of deliberations, it became clear that the jury could not reach a unanimous verdict. Ten of the jurors were convinced that Jeffrey Dahmer had been sane when he killed; two others opted to find him not guilty by reason of insanity. Under Wisconsin law, Dahmer was thus guilty of fifteen counts of murder. At sentencing, a polite, contrite, and articulate Jeffrey Dahmer concluded a lengthy apology by telling the judge, "I know my time in prison will be terrible, but I deserve whatever I get because of what I have done. Thank you, your honor, and I am prepared for your sentence, which I know will be the maximum. I ask for no consideration."[40]

Dahmer was right on both counts. The judge sentenced him to 957 years in prison, and prison was much worse than perhaps even he could have imagined. After serving less than two years in a maximum-security prison, Dahmer was brutally murdered by a mentally ill inmate who crushed Dahmer's skull with a steel bar, later telling authorities "God told me to do it."[41]

⌐13

WOODY ALLEN

AND

MIA FARROW

A Swing of King

Solomon's Sword

⌐

The story of King Solomon tells of two women who each argued that she was the rightful mother of a child. The dispute was brought before the wise king, who was asked to determine which woman should have the child. Presented with equally compelling arguments from both sides, King Solomon drew his sword and declared that he would cut the child in two and give half to each woman. One woman quickly demanded that the king give the child to the other woman, for she was indeed the child's mother. King Solomon then gave the child to the woman who had stopped him from cutting the boy in two. After all, only the true mother would be willing to give up her child so that he could live.

When married couples divorce, a number of issues need to be resolved, including who should have custody of the children. The adverse psychological effects of a divorce on children are minimized when parents are able to cooperate with one another in parenting duties following breakup of their marriage. Therefore, privately negotiated divorces work out better when the parties agree on custody and visitation arrangements for their children. Unfortunately, many divorcing couples are unable to agree on custody matters and the result is often a highly contentious and bitter battle for custody of the children that forces judges to confront issues like those faced by King Solomon. The resolution of child custody disputes is typically guided by the prevailing legal standard of doing what is in the "best interests of the child."

The precise meaning of "best interests of the child" is elusive, and judges making custody decisions have considerable power over determining where to place the children of divorcing couples. Still, the laws of the state where the divorce is granted must guide a judge's decision. However, the best interests of the child include such issues as which parent can provide the best home environment, more effectively foster a child's emotional and intellectual development, attend to basic needs like clothing and shelter, show positive affection, and demonstrate sound judgment when it comes to parenting decisions. Long ago, fathers were often granted custody of their children based on the theory that their offspring were property of the marriage. This approach to granting custody was later replaced by the "tender years" doctrine where mothers were typically granted custody because they were believed to be more nurturing and children would be better cared for emotionally if they were placed with their mothers. Today, neither mothers nor fathers have an assumed right to custody. Rather, judges must consider a number of factors when considering the best interests of the child. Because of concerns about the emotional, psychological, and intellectual development of children from divorced families, judges frequently seek the input of mental health professionals to assist in making difficult child custody decisions.

Forensic psychologists find child custody matters to be among the most difficult and challenging cases they face during their careers. Many professionals simply refuse to get involved in these kinds of cases. When custody evaluations become complicated, such as when a claim of sexual abuse arises, the degree of conflict and animosity intensifies. One of the main reasons that custody cases involving allegations of sexual abuse are so difficult is the sheer number of possibilities that must be considered. There is a very wide range of hypotheses that judges must consider, ranging from the possibility that a child has been abused and is giving an accurate and reliable report of what happened, to the possibility that a child has not been abused and is falsely accusing someone of the abuse.[1] In between these two extremes are a number of alternative possibilities. Some allegations of sexual abuse involve children who provide conflicting accounts of what happened to them or later retract a valid allegation out of fear or shame. Other allegations of sexual abuse may involve children who have not been abused, have misunderstood an innocent interaction with an adult and yet make alarming or misleading statements that suggest abuse because of intellectual or language limitations. Still other allegations of sexual abuse may involve children who were not abused but whose memories and statements are either intentionally or unintentionally contaminated by adults who question the child repeatedly or with leading questions.

When allegations of sexual abuse arise within the context of a child custody dispute, the issues become even more complicated. Various issues must be considered, such as the timing of the allegation. Was an allegation of sexual abuse involving one of the parents the cause of divorce? Did the allegation arise after the initiation, but before finalization of, divorce proceedings? Is the divorce process so hostile that one parent is capable of using an allegation of sexual abuse as a means of getting back at the other parent? Did the allegation of sexual abuse come about long after the divorce was finalized and the child has entered adolescence? Questions about the timing, circumstances, and nature of the allegation must be considered when sexual abuse allegations arise in divorce proceedings. In addition to the highly complicated nature of these types of cases, the level of anger, resentment, and hostility between the parties can often cause all but the most battle-hardened mental health professionals to shy away from becoming involved in helping to resolve the complicated issues.

One of the most visible and highly publicized child custody cases involving an allegation of sexual abuse occurred when filmmaker Woody Allen and actress Mia Farrow dissolved their romantic relationship. Their case was complicated by a number of factors that served to increase not only the public's curiosity and interest in the case, but also the hostility and animosity between these two well-known individuals.

In 1980, Allen and Farrow met and began a romantic relationship.[2] Although they made movies together regularly and had children, they never married but maintained separate residences over the course of their twelve-year relationship. Farrow came into her relationship with Allen with six children from her previous marriage to André Previn. Three of the children from her marriage to Previn—Matthew, Sascha, and Fletcher—were biological and three—Lark, Daisy, and Soon-Yi—were adopted. After Allen and Farrow began their relationship, they adopted two children, a son Moses and a daughter Dylan. The famous couple also had one biological child together, Satchel.

The relationship between Allen and Farrow soured even as Farrow was pregnant with Satchel. In 1987, while she was expecting, Farrow allegedly told Allen not to become too close to the child because she did not think their relationship was "going anywhere."[3]

When Farrow discovered nude pictures of her twenty-two-year-old adoptive daughter, Soon-Yi Farrow Previn, in Allen's apartment, she confronted both of them. Allen had apparently been carrying on a sexual relationship with his adoptive stepdaughter since she was eighteen years old and a senior in high school. When Farrow learned of the relationship, she sought to retain custody of the three children that she and Allen shared together. Soon-Yi was not part of the petition for custody because Allen had not adopted her and the state of New York, where Farrow filed the custody petition, adjudicates custody only for children under the age of eighteen.

When the couple's seven-year-old adopted daughter, Dylan, purportedly told her mother that Allen had touched her in "certain places," Farrow raised a claim that Allen had sexually abused their daughter. Thus, in addition to the high-profile nature of the parties in the case, the fact that they were not married, and that Allen was carrying on an affair with Farrow's adopted daughter from a previous marriage, the case was complicated further by an allegation of sexual abuse.

The manner in which Dylan's allegation came about became a critical issue in the case. Psychological research has shown that when a child is interviewed during a sexual abuse investigation, several factors can often lead to inaccurate, misleading, or distorted statements when children are later called upon to testify in court. Repeated interviewing of a child, leading questions, subtle cues from the interviewer that a child sees as approving or disapproving, and other similar factors can lead to tainted statements from a child.[4] Therefore, the testimony of Monica Thompson, a nanny caring for Farrow's children who was present when Dylan was first questioned by her mother about the alleged abuse, would cast doubt about the veracity of the allegation. Thompson testified that Farrow asked Dylan, "What did Daddy do?" and then followed up with the leading question, "Did Daddy ask you to take off your underwear?"[5] The nanny also testified that Farrow videotaped her interview with Dylan and turned off the camera when the child appeared to lose interest in the conversation; this raised questions about the completeness of the record of Dylan's initial statement to Farrow.

Allen filed a cross-suit against Farrow in which he sought custody of their three children based on a charge that Farrow was an unfit mother.[6] It appeared that Allen's suit was weak from the beginning because he had fostered considerable moral outrage by having an affair with Farrow's adopted daughter. Furthermore, the allegation of sexual abuse added further complications to the already difficult task of determining the specific custody and visitation arrangements that would be in the best interest of the children.

At least one psychologist from whom Farrow sought therapy for Dylan was "fired" after the psychologist stated that it would be "difficult to be certain" if Allen had actually molested the couple's daughter.[7] Dr. Susan Coates, a clinical psychologist who was hired by Allen and Farrow to provide therapy for their children, saw Dylan and Satchel for a period of time and also involved both Farrow and Allen in the treatment process.

Coates testified that she felt Allen was a committed father, particularly to his younger children, but that he also exhibited bad judgment by engaging in an affair with Farrow's adopted daughter. Judge Elliott Wilk, the New York State Supreme Court judge who presided over the case and who would reveal strong negative opinions about Allen, questioned Coates about her view of the relationship between Allen and Soon-Yi Previn and its effect on the other children. Coates admitted that Allen's behavior was "irresponsible and destructive," but she avoided offering an opinion about custody when asked by Wilk. The psychologist admitted that she would need to do more of an evaluation.[8]

Not only was Coates acting properly by refusing to offer an opinion about custody, but it would have been improper for her to conduct an additional evaluation to make such a determination. Her role in the Allen-Farrow case was originally as a treating clinician who was hired to provide therapy to Dylan. Although it was entirely proper for her to be called as a fact witness to testify as to the findings from her evaluation and interviews with Allen, Farrow, and Dylan, she was not originally sought as an expert to offer testimony about custody. A critical distinction exists in forensic psychological cases between a mental health professional who is providing therapy to an individual or family members involved in a legal case and a mental health professional who is hired as an expert to conduct an evaluation that results in an opinion about a legal question. Treating clinicians serve as fact witnesses whereas only an expert witness is qualified by a judge to offer an opinion that goes to a critical legal issue, which in the Allen-Farrow case was custody of and visitation with their children. Therefore, Coates was on safest grounding by testifying as to her findings from the treatment she provided and avoiding formal opinions about custody and visitation.

Still, Farrow's attorney, Gerald Walpin, tried to get Coates to admit that Farrow's hostile feelings toward Allen and the affair with Soon-Yi were reasonable. Walpin asked Coates, "Do you think it was unreasonable that Ms. Farrow considered Mr. Allen evil?"[9] Coates replied, "I wouldn't use that word." Walpin challenged the psychologist further, "Why not?" Coates replied, "I try to understand judgments and I don't make judgments."

Walpin revealed the extent of Farrow's extreme hostility toward Allen when he asked Coates, "Isn't it a fact that it is not unusual for a mother, under the circumstances, to believe that the man she had brought into the family, introduced to the children as a lifetime partner-parent, who was having an affair with one of her daughters, continuing the affair, responsible for her being thrown out of . . . camp and concealing where the girl is, is evil?"[10]

Coates qualified her response to Walpin's description of Allen's behavior in fairly clinical terms, "I would call it an act of extremely bad judgment, but if you wanted to call it evil I could understand that—as long as it did not generalize to a person's whole self."[11]

During her testimony, Coates described how Allen's relationship with his seven-year-old daughter was "inappropriately intense."[12] At times Allen would play with their daughter on his bed while wearing his underwear. However, Coates testified that she did not believe the relationship between Allen and Dylan was sexual. In addition, Coates believed Farrow's rage over Allen's affair with Soon-Yi Previn was so intense that the psychologist feared for Allen's safety. Farrow had apparently stated in sessions with Coates that Allen should be killed or have his eyes stabbed out. However, Farrow later testified that any threats toward Allen were facetious and not to be taken seriously.

Under cross-examination, Coates was challenged by Walpin, Farrow's attorney, about her professional record keeping, professional judgment, and ability to remain objective in the case. The attorney suggested that Coates was "mesmerized" by Allen's celebrity status and chose to obtain most of the information for her evaluation from Allen,[13] creating a bias and thus clouding the psychologist's professional judgment. In the end, Coates concluded that she believed Allen should have regular unsupervised visits with the couple's son, but she was less clear about the conditions of visitation between Allen and Dylan.

The allegation of sexual abuse forced Judge Wilk to seek additional input from mental health experts in an attempt to determine if Allen had, in fact, sexually abused his young daughter. As a result, more expert opinions entered into the case, including not only opinions about whether the sexual abuse allegation was true but also opinions about the quality of the evaluations that were performed to determine the veracity of the allegation. The result was a dizzying array of expert opinions.

Given that the alleged abuse of the couple's child occurred in Connecticut, the state police referred Dylan to the Child Sexual Abuse Clinic at Yale-New Haven Hospital for an evaluation. A team of forensic mental health experts conducted a lengthy examination of Dylan and concluded that Allen had not sexually abused the child. The team's report was never released publicly and remains sealed as part of a confidential court record.[14] Therefore, the conclusions of the Yale-New Haven Hospital study cannot be appraised directly. The only details of the report that are available to the public are those read into the court record by expert witnesses who offered their own opinions about the soundness of the conclusions in the report.

The overall conclusion of the Yale-New Haven study stated that "it is our expert opinion that Dylan was not sexually abused by Mr. Allen."[15] Neither Allen nor Farrow were apparently described favorably in the report, but among the reasons that the sexual abuse allegation was determined to be unfounded was the fact that the team identified problems in Dylan's thinking. She was observed to have difficulty telling a consistent story and her thoughts were sometimes loosely connected to one another.[16] For example, Dylan talked about "dead heads in the attic" and the examiners concluded that her thought disturbances rendered her self-reports about alleged abuse suspect. Of course, there were other factors that undoubtedly entered into the conclusion of the experts from Yale-New Haven, since Allen made himself available for the evaluation. Forensic evaluations in allegations of sexual abuse are on much firmer grounding when both the alleged victim and alleged perpetrator can be independently interviewed and examined.

Despite the positive reputation of the Yale-New Haven clinic and the fact that the experts conducting the evaluation were appointed by authorities in Connecticut and presumed to be neutral and unbiased, attorneys for both Allen and Farrow hired their own experts to cast the findings from the study in a light most favorable to their respective case. The result was a battle of expert opinions concerning the findings of other experts!

Since the findings from the Yale-New Haven investigation were favorable to Allen, his attorneys called a forensic psychologist, Dr. Anne Meltzer, to testify about the merits of the report. Meltzer testified that in her opinion the Yale-New Haven evaluation was "thorough" and conducted in a "sensitive" way.[17] "They reached conclusions that were supported well by the data they collected," Meltzer said of the report that found Allen did not sexually abuse his daughter.[18]

As a rebuttal witness, Farrow's attorney called Dr. Stephen Herman, a child psychiatrist, to testify. Not surprisingly, Herman's opinion held that the report was "seriously flawed" because of questionable investigative methods.[19] Herman claimed that he could identify no evidence of thought disorder in the child based on the examples cited in the Yale-New Haven report because some of Dylan's statements had logical explanations. One of Herman's more ironic criticisms of the report, however, was his claim that the experts at Yale-New Haven had jumped to conclusions about individuals involved in the case who had not been interviewed or examined. Yet, Herman had apparently testified about the likely absence of a thought disorder in Dylan, although public reports of the proceedings fail to provide any indication that Herman had actually examined the child to help prepare his testimony.

However, the most damaging critique of the Yale-New Haven study was the fact that original notes from the interviews and meetings had been destroyed and could not be examined to test the validity of the report's conclusions.[20] The destroying of raw interview notes is a major concern. Most agreed-upon ethical and professional standards for conducting forensic mental health evaluations call for experts to outline the basis for their opinions—which often include findings from interviews—and to preserve their records for examination later in the legal process. When a case is referred for a forensic evaluation, the experts must know that there is a strong possibility their records, opinions, and conclusions will be closely scrutinized in court. As such, forensic experts have an obligation to preserve their notes and records for later review.

Since Meltzer and Herman were hired by attorneys for Allen and Farrow, respectively, it is understandable that they had such divergent opinions about the quality of the Yale-New Haven examination and report in the case. What is more intriguing, however, is why the mental health professionals who actually examined Allen and his daughter and wrote the report did not testify at the child custody trial before Judge Wilk. In his final decision in the case, Judge Wilk noted that the members of the evaluation team were unwilling to testify, although the clinician leading the team gave testimony at a deposition.[21] It remains unclear why the clinicians who performed the direct evaluation of the sexual abuse allegation were unwilling to testify, given the fact that they accepted the task of performing an examination where it was almost certain that they would be asked to testify in court. What is even less clear is the reason that members of the team were not subpoenaed by Allen's attorney. One could speculate that because the child-custody trial took place in New York State and the experts were located in Connecticut, there may have been questions about jurisdiction. Still, the fact that the experts were not willing to testify, along with the fact that they had destroyed their notes, led Judge Wilk to view their conclusion with skepticism. He said in his final decision in the case that these factors, "compromised my ability to scrutinize their findings and resulted in a report which was sanitized and, therefore, less credible."[22]

In his final decision, Judge Wilk had harsh words for Allen as he granted sole custody of the couple's children to Farrow. The highly publicized case created a media frenzy because it involved lurid details of the private lives of two well-known celebrities, complete with allegations of sexual abuse, claims of unfit parenting, and several children caught in the middle of the bitter dispute. Judge Wilk stated in his ruling that he believed Allen "demonstrated no parenting skills that would qualify him as an adequate custodian" for his children and that he lacked "judgment, insight and impulse control."[23] The judge also went on to express his opinion that Allen was "self-absorbed, untrustworthy, and insensitive."[24] Moreover, while the judge did not entirely agree with the report of the team of experts from Yale-New Haven Hospital that Dylan had not been sexually abused, he also stated that it was not likely Allen could be prosecuted for sexual abuse.

With respect to custody, Judge Wilk wrote: "After considering Ms. Farrow's position as the sole caretaker of the children, the satisfactory fashion in which she has fulfilled that function and Mr. Allen's serious parental inadequacies, it is clear that the best interests of the children will be served by their continued custody with Ms. Farrow."[25] The "severe parental inadequacies" in Allen that the judge observed no doubt included the fact that Allen did not know many details of the children's lives (e.g., names of teachers) and, of course, the affair he carried on with Farrow's adopted daughter. Allen was not completely shut out of Dylan's life, since the judge ordered that a therapist be appointed to work with the child to determine if future contact with her father would be harmful. Moreover, the judge ruled that Allen and Farrow's fifteen-year-old son, Moses, would not be forced to see his father and that Allen would be permitted weekly supervised visits with the couple's five-year-old son, Satchel.

Allen continued his relationship with Soon-Yi Previn and they remain involved with one another to this day. His suit for custody was deemed by Judge Wilk to be frivolous and Allen was ordered to pay Farrow's legal fees, in addition to his own. Farrow embraced the final decision and subsequently adopted two other children following her break up with Allen. She later filed a legal claim to have Allen's adoption of her children overturned. Allen found the judge's decision hard to take. In a statement he issued following the final ruling, Allen said, "I think it's tragic for the children that their custody was not awarded to me."[26] Given his behavior in the case, however, it defies credulity to think the judge would have awarded the famous actor, screenwriter, and director sole custody of the children. Nevertheless, Allen was encouraged by the prospect that he might be able to see his daughter in the near future.

Although the child custody dispute between Allen and Farrow was acrimonious, bitter, and filled with strong feelings by those closest to the case, one is left wondering if the best interests of the children were really served—or if they can ever really be served in a case like this. The problem is not necessarily with the final disposition of the case, but with the behavior and opinions of many people involved. The lives of three children were affected, yet several aspects of the case worked against their best interests being served.

For one thing, Allen's affair with Soon-Yi Previn was extremely disruptive to the family relationships and contributed not only to the dissolution of Allen's relationship with Farrow but also added fuel to the fires of rage and hostility surrounding the case. The children not only had to deal with the fact that their parents would never be together again but they also would grow up facing a confusing relationship with their older sister, Soon-Yi. Would she be their sister, quasi-stepmother, or both?

Another factor that worked against the best interests of the children was the fact that that Allen and Farrow leveled sudden claims of parental unfitness against one another. It is common in cases where child custody is disputed that parents try to cast themselves in the most favorable light, with the hope that the judge will grant custody to the more desirable parent. Mothers and fathers who fight over custody of their children often have a distorted view of the standard for granting of custody as the "most favorable parent" test, rather than best interests of the child. Efforts to create favorable impressions often lead to claims by one parent that the other parent is unfit, dangerous, or abusive. When parents raise questions about the fitness of the other parent, absent any evidence of abusive or neglectful behavior, one question that begs an answer is, "If your ex-spouse is such an unfit parent, why did you entrust him or her with the care of your children all the years you were married?"

Children of divorce are best served when their parents are able to set aside hostility, antagonism, and marital conflicts in order to work together to make sure that relationships with both parents are fostered and encouraged. Many divorce cases are able to be resolved without bitter disputes over child custody and spouses are able to agree on the best arrangements for their children. After all, parents should ordinarily determine what is in the best interests of their children.

Finally, the decision in the Allen-Farrow child custody case written by Judge Wilk is laced with strong condemnation of Allen's behavior and skepticism of the purportedly neutral evaluation conducted by the professionals at the Yale-New Haven clinic who evaluated the veracity of the sexual abuse allegation against Allen. Although the judge's condemnation of Allen's affair with Soon-Yi Previn is warranted, the judge's expressed doubt about the conclusion of the experts who evaluated the veracity of the sexual abuse allegation against Allen led to visitation arrangements that added further disruption to seven-year-old Dylan's life. Judge Wilk cited several examples of Allen's behavior that supported the overall decision to grant custody to Farrow, including the fact that Allen did not know the names of his son's teachers or which children shared bedrooms in Farrow's apartment. However, the judge made it clear in his decision that he was not certain that Allen had not abused Dylan and ordered further psychological treatment of the child before Allen would be allowed to have visitation with his daughter.

In child custody cases involving allegations of sexual abuse where the abuse is unfounded or proven to be false, judges are often left in a position of having to decide about visitation arrangements with the accused parents. Undoubtedly, one of the questions that looms large in a judge's thinking is, "What if the abuse really happened but it just couldn't be proven in court?" In these instances, a cautious decision that some judges make is to rule the abuse to be unfounded but then order custody and visitation arrangements that protect the children in case the allegations happened to be true. Therefore, a completely innocent parent who has been the target of an unfounded or completely false allegation of abuse may be granted only supervised visitation with a child in order to protect the child. In Allen's case, this is exactly what occurred because the sexual abuse allegation was unfounded; there were presumably no facts proven at trial to substantiate the need for supervised visitation. Nevertheless, given the apparent existence of questions in the judge's mind, supervised visitation was granted nonetheless.

Of course, in cases where there is clear or even equivocal evidence of abuse (e.g., an expert opinion that the abuse could be neither substantiated nor disproved), supervised visitation would seem to be a likely choice. However, in cases where the accused parent is innocent, one must question the impact a decision of supervised visitation would have on a child who had not been sexually abused. Somewhere along the way, the child may pick up cues from the parent who remains convinced the abuse occurred or from questions asked by therapists or case workers who monitor the supervised visitation that the accused parent has "done something wrong." These outcomes beg the question of whether supervised visitation in cases where an allegation of sexual abuse has been unfounded adds to, rather than helps, the child adjust to divorce. Other than the tragic physical injuries to an abused child, one can only wonder if there are real differences in the psychological and emotional injuries suffered by children who are actually abused and children who have not been abused but treated by the legal system as though they have been abused.

Given the fact that divorce and custody arrangements are disruptive to the lives of children, it is perhaps more appropriate to view child custody cases as resulting only in what is in the "*better* interests of the child," since "best interests of the child" may be an elusive ideal that can never really be attained in these difficult and challenging cases. Furthermore, some of the more probing psychological questions in child custody cases are those pertaining to the motives of the parents. For instance, why do some divorcing parents fail to put their animosities aside when it comes to their children in order to work toward making their post-divorce lives ones that will allow their children to continue growing, thriving, and developing into happy, well-adjusted, and productive adults?

▸14

GARY AND
HOLLY RAMONA

Recovered Memories

or False Allegations?

◢

B y 1988, forty-four-year-old Gary Ramona found himself in a life situation most people could only envy. After two decades of hard work,
he had moved up the corporate ladder to become a top executive at one of
America's leading wineries and was earning nearly half a million dollars a
year. He was married to a glamorous woman, had three bright and attractive
teenage daughters, and lived in a luxurious home in California's exclusive
Napa Valley.

But all was not entirely well with the Ramona family. Ramona's oldest daughter, Holly, a high school senior, was struggling with depression and
what appeared to be an eating disorder. She was withdrawing from family and
friends and spending more and more time alone. Though she stood only five
feet, four inches tall, her weight had ballooned from 120 to 155 pounds. Her
mother, Stephanie Ramona, wanted her in psychotherapy but Gary did not
like the idea. Holly was about to enter her freshman year at the University
of California at Irvine, and it was not unreasonable to think that perhaps a
change of scenery would be beneficial for the eighteen-year-old.

Sadly, Holly's condition continued to deteriorate during her first year of
college. She became anorexic and bulimic, alternating between rigid dieting
and a regimen of bingeing and purging. With her parents only suspecting
the worst, Holly's eating disorder continued to dominate her life during the
summer after her freshman year. Just as she was about to return to UC Irvine

for her sophomore year, she confided in her mother, who immediately sought psychological help for the ailing teenager.

By the time Holly was back at Irvine for the fall semester, Stephanie had arranged for her to begin seeing a counselor, Marche Isabella at the Irvine Family Psychological Services, an off-campus private practice. Isabella, a newly licensed marriage and family counselor, had little experience with eating disorders. When Stephanie Ramona asked Isabella what could have caused her daughter's bulimia, Isabella told her that 70 to 80 percent of bulimic women have been sexually abused.[1] Stephanie then confronted Holly and asked if she had ever been molested. Holly said she was not sure but thought she had. Stephanie asked if Gary had been the perpetrator and Holly replied that he was not.

Holly's treatment with Isabella began uneventfully but she soon asked Holly to join a therapy group she was conducting for women with eating disorders, some of whom had been sexually abused.

In December, after a semester of college and psychotherapy, Holly returned home for the holidays. Later she would report that during the Christmas break her father had stared at her in a sexual way. Shortly thereafter, she would later say, she began having "flashbacks" of her father sexually abusing her.[2] The flashbacks continued and became more vivid, going from thoughts of fondling to vaginal, oral, and anal intercourse, and ultimately to bestiality—Gary having sex with the family dog and Holly performing oral sex on the animal.[3]

Initially Holly had told no one about what she was experiencing. But her bulimia worsened and, by mid-January, she told Isabella about her father's "sexual" look, which Isabella labeled "emotional incest."[4] Soon, Holly was seeing Isabella three or four times weekly and sharing her flashbacks with the therapist. Isabella suggested that Holly confront Gary. Holly wanted to do so but wanted to be absolutely sure that what she was experiencing were memories of actual abuse. Having heard from a fellow group member that a drug called sodium amytal could be used in such cases as a sort of "truth serum," Holly pressed to have the drug administered.[5]

Isabella initially resisted the idea but then gave in and consulted a psychiatrist, Dr. Richard Rose. Rose agreed that if Holly were to confront Gary, the confrontation should take place in the safety of a psychiatric ward. On March 12, Holly was admitted to such a ward at the Western Medical Center where, after a forty-five-minute interview, Rose determined that she was a good candidate for a sodium amytal interview.

Two days later, Rose administered the drug to Holly and asked her to try to recall the events she had been discussing with him and Isabella. No record was made of the session but it would later be reported that Holly readily described the sexual abuse she had been reliving in her mind for the past several months and added that she now recalled actually being raped by her father.

Following the interview, Isabella contacted Stephanie Ramona and told her that her daughter had been raped. The next day, Isabella reassured Holly that she had been truthful while under the drug's influence "because usually you need to be trained to lie under sodium amytal."[6] Isabella added that "given my experience and analysis of you during the interview, you were not lying."[7]

Later that day, having been summoned to Isabella's office, Gary Ramona was confronted by Holly, who told him flatly, "You raped me."[8] When Ramona denied ever having done any such thing, Isabella told him "we have proof" and explained that sodium amytal was "kind of like truth serum in the movies."[9] When Ramona asked how it could be that his daughter had been repeatedly sexually abused and had only recently recalled it, Isabella explained that Holly had repressed memories of the abuse because the emotional pain had been too great to allow her to deal with them.

Sued for divorce and cut off from virtually any contact with his wife and daughters, Ramona soon discovered that the impact of Holly's accusations would not stop there. Before long, rumors of the alleged abuse made it to Ramona's employer: he was placed on paid leave, then demoted, and finally eased out of his job altogether. Meanwhile Ramona began seeking legal advice, asking lawyers if he could sue the mental health professionals he felt had somehow caused his daughter to believe that he had abused her.

The lawyers were blunt, and with good reason. Ramona, they said, could not sue Isabella or Rose for malpractice because under then-existing California law, neither professional had any duty to him because he had not been their patient. Additionally, the lawyers noted that, as a practical matter, such a lawsuit would not succeed because all of Holly's medical and mental health records were confidential, and without access to those records no malpractice could be proven.

Meanwhile, as the flashbacks continued and Holly's mental health continued to deteriorate, she gave increasing thought to initiating her own lawsuit—one in which she would sue her father for the psychological damage she believed had been caused by his sexual abuse.

Holly's lawsuit would be far from the first such legal action taken by an alleged victim of child sexual abuse. In the 1980s, a number of adult women began confronting men they claimed had sexually abused them during childhood. Many of these cases involved the alleged perpetrator being sued for damages incurred as a result of sexual abuse that had occurred years, some-times even decades, earlier. Although confrontation of the perpetrator, and even litigation itself, was believed by some therapists to facilitate recovery, one of the legal hurdles in these cases was the statute of limitations.

Seen as a safeguard against stale evidence, these statutes impose strict time limitations on the filing of lawsuits. However, certain exceptions have long allowed civil plaintiffs to overcome the statute of limitations, such as when an injury is not discovered until months or years later. For instance, minors are typically allowed to wait until their age of maturity (e.g., eighteen years old) before bringing suit; also, people who do not know they have been injured until years later (e.g., the patient who finds out that a surgeon left a sponge in the body cavity) are permitted to sue after the statute of limitations has passed.

Consulting an attorney, Holly learned that three years earlier, in 1987, the California legislature had joined numerous other states in enacting laws liberalizing the statute of limitations in cases of alleged sexual abuse.[10]

Responding to a growing number of lawsuits brought by people with so-called recovered memories of distant sexual abuse, California lawmakers had made it possible for alleged victims of child sexual abuse to bring lawsuits within three years of reaching adulthood, no matter how much earlier the alleged abuse had occurred. Several years later, the legislature had also made it possible for alleged sexual abuse victims to bring lawsuits within three years of discovering the psychological harm done them by the abuse, regardless of whether they had ever forgotten the abuse.

Ultimately Holly decided to sue her father and, when she did, she unwit-tingly made possible the lawsuit Gary Ramona's lawyers had previously said could not be brought or won.

By claiming that she had been psychologically harmed by the sexual abuse allegedly inflicted upon her by her father, Holly had, in legal terms, placed her mental condition at issue. To win the monetary damages she was seeking she would have to prove not only that the abuse had occurred but that it had impaired her psychologically. That would require evidence from the mental health professionals, including Isabella and Rose, who had treated her. Moreover, the rules of discovery meant that, in order to enable Gary Ramona to defend himself against Holly's charges, he and his lawyers would have to be granted access to Holly's records.

Emboldened by the knowledge that he would now have the evidentiary ammunition needed to pursue his claims against Isabella, Rose, and the hos-pital in which the sodium amytal interview had been conducted, Ramona filed an $8.5 million lawsuit. Ramona would still have to get a court to agree that

Isabella and Rose owed him a duty of care, but his attorneys now had an encouraging theory about that.

Ten years earlier the California courts had dealt with a case in which a woman was misdiagnosed as suffering from a sexually transmitted disease (STD).[11] The woman's physician, who had made the erroneous diagnosis, had also suggested that she inform her husband so that he, too, could be tested for the STD. The wife's revelation to her husband led to the couple's divorce. When they learned that the diagnosis had been faulty, they sued the physician and won. The California Supreme Court upheld the verdict, ruling that:

> In the case at bar the risk of harm to plaintiff was reasonably foreseeable to defendants. It is easily predictable that an erroneous diagnosis of syphilis and its probable source would produce marital discord and resultant emotional distress to a married patient's spouse; Dr. Kilbridge's advice to Mrs. Molien to have her husband examined for the disease confirms that plaintiff was a foreseeable victim of the negligent diagnosis. Because the disease is normally transmitted only by sexual relations, it is rational to anticipate that both husband and wife would experience anxiety, suspicion, and hostility when confronted with what they had every reason to believe was reliable medical evidence of a particularly noxious infidelity.
>
> We thus agree with plaintiff that the alleged tortious conduct of defendant was directed to him as well as to his wife. Because the risk of harm to him was reasonably foreseeable we hold, in negligence parlance, that under these circumstances defendants owed plaintiff a duty to exercise due care in diagnosing the physical condition of his wife.[12]

When attorneys for Isabella and Rose claimed that Ramona's suit should be dismissed because their clients owed him no duty of care, Ramona's legal team argued that this case was similar to that of Mr. and Mrs. Molien. In allowing Gary Ramona's lawsuit to continue, the judge agreed, finding Isabella and Rose did owe Gary Ramona a duty of care because they directed Holly to confront her father and it was foreseeable that being confronted with the allegations of incest would harm him.[13]

Meanwhile, Holly's lawsuit against her father would eventually be doomed by her allegation that her memories of molestation were confirmed by the sodium amytal interview arranged by Isabella and administered by Rose. In unanimously ordering her lawsuit dismissed, a California appeals court held that Holly's own testimony about the alleged abuse (essentially the only evidence that it occurred) was inadmissible because it had been "tainted"

by the sodium amytal interview, a technique the court found to be scientifi-
cally unreliable.[14] Ironically, in arranging and conducting the sodium amytal
interview, Isabella and Rose had not only opened the door to a lawsuit against
themselves but also precluded their patient from suing her alleged abuser.

Though Holly Ramona had been denied her day in court, when Gary
Ramona's lawsuit finally went to trial, it was clear that the case would turn
on the question of whether Holly's allegations of sexual abuse were true.
Although officially the defendants were Marche Isabella and Richard Rose,
there could be little question that the true parties in interest were Gary and
Holly Ramona or that the trial would turn more on the legitimacy of repressed
memories than the technicalities of professional malpractice law.

A verdict for the defense would vindicate not only the professionals, but
Holly as well. A verdict for the plaintiff would not only vindicate Gary but
drive a dagger into the heart of the controversial repressed-memories move-
ment that had grown so rapidly over the preceding decade and had fueled
so many other lawsuits against (and criminal prosecutions of) alleged sexual
abusers.

Given the stakes, it came as no surprise that the witness list in the trial read
like a who's who in the fields of sexual abuse, eating disorders, and repressed
memory. Dr. Park Dietz, the forensic psychiatrist who had previously testified against presidential assassin John W. Hinckley, Jr., and Milwaukee serial
killer Jeffrey Dahmer, led off the parade of experts for Gary Ramona. Dietz
testified that there was "no credible evidence" for the existence of repressed
memories such as those claimed by Holly, and that Holly was "reporting, sin-
cerely, false memories caused by the treatment she received."[15] Dietz added
that, "She started with obsessional intrusions and dreams and through the
'magic' of truth serum, she was led to believe that she was sexually abused by
her father."[16] It was only after the sodium amytal interview, Dietz testified,
that "Holly becomes persuaded that she was raped by her father."[17] Finally,
Dietz faulted Isabella and Rose, concluding that their failure to videotape or
audiotape the sodium amytal session fell below the professional standard of
care. Confronted on cross-examination with a statement he had made a couple
of years before the Ramona trial regarding the possible existence of repressed
memories, Dietz replied: "I've learned more, changed my mind."[18]

Next came the testimony of Dr. Robert Gerner, a prominent California
psychiatrist selected by Ramona's legal team to conduct the only examination of Holly Ramona that the plaintiff's side would be allowed by the court.
Gerner offered the opinion that Holly had difficulty differentiating reality
from fantasy, had significant personality disorders, and had projected her
sexual fantasies onto her father. However, on cross-examination, Gerner's

objectivity was called into question when he was forced to admit that, like Gary Ramona, he too had come under investigation for engaging in sexual improprieties. Pressed further by one of the attorneys for the defense, Gerner acknowledged that in the course of counseling a couple regarding their marriage he had accepted oral sex from the wife in his office.[19]

The next psychiatric expert to testify was Dr. James Hudson, a Harvard Medical School professor and founder of the Academy for Eating Disorders. Hudson testified that he knew of no evidence that childhood sexual abuse caused bulimia; he also asserted that the sorts of behaviors demonstrated by Holly (e.g., her obsession with weight, preoccupation with food, and aversion to certain foods such as bananas and mayonnaise) were symptoms of bulimia and not "evidence of childhood sexual abuse."[20]

Asked whether "there [was] any evidence at all that a person who has been sexually abused from age five to age sixteen [as Holly claimed she had been] could have repressed it and forgotten the whole thing," Hudson replied: "No. People who have been forcibly raped over an eleven-year period from age five to age sixteen just don't forget."[21] Asked on cross-examination if, in light of his direct testimony, he thought Holly had been lying about the alleged abuse, Hudson said, "I don't think she's consciously lying but saying things that I think are untrue."[22]

Next, after the jury heard from two local doctors, a psychologist and a psychiatrist, that Isabella and Rose had failed to meet the standard of care in their respective professions, Dr. Elizabeth Loftus took the stand. Loftus, a world-renowned experimental psychologist and the pre-eminent authority on human memory agreed with Hudson. Citing her own studies and others, Loftus testified that "there is no scientific support for the idea that you can be raped, molested, anally raped—bestiality—spanning an eleven year period, and totally forget about it, block it into your subconscious, and then reliably recover it later."[23]

Loftus also described the mechanisms by which false memories may be created. As an example, she detailed a study she and a colleague had conducted. In this research, twenty-four adult subjects (ages eighteen to fifty-three) were asked to try to remember a number of childhood events they were told had been recounted by their parents, older siblings, or other close relatives. Each subject was presented with three incidents that had actually occurred and one that was entirely fictional—a scenario in which the subject reportedly had been lost for a long period of time in a shopping mall at about age five. The description included the subject crying, being assisted by an elderly woman, and then reunited with family. After reading accounts of the events, both true and false, seven of the twenty-four subjects (29 percent) reported partially or fully recalling the fictional shopping-mall event; in follow-up interviews, six subjects (25 percent) continued to claim recall of the fictitious event.[24]

Could Holly Ramona's "memories" have been the product of suggestion? Loftus believed so. After all, her therapist and psychiatrist had not only accepted and nurtured Holly's beliefs that she had been sexually abused by her father, but had fueled them through repetition and the use of suggestive terms such as "emotional incest" and "truth serum."

On cross-examination, defense counsel were quick to establish that Loftus was an experimentalist and not a clinician; she had never treated patients and based her conclusions on academic studies rather than real-world experience; the subjects in her research were healthy college students, not sexually traumatized children; and she could not rule out the possibility that Holly Ramona had been sexually abused by her father. Asked whether she believed Holly had been lying about the alleged abuse, Loftus echoed what Dietz and Hudson had already told the jury: "I see no evidence that she was deliberately lying. False beliefs, false memories, false constructions—we're talking about people who are trying to tell the truth."[25]

In an effort to counter the compelling expert testimony of Drs. Dietz, Hudson, and Loftus, defense attorneys pinned their hopes on the testimony of the two defendants, Isabella and Rose, and the expert testimony of Dr. Thomas Gutheil and Dr. Lenore Terr.

Isabella testified that she "believe[d] everything" Holly told her and that she had "no reason not to believe" what Holly said while under sodium amytal.[26] She acknowledged that it had never occurred to her to tape the interview and she admitted referring to sodium amytal as "kind of like a truth serum."[27] She had taken no notes of the interview, she testified, because "I hate notes."[28]

Cross-examination was even worse for the defendant. Contradicting her earlier testimony, Isabella then said, "I did not tell them [sodium amytal] was a truth serum. I never believed it was a truth serum."[29] Acknowledging that at the time she understood that one could not lie while under the drug unless trained to do so, Isabella now admitted that she was mistaken in that belief. Asked about her admitted assertion that 70 to 80 percent of people with eating disorders had been sexually abused, Isabella could not identify the source for that purported statistic, except to say that she had read it in a "big book."[30] Finally, when asked if she would believe a patient who reported incidents of witchcraft while under sodium amytal, Isabella replied "I would accept that as true if the patient reported that under a sodium amytal interview."[31]

Rose proved not much better as a witness on his own behalf. The psychiatrist played down his support for the sodium amytal interview, acknowledging that he had relented and given Holly the drug because "She thought she was going crazy."[32] Rose admitted telling Holly after the interview that he did not think she was lying but when asked if he was concerned that the sodium amytal might have led to false memories, he replied, "Yes."[33]

To meet allegations that Rose had not met the standard of care in psychiatry when he administered sodium amytal to Holly, the defense called Dr. Thomas Gutheil as an expert witness. Gutheil, another Harvard Medical School professor, had written extensively on psychological and legal issues including "the tendency of . . . poorly trained counselors to seize upon childhood sexual abuse as a single cause for all adult psychopathology" and "therapist[s] testifying in court to reasonable medical certainty that something really happened . . . based solely upon what the patient said."[34] Gutheil had also written approvingly of Loftus's work on the creation of false memories. But in the confines of psychotherapy, Gutheil testified, "you have to immerse yourself in your patient's belief," adding that "If he told you a spaceship came down, you didn't tell him you believed it really happened. You asked 'What is the spaceship trying to tell us about your inner life?'"[35] Nonetheless, in Gutheil's view, Rose had met the standard of care because the psychiatrist had been "try[ing] to help someone who was really torn between the memories and the wish that they were not true."[36] Administering sodium amytal to Holly, Gutheil testified, responded to her needs and helped her to clarify her experience.

The last psychiatric expert to testify was Dr. Lenore Terr, a San Francisco psychiatrist who had spent thirty years working with traumatized children and had recently been involved as an expert in two sensational cases. Terr was best known for her groundbreaking study of a group of twenty-six children who had been kidnapped from their school bus in Chowchilla, California and held underground for twenty-seven hours. Terr, who later interviewed twenty-five of these children, concluded that they, as well as other youngsters who had been traumatized, had lasting memories of the trauma.[37]

But Terr was also well known for her more recent role as an expert witness in an unprecedented California criminal case. In 1989, twenty-eight-year-old Eileen Franklin-Lipsker experienced a "flashback." Suddenly, in her mind's eye, it was twenty years earlier and her father was raping and beating her best friend to death. In this allegedly recovered memory, Franklin-Lipsker's father also threatened to kill her. Soon, Franklin-Lipsker also claimed to have recovered memories of her father and others repeatedly sexually abusing her from the age of five on.

After Franklin-Lipsker revealed her "flashback" to the authorities, her father, George Franklin, was charged with murder in the twenty-year-old unsolved killing of his daughter's childhood friend. Lacking other direct evidence, prosecutors relied upon Franklin-Lipsker's purported recovered memory as proof of George Franklin's guilt. Testifying for the prosecution, Terr, who had examined Franklin-Lipsker, told the jury how Franklin-Lipsker would have been able to completely forget such a horrific trauma and then recall it vividly and accurately twenty years later. Franklin was convicted and sentenced to life but his conviction was later overturned on appeal and he was freed after spending more than six years in prison.[38]

In the Ramona trial, Terr seemed to reconcile the apparent conflicts between the Chowchilla kidnapping and the Franklin case. Chowchilla, she testified, involved "a single blow" trauma, as compared with the sort of "multiple blow" trauma alleged in the Franklin and Ramona cases.[39] With "single blow" or "Type I" trauma, as Terr called it, the traumatic event would be remembered well. But with "multiple blow" trauma, "Type II" in Terr's schema, memory loss followed by later recovery would be more likely. The key distinction, she told the jury, was "anticipation"; children subjected to repeated abuse, as Eileen Franklin-Lipsker and Holly Ramona allegedly had been, "know it's going to happen" and "can suppress" the memories.[40]

Terr claimed that this distinction, which she developed, was "generally accepted" and "being taught in medical schools."[41] Though there are no systematic empirical data to support the theory or her assertions about its acceptance, Terr pointed to "something like eighty-five years of single case reports."[42] Terr added that in her own "very strong opinion" those who had gone through many traumatic events remembered the events less well than people who had gone through just one event.[43]

But Terr went even further than educating the jury with regard to repressed memories. She as much as told the panel that Holly had been sexually abused. Holly's trauma, Terr testified further, was validated by the "symptoms and signs" she demonstrated.[44] Holly's fears of men and sex, her dislike for movie idol Tom Cruise because he had teeth like her father's, her avoidance of foods that reminded her of penises, semen, or sex (e.g., mayonnaise, cream sauce, and uncut bananas and pickles), and her enjoyment of games such as "Charlie's Angels, Bionic Woman, Wonder Woman (which involved destroying 'villainous men')" all constituted a cluster of symptoms indicating that she had been sexually abused.[45] Finally, Terr testified that Isabella, Rose and the hospital had all met the standard of care in their treatment of Holly. "I don't see that any major mistakes were made," she told the jury.[46]

After about two days of deliberations, the jury found in favor in Gary Ramona, responding in the affirmative to three questions posed to them in their instructions from the judge. First, the jury concluded that Isabella and

Rose were negligent in providing health care to Holly Ramona by implant-ing or reinforcing false memories that her father had sexually molested her. Second, the jury determined that Holly's therapists had caused Gary Ramona to be personally confronted with the accusation that he sexually abused his daughter. And, finally, the jury found that Ramona suffered damages that were caused by the negligence of Holly's therapists. In a rather surprising move, however, the jury awarded no money damages to Gary Ramona for the emotional harm he had incurred. Overall, the jury awarded Ramona $500,000 in economic damages, apportioning 40 percent of the responsibility to Isa-bella, 10 percent to Rose, 5 percent to the hospital, and 40 percent to others named by the jury—people in the community whose loose lips and point-ing fingers had cost Ramona his reputation and his livelihood. The jury also assessed 5 percent of the blame to Ramona himself, not for molesting Holly but for his failure as a parent.

In the end, Gary Ramona had spent millions to come away with only $500,000, something very few litigants could afford. But in addition to win-ning the vindication he sought, his lawsuit paved the way for dozens of others from coast to coast. In the years since the Ramona verdict, courts across the nation have become receptive to suits of this sort and many parents have suc-cessfully sued their children's psychologists, psychiatrists, and other counsel-ors, alleging that these professionals implanted false memories of abuse that destroyed their families.

The question of whether and, if so, to what extent repressed and recov-ered memories exist remains unresolved and continues to be the subject of great controversy among and between clinicians and behavioral scientists. But, out of financial and professional self-defense if nothing else, since the Ramona verdict many therapists have taken a more reasoned, cautious, and skeptical approach to allegations of recently uncovered memories of tempo-rally remote sexual abuse.

15

COLIN

FERGUSON

A Fool for a Client?

A ccording to the old adage, "He who has himself for an attorney has a fool for a client." While the folly of representing oneself legally, especially in court, has long been recognized, so too has the legal right to do so. The right to self-representation has a long history in Anglo-American jurisprudence. Prior to the establishment of colonial America, only one British tribunal had ever forced a defendant to be represented by anyone other than himself. That tribunal was the notorious sixteenth- and seventeenth-century Star Chamber, which has since come to symbolize disregard for legal rights.

In the U.S. federal courts, self-representation has been guaranteed since 1789, when the First Congress passed the Judiciary Act, which provided that "in all the courts of the United States, the parties may plead and manage their own causes personally or by the assistance of . . . counsel."[1] Additionally, the right to self-representation is guaranteed by the Constitutions of thirty-six states and by statute and/or case law in numerous other states.

In 1975, the U.S. Supreme Court held that a criminal defendant's right to represent himself in court is also guaranteed by the Sixth Amendment. In elevating this right to constitutional stature, the Court held in *Faretta v. California* that:

> The Sixth Amendment does not provide merely that a defense shall
> be made for the accused; it grants to the accused personally the

right to make his defense. It is the accused, not counsel, who must be "informed of the nature and cause of the accusation," who must be "confronted with the witnesses against him," and who must be accorded "compulsory process for obtaining witnesses in his favor." Although not stated in the Amendment in so many words, the right to self-representation—to make one's own defense personally—is thus necessarily implied by the structure of the Amendment. The right to defend is given directly to the accused; for it is he who suffers the consequences if the defense fails.[2]

In *Faretta* the Court recognized that while choosing to represent oneself in court may be foolish and even detrimental to a defendant's own interests, such a choice must be respected. As the Court explained:

It is undeniable that in most criminal prosecutions defendants could better defend with counsel's guidance than by their own unskilled efforts. But where the defendant will not voluntarily accept representation by counsel, the potential advantage of a lawyer's training and experience can be realized, if at all, only imperfectly. To force a lawyer on a defendant can only lead him to believe that the law contrives against him. Moreover, it is not inconceivable that in some rare instances, the defendant might in fact present his case more effectively by conducting his own defense. Personal liberties are not rooted in the law of averages. The right to defend is personal. The defendant, and not his lawyer or the State, will bear the personal consequences of a conviction. It is the defendant, therefore, who must be free personally to decide whether in his particular case counsel is to his advantage. And although he may conduct his own defense ultimately to his own detriment, his choice must be honored out of "that respect for the individual which is the lifeblood of the law."[3]

Not all of the justices agreed with the Court's conclusion in *Faretta*. Three dissenters noted, among other concerns, the inability of most laymen to represent themselves in court, quoting the Supreme Court's opinion in the 1932 case of *Powell* v. *Alabama*:

Even the intelligent and educated layman has small and sometimes no skill in the science of law. If charged with crime, he is incapable, generally, of determining for himself whether the indictment is good or bad. He is unfamiliar with the rules of evidence. Left without the aid of counsel he may be put on trial without a proper

charge, and convicted upon incompetent evidence, or evidence irrelevant to the issue or otherwise inadmissible. He lacks both the skill
and knowledge adequately to prepare his defense, even though he
may have a perfect one. He requires the guiding hand of counsel at
every step in the proceedings against him. Without it, though he
be not guilty, he faces the danger of conviction because he does not
know how to establish his innocence. If that be true of men of intelligence, how much more true is it of the ignorant and illiterate, or
those of feeble intellect.[4]

Nine years after deciding *Faretta*, the U.S. Supreme Court tackled the
question of how courts must respond when a mentally troubled defendant
wishes to waive counsel and represent himself. In *Godinez v. Moran* (1993),
capital defendant Allan Moran waived his right to be represented by an attorney, pleaded guilty, and ultimately was sentenced to death. The trial court
held that Moran's waiver of counsel was legal because he was competent to
stand trial. A federal district court reversed Moran's conviction, holding that
competence to waive counsel requires a higher degree of understanding and
reason than does mere competence to stand trial, the standard for which is
simply that the defendant understand the charges against him and be able to
assist counsel in his own defense. After a federal appeals court rejected the
district court's decision and sided with the trial court, the U.S. Supreme Court
also essentially agreed with the trial court that if a defendant is competent to
stand trial he is competent to waive counsel and to represent himself if he so
chooses. As the Court concluded:

There is no reason to believe that the decision to waive counsel
requires an appreciably higher level of mental functioning than the
decision to waive other constitutional rights. Respondent suggests
that a higher competency standard is necessary because a defendant
who represents himself " must have greater powers of compre-
hension, judgment, and reason than would be necessary to stand
trial with the aid of an attorney." But this argument has a flawed
premise; the competence that is required of a defendant seeking
to waive his right to counsel is the competence to *waive the right*,
not the competence to represent himself. In *Faretta v. California*,
(1975), we held that a defendant choosing self-representation must
do so "competently and intelligently," but we made it clear that the
defendant's "technical legal knowledge" is "not relevant" to the
determination whether he is competent to waive his right to counsel, and we emphasized that although the defendant "may conduct

his own defense ultimately to his own detriment, his choice must be honored." Thus, while "it is undeniable that in most criminal prosecutions defendants could better defend with counsel's guidance than by their own unskilled efforts," a criminal defendant's ability to represent himself has no bearing upon his competence to *choose* self-representation.[5]

Writing in dissent for himself and Justice Stevens, Justice Blackmun challenged the Court's reasoning in *Moran*:

> The majority "reject[s] the notion that competence to plead guilty or to waive the right to counsel must be measured by a standard that is higher than (or even different from)" the standard for competence to stand trial. . . . But the standard for competence to stand trial is specifically designed to measure a defendant's ability to "consult with counsel" and to "assist in preparing his defense." A finding that a defendant is competent to stand trial establishes only that he is capable of aiding his attorney in making the critical decisions required at trial or in plea negotiations. The reliability or even relevance of such a finding vanishes when its basic premise—that counsel will be present—ceases to exist. The question is no longer whether the defendant can proceed with an attorney, but whether he can proceed alone and uncounseled.[6]

The Supreme Court's rulings in *Faretta* and *Moran* were put to a practical test perhaps most dramatically in the 1994 murder trial of Colin Ferguson.

In the fall of 1993, Colin Ferguson, a thirty-five-year-old divorced black Jamaican immigrant was living alone in a single room in the Flatbush section of New York City. For years, since coming to the United States in 1985, Ferguson had moved from job to job, had attended two colleges (Nassau Community College and Adelphi University), and had become embroiled in controversies with the Worker's Compensation Board, the Equal Employment Opportunity Commission (EEOC), and various law enforcement agencies. Ferguson had been unable to remain in the same job or attend college for long because he believed that he was the victim of racism wherever he worked or studied. His marriage ended after he concluded that the U.S. Immigration and Naturalization Service (INS) was harassing him, in part because the INS had shown his wife a picture of another man and she had failed to identify that man as Ferguson, her husband.

In December 1993, Ferguson's landlady began to notice a change in his behavior; he was "acting funny" and praying loudly.[7] On December 7, around

4:00 P.M., Ferguson left his room, carrying a bag. Nearly two hours later, the bag still in hand, Ferguson boarded a rush-hour commuter train packed with commuters heading home to Long Island from New York City.

Ferguson chose a seat at the end of the third car, where he had a full view of all twenty-six rows of seats. But Ferguson wasn't seated long. After two stops, he pulled a 9-mm semiautomatic pistol from the bag, stood up, and shot the passenger on his right five times. He then turned and fired at a passenger to his left. Other passengers began to cry and scream as Ferguson made his way down the aisle, shooting one commuter after another, stopping only long enough to reload his pistol.

When Ferguson stopped, apparently to reload the gun a second time, he was rushed and tackled by two passengers. While they pinned Ferguson to the floor, he mumbled incoherently and did not resist.

In less than three minutes, Colin Ferguson had killed six passengers and wounded nineteen others. Although one passenger remarked that Ferguson ought to be shot, others held him for the police. Arrested at the scene and positively identified as the shooter, Ferguson claimed that the killer was not him but another man who looked just like him. In Ferguson's pockets, police found numerous handwritten notes listing "reasons for this."[8] Among the "reasons" listed in Ferguson's notes were "Adelphi University's racism, the EEOC's racism, Worker's Compensation's racism, NYC Transit Police, NYC Police, [and] the racism of Governor Cuomo's staff."[9] "Additional reasons for this" were listed as: "The sloppy running of the #2 train. It is racism by Caucasians and Uncle Tom Negroes. Also the false allegations against me by the filthy Caucasian racist female on the #1 line."[10]

After Ferguson's arrest and arraignment on multiple counts of murder and attempted murder, a court-appointed psychologist, Dr. John D'Alessandro, and psychiatrist, Dr. Allen Reichman, jointly examined Ferguson's competence to stand trial and found that that he was intelligent but "evasive, defensive and misleading,"[11] was "able to understand the charges against him and to cooperate with his attorney" and was "malingering in an attempt to create an impression that he is unable to do so."[12] D'Alessandro and Reichman felt that Ferguson was suffering from a paranoid personality disorder but was not delusional or psychotic. They characterized him as an overly suspicious man who had difficulty getting along with others, had a "chip on his shoulder," and made a "big issue out of little things."[13]

Meanwhile, while they were still representing him, Ferguson's attorneys maintained that Ferguson was mentally ill and had a possible insanity defense. A psychiatrist selected by the defense, Dr. Richard Dudley, examined Ferguson and found him to be suffering from a delusional disorder (persecutory type). In his lengthy report, Dr. Dudley wrote that Ferguson's " belief that he has been and continues to be surrounded by and constantly persecuted by racist whites and non-whites who have been influenced by white racism is so extreme (and out of line with reality) and so resistant to change by available evidence that it meets the definition of a delusion."[14] Dudley also concluded that as a result of this mental illness, Ferguson had been insane at the time of the killings and that he was, at the time of trial, not competent to be tried.

In view of the conflicting psychological and psychiatric reports, the judge conducted his own in-court questioning of the defendant. Though his responses to the judge's questions were at times polemic and often laced with bitterness toward the criminal justice system, they demonstrated knowledge of the charges and the system under which he would be tried. For example, Ferguson and the judge engaged in the following colloquy aimed at determining whether Ferguson understood the role of the Assistant District Attorney prosecuting him:

> *The Court:* Do you know what his role is?
> *The Defendant:* Yes, I suspect, if you would permit me to express myself fully—
> *The Court:* I'm sorry?
> *The Defendant:* Simply, in a monstrous and evidently wounded criminal justice system—
> *The Court:* No. I don't want a speech. I just want an answer what his role is.
> *The Defendant:* Well, I think it's appropriate for me to speak on this because—
> *The Court:* I'll make that decision. What is his role?
> *The Defendant:* To perpetrate injustice against me.
> *The Court:* Is it to prosecute you?
> *The Defendant:* Inasmuch as the description of that term is, yes.[15]

The judge felt that Ferguson clearly understood the nature of the charges against him and the process by which he would be tried. There remained, however, the question of whether Ferguson was capable of assisting counsel in his own defense. His two court-appointed attorneys, William Kunstler and Ronald Kuby, believed that he was not capable of assisting them. Ferguson not only disagreed but told the judge that he wanted to represent himself, in part because he was troubled by an article that had just appeared in *Newsday*, a widely read local newspaper. "Having read that article," Ferguson explained to the judge, "it suggests that substantial damage has been done to my case. . . . It seemed to me that what appeared in the media would severely harm my case if I were not to go psychiatric [i.e., plead insanity]."[16]

The article to which Ferguson referred quoted defense attorney Ronald Kuby as describing Ferguson as extremely mentally ill: "Clearly he's deteriorated dramatically since even March when we entered into the case. The man is crazy."[17] The article also quoted Kuby and Kunstler as having informed the court that Ferguson "has begun to assert that he, in fact, did not do the shooting."[18] "These assertions," the defense lawyers said, "obviously are totally at variance with the evidence and with reality."[19]

Ferguson rejected the notion that he was mentally ill and refused to go along with an insanity plea premised upon what his lawyers called "Black rage."[20] Ferguson was in good company. Both Dr. D'Alessandro and Dr. Reichman agreed that he was not seriously mentally ill or insane.

As the prosecution would later point out, Ferguson's lack of trust in his court-appointed attorneys was not delusional but based in reality:

> Defendant's distrust of his attorneys in this case also germinated
> from actual events. . . . Defendant . . . repeatedly told his attorneys
> that he did not want to use a "black rage" or insanity defense. But
> his attorneys, neither of whom was confronted with spending the
> rest of their lives in a mental institution, did not heed their client's
> wishes. Instead, they continued to advance these theories, over their
> client's objection. Defendant's trust in his attorneys was further
> eroded when his private communications with them were published
> in *Newsday*. In that article, defendant's attorneys, referring to
> recent conversations with defendant, derogatorily referred to him as
> "crazy" and tacitly conceded he had committed the crimes.[21]

Ferguson's attorneys not only argued that he was incompetent but one of them, Ronald Kuby, cited Ferguson's refusal to plead insanity as evidence that he was not competent to stand trial, much less defend himself. Kuby told the court that "Colin Ferguson has never permitted any lawyer to stand up in court and argue his insanity. He's too crazy."[22] Kuby concluded his argument in Ferguson's competency hearing by predicting that if found competent and allowed to represent himself, Ferguson's trial would be "an obscene and tragic spectacle."[23] Ultimately, the judge rejected Kuby's arguments and concluded that Ferguson not only understood the charges against him but was capable of assisting in his own defense and, thus, both competent to stand trial and to waive his right to legal representation. As a result, Colin Ferguson went to trial representing himself, joining a host of other "celebrity" defendants who had chosen and been allowed to take the same legal path: serial killer Ted

Bundy, mass murderer Charles Manson, assisted-suicide specialist Dr. Jack Kevorkian, accused terrorist Zacarias Moussaoui, and former U.S. Congressman James Trafficant—not to mention Jesus Christ, Socrates, Thomas More, and Joan of Arc, who also defended themselves.

Attorney William Kunstler criticized the court's decision, labeling Ferguson "a delusional paranoid."[24] Kunstler also decried Ferguson's refusal to plead insanity: "He thinks he is sane, I'm sure. He thinks and believes thoroughly that he did not shoot anyone, that he was sleeping, and some white man took a gun out of his bag and then massacred everybody. He's clearly insane. And that's unfortunate, that he's in there doing the one thing that's sure to convict him. He's giving up an insanity defense, which clearly applies here."[25]

As the highly publicized and nationally televised trial unfolded, many observers echoed Ronald Kuby's sentiments and criticized a system that would allow an obviously troubled if not seriously disturbed mass murderer to represent himself. Certainly the trial was more traumatic for some witnesses than it would have been had Ferguson been represented by counsel; many who survived Ferguson's rampage were forced not only to face him in court but to be cross-examined by him. But was Ferguson's trial as detrimental to his chances for acquittal as Kuby, Kunstler, and others predicted? And was the trial the bizarre and grotesque mockery of the American criminal justice system that Kuby, Kunstler, and many other critics claimed?

To answer those questions requires first a look at what Ferguson's chances were even if represented by Kunstler and Kuby (then two of America's top criminal defense lawyers), then, second, an examination of how Ferguson performed as a lay attorney representing himself in this high profile trial, and, third, a consideration of the benefits Ferguson and society derived from his self-representation.

After representing himself at trial, claiming that he was not the shooter, the jury quickly and easily convicted him of multiple counts of murder and attempted murder and he was sentenced to six consecutive terms of twenty-five years to life in prison, making him theoretically eligible for parole in 150 years. Would an insanity plea presented by professional legal counsel have brought a different or more desirable result? Almost assuredly not.

To begin with, the chances of acquittal by reason of insanity in any prosecution are minuscule; some studies have found that as few as 1 percent of those who raise this plea are actually acquitted. But the chance that Colin Ferguson would be found not guilty by reason of insanity was virtually nil, regardless of who represented him in court. A court-appointed psychologist and psychiatrist who examined him prior to trial agreed that while Ferguson suffered from a paranoid personality disorder, he was evasive, misleading, inconsistent, and attempting to fake a mental illness. Their opinions would have been pitted against a single psychiatrist, hired by defense counsel, who opined that Ferguson was "suffering from a Delusional Disorder, persecutory type on 7 December 1993, and that as a result of this disorder he lacked substantial capacity to understand that what he was doing was wrong."[26]

Even in the extremely unlikely event Ferguson had been found not guilty by reason of insanity, under New York law he would almost certainly have spent the rest of his life incarcerated along with the most dangerous and deranged offenders in a secure state mental institution—a hybrid facility where treatment for mental illness is available but in a prison-like setting. In that case, by statute, Ferguson could never be released from state custody until he was proven to be no longer dangerous or mentally ill. Having deliberately killed six and wounded nineteen railroad passengers, Ferguson would be extremely hard pressed to ever establish that he posed no danger to others.

Though many commentators who observed Ferguson's trial felt he would have been better served by accepting representation from an attorney, at least one reporter who sat through the trial described Ferguson as "smooth" and his lawyerly performance as "polished, calm, articulate."[27]

Even before the prosecution presented its case, Ferguson took actions that most lawyers would have approved. First, though he claimed he had been assaulted by other inmates while in jail awaiting trial, he declined to testify against his assailants for fear that to do so might prejudice his own chances for acquittal. He told an assistant district attorney prosecuting that case that he preferred to wait until after his own trial was complete because testifying earlier might have allowed defense lawyers in the assault case to cross-examine him about what the law calls "prior bad acts," including the allegations that he shot twenty-four people in the Long Island Railroad. It should also be noted that by representing himself at trial, Ferguson was able to "testify" (essentially tell the jury his story) without being sworn in or facing any cross-examination.

Second, during the *voir dire*, the jury selection process, Ferguson repeatedly and astutely tried to question potential jury members about their racial biases. Among other questions, Ferguson asked potential jurors:

> Judge Belfi read the charges as stated in the indictment . . . And you understand that the charges suggest racial overtones? Would you agree on that?
>
> How do you think you would react if you were to see, for instance, the portrayal of [the crime] scene involving only people of your race?

If you are ... seated in [this] trial as a juror, you will be asked to make judgments concerning specific charges of civil rights violations. This is something you'll have to deal with here during the trial. Therefore, I just need to ask what are your impressions of people of African descent?

If I may read directly from the indictment ... "The defendant, Colin Ferguson ... subjected and attempted to subject another person to physical contact, to wit: Alfred Casazza because of the race, color or nation of Alfred Casazza" ... Therefore I will make one more attempt to ask you, and this is not a reflection of you because you have made no decision to bar the question, what impressions do you have of people of African descent in general?[28]

While these questions and others of a similar vein were all objected to and disallowed by the court, they are precisely the kinds of questions even a seasoned criminal defense attorney would have asked as part of the effort to select a racially unbiased jury. As noted by the attorney who later appealed Ferguson's conviction in part on the grounds that these questions were not permitted by the trial judge:

[Ferguson's] initial question—You understand that the charges suggest racial overtones? —was not an objectionable question and the judge should have allowed the juror to answer. In the first place, it was an accurate statement. The crime [with which Ferguson was charged] plainly does have racial overtones and it was vital to [his] right to a fair trial that he sound out potential jurors as to their preconceptions about crimes committed by African-Americans against Caucasians.[29]

Once the jury was selected, the prosecutor and Ferguson each made opening statements to the jury. Among other things, Ferguson told the jury that "Mr. Ferguson did not fire a gun. He simply is the victim of a shooting on a train, like any other victim."[30] Ferguson also told jurors that "there were ninety-three counts to that indictment. Ninety-three counts only because it matches the year 1993. Had it been 1925, it would have been twenty-five counts."[31] While some commentators regarded this statement as delusional, that is unlikely. Throughout the trial, Ferguson made it plain that he understood the charges contained in the indictment. Indeed, at times he read from the indictment in open court. A more likely explanation for this reference is that Ferguson was mocking the indictment. His opening statement may have been somewhat stilted and arrogant but it does not appear to have been delusional.

Critics of Ferguson's self-representation also complained that his cross-examinations were often not helpful because some prosecution witnesses were able to make him look foolish by resisting his use of the third person and identifying him directly as the gunman. For example:

> *Colin Ferguson:* It was your statement that you played dead?
> *Maryanne Phillips:* Yes.
> *Colin Ferguson:* And did that involve closing your eyes?
> *Maryanne Phillips:* Yes, it did.
> *Colin Ferguson:* So you wanted the person who was doing the
>   shooting to think that you were dead?
> *Maryanne Phillips:* Yes. I didn't want you to shoot me again. I saw
>   you shoot me and I played dead.[32]

Still, with this witness and others, Ferguson managed to point out that given what he called the "pandemonium" and "chaos" that ensued once the shooting began, much of the eyewitness testimony against him was at least questionable.[33]

At least one law professor who reviewed Ferguson's performance as an examiner and cross-examiner of witnesses felt he did a reasonably good job of mastering the technical aspects of trial practice. Reflecting on the job Ferguson did representing himself, Marianne Wesson, who teaches evidence, criminal law, and trial practice at the University of Colorado School of Law, said:

> Every observer at that trial thought that Colin Ferguson suffered
> from fairly severe mental illness; not so severe that he couldn't
> stand trial and couldn't represent himself. By many accounts, he did
> a pretty credible job of employing a lot of standard lawyerly advo-
> cacy techniques. He mastered the art of impeaching witnesses with
> prior inconsistent statements. He made hearsay objections, objected
> that counsel was leading the witness, that sort of thing.[34]

Other legal commentators also made much of Ferguson's "rambling three hour closing argument."[35] Specifically, they pointed to Ferguson's comparison of himself to a Biblical martyr: "John the Baptist lived in the wilderness, a humble man, and he was put into prison for no reason. He was beheaded by a criminal justice system similar to this."[36]

The critics and pundits also pointed to Ferguson's affected use of the third person:

Vindicate Mr. Ferguson. Do not destroy his life more than it has already been destroyed. . . . Come back with a verdict of not guilty. Not guilty. That will be the most joyful day, I believe, for me and not only for yourselves. Mr. Ferguson is willing to be patient as long as you need to deliberate. It is appreciated. I thank you ladies and gentlemen.[37]

Again, Ferguson's presentation may have been somewhat stilted and may not have been very persuasive, but it was neither delusional nor without substance. In a nationally televised discussion of the case, a well-known defense lawyer and a criminal law professor both gave Ferguson good grades for his closing argument. Criminal defense attorney and former federal prosecutor Michael Nasatir said, "The final argument, I thought, was a passable final argument. I mean, I think that the three of us could maybe do better and that better lawyers could do better, but it was really astounding how well he did do."[38] Law professor Stanley A. Goldman, who teaches criminal justice, criminal procedure, and evidence at Loyola Law School, had even more praise for Ferguson's closing argument: "His closing argument was more fluid than the prosecution. And given the case he had, he did about as well as the prosecution did in the closing argument."[39]

It is difficult if not impossible to regard Colin Ferguson's self-representation as having had any significant value to society, other than perhaps vindicating a centuries-old legal tradition that is rooted in the ideal of personal autonomy. It is much easier, however, to see what good representing himself did for Ferguson.

Of course, Ferguson "lost" the trial and was convicted of many of the charges against him. But, given the evidence against him, those convictions seemed to be foregone conclusions regardless of who represented him. By representing himself, Ferguson not only gained a number of potential strategic trial advantages but also achieved a measure of self-satisfaction that would have been impossible to attain had he been represented by counsel.

In terms of trial strategy, representing himself gave Ferguson many of the advantages identified in a 2000 study of criminal defendants who dismissed attorneys and appeared in court on their own (*pro se*). Psychiatrists Douglas Mossman and Neal Dunseith examined fifty-four such cases and identified several "potential advantages of *pro se* representation," all of which appear to have redounded to Colin Ferguson's benefit, even though he was convicted:

Being a *pro se* defendant allowed defendants to confront directly and cross-examine their accusers . . . and introduce information at trial without being cross-examined. In a few cases, defendants appeared to benefit from the rapport they established with jurors who got to know the defendants from the beginning of the trial and therefore had more opportunity to understand *pro se* defendants as persons than would have been the case had the defendants used lawyers.[40]

On a personal level, this troubled man, who believed that he had been disrespected most of his adult life, was given the chance to command the attention not only of the judge and jury but also of the media and thousands of Americans who watched his trial on Court TV. Moreover, by representing himself, he was able to show a skeptical world that he was, in fact, intelligent and articulate and not nearly as mentally ill as he had been made out to be.

◤16

RALPH
TORTORICI

A Question

of Competence

◢

Ralph Tortorici was born in 1968 with a rare condition known as hypospadias. This congenital deformity of the urethra results in an opening near the base rather than at the tip of the penis. The condition embarrassed Tortorici as a youngster and likely contributed to his later mental illness.

Three separate operations failed to correct the problem but clearly seemed to influence Tortorici's psychiatric symptoms. By the time Tortorici reached adolescence, he was convinced that the government had placed a listening device in his penis. Diagnosed as suffering from paranoid schizophrenia, he was hospitalized numerous times. As psychiatric treatment also proved unsuccessful, Tortorici's delusions expanded and he came to believe that the government was controlling his behavior through a second microchip implanted in his brain. For years, Tortorici complained of a conspiracy against him and kept a list of those he suspected were involved, including his parents and brother.

Despite his physical and mental abnormalities, Ralph Tortorici was a bright young man who eventually was accepted as a psychology major and functioned for awhile as a "B" student at the State University of New York at Albany (SUNY Albany). Still troubled by his delusions, however, Tortorici continued to complain that his mind was under government control. In August 1992, for example, a nurse at the SUNY Albany Student Health Services noted that:

Ralph came in and said that he could no longer handle what was
happening, he couldn't take the pressure of what was going on in
his head and just couldn't take it any longer. . . . And he told me that
he had had an X-ray, the X-ray was negative, and that he still was
sure he had an implant, a microchip in his penis, and that was forc-
ing him to do things he didn't want to do. He felt that the government was speaking to him through the microchip and he couldn't
handle the pressure.[1]

Later that day, Tortorici was admitted to a local psychiatric hospital. His
record upon admission contained the following "impression":

24-year old male presents with a fixed delusion accompanied by
suspiciousness. After eight years of dealing with this experience
privately, he comes to attention. Because of increased stress in his
life, he believes more conspiracy activity is taking place and, so, out
of desperation he seeks to expose the conspiracy.[2]

On another occasion, in December 1992, Tortorici took his concerns to
the New York State Police, complaining that the microchip in his penis was
transmitting voices directing him to molest young girls. The state trooper
who listened to Tortorici's rambling diatribe later said, "I wanted to get him
under control. I decided I was going to take him into custody and deliver him
to the psych center at that point."[3] Admitted to the Capital District Psychiatric Center, the growing urgency of Tortorici's delusions was described in detail
by hospital staff:

Patient states that he had baby-sat for his sister's child and a few
other children and admits to holding the seven-year-old female
and kissing her. Patient states that the penis implant emits beeping
sounds in a code that he has managed to break and they are now
giving him instructions to fuck the girl, as per Trooper McDonald.
Patient informs Trooper McDonald that he was getting frustrated
and wanted the investigation out in the open and threatened, "Do I
have to do something drastic?"[4]

Apparently to get the kind of attention he felt he needed, Ralph Tortorici
did need to do something drastic. In November 1994, despite his lengthy psychiatric history, Tortorici was able to purchase a Remington rifle at a local
discount department store. Several weeks later, on December 14, 1994, Ralph
Tortorici stormed into a lecture hall at the university. Dressed in military
fatigues and armed with the semiautomatic rifle, eighty rounds of ammuni-

tion, and a hunting knife, he terrorized a class of thirty-five students. After yelling "Stop government experimentation," Tortorici demanded to see both the governor and the president, threatened to kill his hostages, and fired the rifle at a projection screen.[5]

After a two-hour standoff, several student hostages overpowered Tortorici. During the struggle with Tortorici, one student was shot in the scrotum and severely maimed. Another student suffered superficial knife wounds. Police officers rushed the classroom and arrested Tortorici, charging him with attempted murder, assault, kidnapping, reckless endangerment, and criminal use and possession of a firearm.

Following his arraignment the next day, two psychiatric examiners found Tortorici incompetent to stand trial—that is, unable to understand the charges against him and to assist in his own defense. As a result, he was remanded to the Mid-Hudson Psychiatric Center, a secure state forensic hospital where, upon admission, he was noted to be delusional and "very psychotic with paranoid beliefs."[6]

While hospitalized, Tortorici received counseling but refused all medication. During his stay he was described as "rational and logical in speech and thought . . . very cooperative to the interview situations [and] able to follow the rules and regulations of the hospital."[7] The staff found that he had "satisfactory knowledge of courtroom procedure and the duties of court officials . . . [knew] his lawyer . . . and state[d] he is going to go along with his lawyer's suggestions."[8] On March 20, 1995, after ten weeks as an inpatient, Tortorici was returned to the court as competent to stand trial.

From that date until the start of jury selection in his trial the following January, Tortorici appeared in court on several occasions, each time speaking only briefly to the judge and asking to be excused from the proceedings. For example, at a pretrial hearing on November 16, 1995, Tortorici's attorney indicated that the defendant wanted to waive his presence. Questioned by the judge, Tortorici made just two statements. The first was "I speak English, Judge. I don't desire to be present. I made that point clear. That is all."[9] The second was "I do not desire to be present. No further comments."[10]

On January 3, 1996, at the beginning of jury selection, defense counsel informed the court that Tortorici wished to waive his right to be present throughout the course of the trial. The judge questioned Tortorici about his wishes, and Tortorici replied, "Let me make this clear, please. This trial, the bad memory, it's a nuisance to me. I want to have as little to do with these proceedings as possible."[11]

The next day, while jury selection proceeded, Tortorici was examined by a psychiatrist retained by the prosecution in an effort to rebut Tortorici's claim that he was insane at the time of his crimes. Based on this examination, which defense counsel and the prosecutors attended, the psychiatrist, Dr. Lawrence Siegel, reported that he was unable to assess Tortorici's mental state at the time of the offense, but that Tortorici was "incapable of rational participation in court proceedings"[12] and "not fit to proceed to trial."[13]

Siegel concluded that "[Tortorici's] mental condition does not appear sufficiently stable to enable him to withstand the stresses of a trial without suffering a serious, prolonged or permanent breakdown. [H]e has deteriorated into a psychotic state."[14] Siegel further concluded that:

> Mr. Tortorici is currently exhibiting signs and symptoms of acute psychosis. He is incapable of rational participation in court proceedings. He requires hospitalization and treatment with medication to restore him to fitness. . . . Based upon the information available at this time, it is my professional opinion with a reasonable degree of psychiatric certainty that Mr. Tortorici is not fit to proceed to trial.[15]

Dr. Siegel also reported that Tortorici knew the names of the charges against him, the date and place of the alleged offense, the name of his attorney, and the roles of the major participants in the trial, and had more than a rudimentary understanding of the trial process. Siegel added, however, that "this understanding is tainted by his conviction that there are external governmental forces influencing these persons through waves."[16] Siegel also said of the defendant: "While he is capable of forming a relationship with his attorney (and appears to have formed one), his delusional system is such that there cannot be a joint understanding of the meaning of the trial currently going on."[17]

After Dr. Siegel's report was distributed, defense counsel told the court that "the law of this case is that there had been a previous determination, after Mr. Tortorici's [hospitalization], that he was in fact fit to proceed. . . . Ralph Tortorici is in fact suffering from a mental illness, paranoid schizophrenia. Notwithstanding the mental illness, your Honor, we are ready to proceed with the defense. And I'm not making any motions at this time."[18]

The prosecutor advised the court that "a review of the jail records . . . would not in any way contradict the fact that [the defendant] appeared at all times fit to proceed as of yesterday."[19] That statement was made on January 5, 1996, so the "yesterday" referred to by the prosecutor was the day the state's own expert, Dr. Siegel, had examined Tortorici. Later the prosecutor would explain that while she was well aware of Dr. Siegel's conclusions, she did not resist going forward with the trial because "I think we thought he was as competent as he ever was," adding that "somebody described competent once as knowing the difference between a judge and a grapefruit and that was about the standard for competency. I think [Tortorici] knew that."[20]

Hearing no objections from either the defense or the prosecution, the judge then observed that in light of his own observations of Tortorici and representations by both counsel that they were ready to proceed: "Nothing has occurred in this court and to this court's observation that would lead it on its own initiative to review the expert determination made by the psychiatrists of Mid-Hudson earlier on, that this defendant is in fact fit to proceed. And therefore, we will proceed."[21]

Proceed they did and the jury heard from a bevy of witnesses, both lay and expert, about just how psychotic Ralph Tortorici had been for years and was at the time of his classroom siege at SUNY Albany. The prosecution presented no evidence to the contrary, and certainly no expert testimony to indicate that Tortorici was sane at the time of the crimes. Instead, the prosecutor argued to the jury that, while Tortorici was mentally ill, he did not meet the stringent legal definition of insanity:

> The issue is not whether Ralph Tortorici is crazy, insane, whatever you want to call it. The issue is not, as it is understandably for Ralph's Tortorici's family, whether or not he needs treatment or medical attention, as opposed to punishment. The punishment issue is whether Ralph Tortorici's mental illness is so pervasive, so profound, so all consuming that it prevented him from knowing either of those two things that I told you about: the physical nature, consequences of his acts, that his conduct was wrong, legally, morally.[22]

On February 16, 1996, after deliberating for just an hour, the jury rejected Ralph Tortorici's insanity plea and convicted him of all charges. Though the judge had the authority to set aside the jury's verdict and impose a finding of legal insanity, he declined defense counsel's request that he do so. As the defense lawyer explained, "I can recall Judge Rosen basically commenting to me that the insanity defense in Albany County [is] essentially dead because if I didn't win this case on legal insanity, what possible case could you win? Of course, I responded to him, 'Well, then, why don't you set the verdict aside?' which he refused to do."[23]

Indeed, not only did the judge refuse to alter the verdict, he sentenced Tortorici to the maximum term of incarceration allowed under New York law: a prison term of twenty to forty-seven years. As the judge would later explain, he doubted that any other judge would have imposed any lesser sentence despite Tortorici's obvious mental illness, adding, "When you have 37 victims as you had here, I felt the hammer had to be utilized."[24]

Tortorici appealed, claiming that, in light of Dr. Siegel's report, the judge erred in not ordering a competency hearing prior to trial. In support of this claim, Tortorici's appellate attorney cited *Pate v. Robinson*, a 1966 U.S. Supreme Court decision and the 1957 New York Court of Appeals decision in *People v. Smyth*. In *Pate*, the U.S. Supreme Court held that "Where the evidence raises a 'bona fide doubt' as to a defendant's competence to stand trial, the judge on his own motion must . . . conduct a hearing."[25] And in *Smyth*, the New York Court of Appeals held that:

> if at any time before final judgment in a criminal action it shall
> appear to the court that there is reasonable ground for believing
> that a defendant is in such state of idiocy, imbecility or insanity that
> he is incapable of understanding the charge, indictment or proceed-
> ings or of making his defense, it is the duty of the court to direct
> him to be examined in these respects.[26]

The first court to hear Tortorici's appeal affirmed his conviction by a vote of 3–2.[27] The Court of Appeals, New York's highest court, also affirmed the conviction by a 5–1 margin.[28] The Court of Appeals explained that in making a decision as to whether to order a competency examination, a trial judge may consider all the evidence, including his or her own observations. Additionally, the court noted that nearly a year before the trial, mental health professionals at the Mid-Hudson Psychiatric Center had pronounced Tortorici fit to proceed. The court also relied on the fact that Tortorici's own attorney, who had attended Dr. Siegel's examination, had not asked for another competency examination, indeed had repeatedly told the court he was ready to proceed. The court emphasized that defense counsel was in the best position to assess Tortorici's capacity, raise the issue of Tortorici's fitness to proceed, or request another examination, but instead consistently made it clear that Tortorici was competent and that the defense was ready to proceed. In that regard, the court expressed the belief that the attorney may have been acting out of some defense strategy and might well have viewed a finding of incompetence as interfering with his presentation of an insanity defense. Finally, the court emphasized that some of the evidence in Dr. Siegel's own report supported the belief that Tortorici was competent.

Confined in a maximum-security prison with virtually no hope that the U.S. Supreme Court would agree to hear his case and overturn his conviction,[29] Ralph Tortorici's mental illness made it impossible for him to adjust to incarceration. For three years he was shuttled back and forth between the regular prison population and a special prison unit for the severely mentally ill. In August 1999, Tortorici committed suicide by hanging himself from a bed sheet tied to a shelf in his cell.

Following Tortorici's suicide, one of the two assistant district attorneys who prosecuted him wrote,

> As prosecutors, we were satisfied we had done the right thing. We had a totally innocent victim, an incredibly dangerous, albeit insane, defendant, and a law that was clearly on our side. . . . The public would be protected from Ralph for a long, definite time period, and Ralph would be protected from himself. . . .
>
> Unfortunately, securing Ralph's conviction only accomplished the former. Incredibly enough, to the officials at [the state corrections department], the guilty verdict equaled a determination that Ralph was not insane. Nothing, of course, could have been further from the truth. Into population he went. Within the year, he did a good job hanging himself. He was then transferred to a psychiatric hospital, and subsequently returned to prison. This time, he did a much better job. His death haunts me more than I can explain.[30]

The crimes, prosecution, conviction, and suicide of Ralph Tortorici all reflect the failure of the criminal justice system to deal appropriately with offenders and potential offenders who are mentally ill.

Despite his obviously severe mental illness, Tortorici was never able to secure the kind of treatment that might have prevented him from harming others and himself. Civil commitment laws in New York and elsewhere allow involuntary confinement of the mentally ill only when they pose an imminent danger to themselves or others. Even when Tortorici complained to the police that voices were telling him to molest children, he was not regarded as sufficiently dangerous to warrant hospitalization against his will. Moreover, even with his long history of mental illness, psychiatric care, and numerous hospitalizations, he had the same right as any other adult citizen to purchase a rifle from a department store.

The danger Ralph Tortorici posed (at least to others) was, of course, recognized when he committed the crimes for which he was convicted. But even then, the criminal justice and mental health systems continued to fail him. Under New York law, had Tortorici been judged incompetent to stand trial, he would have been returned to the secure forensic psychiatric hospital and would have remained there until his competence was restored or he had been confined for a period equal to two-thirds of the maximum sentence he faced if convicted. Thus, had he not been restored to competency sooner, Tortorici could have been retained behind locked doors at the secure forensic hospital for at least thirty-one years.

Yet, despite obvious signs that he was not competent to stand trial, the trial judge, prosecutor, and his own attorney allowed Tortorici to be tried without ever even requesting a hearing on competency. Why?

Surely much of the blame has to be placed on the law itself. In New York, as in virtually all states, the threshold for competence to stand trial is relatively low. In 1960, in *Dusky v. United States*, the U.S. Supreme Court concluded that competency to stand trial encompasses only two questions: (1) Does the defendant have "sufficient present ability to consult with his lawyer with a reasonable degree of rational understanding"?[31] (2) Does he have a "rational as well as factual understanding of proceedings against him"?[32] Thus, even a severely psychotic defendant might be held competent to stand trial if he were able to understand the charges against him and assist counsel in his own defense.

But did the key players in this tragedy fully understand and apply the law as intended by the Supreme Court? Consider first the prosecutor who, at the very least, had serious doubts about Tortorici's competence to stand trial. After describing the "grapefruit" test mentioned earlier, she stated: "Was he competent to help his counsel? Of course he wasn't. . . . He was certainly less able to help in his defense than most. So in the spirit of competence, was he competent? No. Did he fit the legal definition of competency? Yes, probably."[33] That ambivalent appraisal, of course, came after the prosecutor's own expert had examined Tortorici at the time of trial and opined that Tortorici was grossly psychotic and clearly not competent to stand trial.

As a matter of trial strategy, the prosecutor's failure to raise the issue of competency despite her own expert's report that Tortorici was incompetent is not surprising. Delay of any sort usually works to the detriment of the prosecution in a criminal case; witnesses move or even die, public indignation wanes, and the defense has more time to prepare. What is less understandable, if understandable at all, is the prosecutor's unwillingness to stipulate to a verdict of insanity in this case. Had the prosecutor agreed that Tortorici met the legal criteria for insanity, there would have been no need for a trial; the court would have simply entered such a judgment.

By her own acknowledgment, the prosecutor was concerned that a finding of insanity might result in Ralph Tortorici being returned to the community prematurely and thereby posing a serious threat to others. What she was either unaware of or unwilling to acknowledge is that such a scenario had virtually no chance of ever occurring. In New York, as in most other jurisdictions, a finding of insanity requires state experts to determine whether the acquitted defendant is mentally ill and dangerous. A finding that the defendant is both mentally ill and dangerous—a foregone conclusion in this case—results in an indefinite commitment to a secure state forensic hospital. Release from such a commitment requires proof that the defendant is no longer dangerously mentally ill. As a result, defendants acquitted by reason of insanity often spend much more time in state custody than they would have had they pleaded guilty or been convicted. Indeed, in many cases where defendants have committed serious crimes, a finding of insanity results in a lifetime of confinement.

The prosecutor here was also purportedly concerned about what would happen to the defendant. A conviction, she believed, would be a "win-win" situation in which the public would be protected from a dangerous, mentally ill offender and Ralph Tortorici would be protected from himself.[34] What she either did not know or failed to acknowledge is that New York state prisons, like those in most states, treat convicted defendants as convicts, not as patients. When an inmate like Ralph Tortorici becomes a management problem in the regular prison population, he is likely to be segregated and may even be briefly treated. However, such treatment is aimed at maintaining order in the prison, not at rehabilitating the troubled inmate. Having been convicted rather than found not guilty by reason of inanity, Tortorici had no right to any other treatment than what he received.

The actions of Tortorici's defense counsel are another story. Unlike the prosecutor whose ethical duty is not to "win" but to make every effort to see that justice is done, criminal defense attorneys are legally and ethically obligated to zealously represent their clients' interests within the bounds of law. In its decision in the Tortorici case, the New York Court of Appeals suggested that the defense counsel's failure to raise the issue may have been an indication that he believed his client was competent to stand trial. At the same time, the appeals court also suggested that defense counsel's failure to raise the issue may have been the result of a strategic decision not to prevent Tortorici's insanity defense from being heard by a jury; had Tortorici been declared incompetent he would have been denied an immediate trial and may have been denied trial altogether.

Apparently the appeals court was at least partially correct in these speculations. Interviewed after the conviction had been affirmed by the appeals court, Tortorici's defense attorney explained that he had felt he had "no ability" to move for another hearing on Tortorici's competence to stand trial, despite Dr. Siegel's conclusions, because "I had no authority from Ralph."[35] According to the attorney, he did not press for further review of Tortorici's competence at the time of the trial because "Ralph didn't want to go back to Mid-Hudson [the secure forensic hospital to which Tortorici had been earlier been committed for evaluation]. He did not like it at Mid-Hudson. He wanted to move on with the process."[36] The attorney added that "I had to make a judgment call. . . . I went forward on the basis of the fact that we had put together a very significant [case] to support the legal insanity defense."[37]

The defense attorney's rationale in this regard is somewhat puzzling. Assuming he genuinely believed that his client was competent to stand trial, even in the face of overwhelming evidence that he was not, his duty was to zealously represent his client's interest. Thus, since he says Tortorici wanted to go to trial, he would have been both legally and ethically justified in doing whatever he could to ensure that Tortorici was not found incompetent. At the same time, however, he would be legally and ethically bound to make sure that his client was properly advised regarding the consequences of going to trial. The attorney said that at least part of Tortorici's motivation for wanting to go to trial was a desire to avoid going back to Mid-Hudson Psychiatric Center. Ironically, a trial in this case had only two possible outcomes. If convicted, Tortorici would be sent to prison. If acquitted by reason of insanity he would be committed indefinitely to a secure state forensic mental hospital, in all likelihood Mid-Hudson Psychiatric Center. Even the attorney appeared to have some doubts about his client's reasoning regarding going to trial: "Do I know whether or not Ralph's telling me he wants this case to get behind him [is] part of the delusion or not? I don't know the answer to that."[38]

Like the prosecutor, whose "grapefruit" test clearly understates the legal standard for competence to stand trial, the defense attorney in this case may also have further minimized what was already admittedly a rather low legal standard. As he later explained, in his view a defendant in New York was likely to be found competent by forensic mental health professionals if he had a "bare-bones understanding" of the number of counts with which he is charged and the general roles of the judge, prosecutor, and defense counsel.[39] Ironically, Dr. Siegel's report on Ralph Tortorici belies such reasoning. The psychiatrist reported that, upon examination at the time of trial, Tortorici was "aware of the names of the charges against him and [had] an understanding of what he is alleged to have done." Moreover, Siegel found that Tortorici had "more than a rudimentary understanding of the process of trial and the roles of the judge, jury, prosecutor, and defense attorney."[40] Nevertheless, based on Tortorici's mental state at that time, Siegel concluded that he was clearly not competent to stand trial.

While the Court of Appeals clearly defended the judge's failure to pursue the question of Tortorici's competence in light of Dr. Siegel's eleventh-hour report, he was clearly the one key player in this trial who had both the duty and the power to stop the proceeding at any time if he felt there was legitimate doubt about Tortorici's competence. As noted earlier, under both the U.S. Constitution and New York case law, the judge was obligated to conduct a hearing on the issue if at any time he had any "bona fide doubt" or any "reasonable ground" to question Tortorici's competence to stand trial. There can be no question that Dr. Siegel's detailed, nine-page report would have given any reasonable jurist pause with regard to Tortorici's competence.

While Siegel reported to the judge that Tortorici was able to relate to his attorney and had a basic understanding of the charges against him and the roles played by the attorneys, judge, and the psychiatrist, he clearly and graphically qualified these findings by reference to Tortorici's severe psychosis:

> Much of Mr. Tortorici's communication regarding his legal situa-
> tion makes sense. He is aware of the names of the charges against
> him and has an understanding of what he is alleged to have done.
> However many of his ideas concerning how he should deal with his
> legal situation, and how others might perceive his ideas, betrays his
> problems with his thinking. His thought that his current criminal
> trial is a test prior to his being made a "leader" is clearly erroneous.
> His thought that persons in the court are influenced through "air
> waves" and "power waves," interferes with his capacity to under-
> stand the true nature of the proceedings.
>
> The defendant is oriented to time and place. He has more than
> a rudimentary understanding of the process of trial and the roles
> of the Judge, jury, prosecutor and defense attorney. However this
> understanding is tainted by his conviction that there are external
> governmental forces influencing these persons through waves. His
> mental condition does not appear sufficiently stable to enable him
> to withstand the stresses of a trial without suffering a serious, pro-
> longed or permanent breakdown. Based upon the examination he
> has deteriorated into a psychotic state.
>
> His abilities to perceive, recall and relate are variably impaired.
> His perceptions are filtered by his psychotic beliefs. For instance he
> perceives that the examiner has moved in a manner that proves the
> examiner has been subjected to power waves. He appears able to
> recall, but much of his recollections are of psychotic material. His

ability to relate is impaired by difficulty expressing himself in a rational manner. While he is capable of forming a relationship with his attorney (and appears to have formed one), his delusional system is such that there cannot be a joint understanding of the meaning of the trial currently going on. He does seem able to consider advice given to him by his attorney.[41]

Both the trial judge and the appellate courts pointed to the Mid-Hudson report of March 1995 as evidence that Tortorici was competent to be tried at the time of trial. The trial, of course, took place nearly nine months after doctors at Mid-Hudson Psychiatric Center found Tortorici competent to stand trial. Under both state and federal law, competence to stand trial is not a static concept that can be finally determined at any given point prior to the conclusion of the trial; a defendant must be competent to stand trial at all times throughout the proceedings against him. Thus, the Mid-Hudson report had little if any bearing on Ralph Tortorici's competence in January 1996.

In affirming Tortorici's conviction, the appellate courts also pointed to the judge's independent capacity to observe and evaluate the defendant's competence:

> The Trial Judge additionally could consider his "progressive personal observations of defendant," during which defendant clearly indicated that he understood his right to be present in the courtroom and consult with counsel, and also understood the proceedings that would ensue in his absence. These observations included the court's questioning of defendant on January 3, 1996, *the day before* Dr. Siegel examined him. Furthermore, it is significant that the court continued to monitor defendant's understanding of his rights and the proceedings against him throughout the duration of the trial, even though defendant himself did not appear in court. Every day during the trial, before the jury entered the courtroom, the Trial Judge asked defendant's lawyer if defendant still wished to be absent from the courtroom. Counsel always responded in the affirmative, indicating that he had spoken with defendant regarding the defense.[42]

Even assuming that the very limited and formal contact the judge had with Tortorici on a few occasions in the courtroom were sufficient for the judge (who is not a trained mental health professional, much less a forensic psychiatrist or psychologist) to evaluate Tortorici's competence, as the dissenting Judge on the Court of Appeals noted: "The trial record is undisputedly devoid of any indication that the trial court, after having received the nine-page communication from the People's forensic psychiatrist, undertook any further contact, communication with, or observation of defendant prior to rendering its decision."[43]

MIKE TYSON

Predicting

the Violence of a

Professional Fighter

O n June 28, 1997, Mike Tyson and Evander Holyfield met in a highly touted boxing match for the heavyweight championship of the world. During the fight, Tyson committed a major foul by biting Holyfield. Boxing observers speculated that Holyfield was winning the fight and Tyson's act may have resulted from frustration over the prospect of losing. After Tyson had two points deducted from his score, the fight resumed, but Tyson again bit Holyfield, this time taking off a piece of the defending champion's ear. As thousands of spectators at the event and millions of people tuning in on pay-per-view television watched, Holyfield jumped up and down in pain as blood dripped from his ear.[1] The referee disqualified Tyson and declared Holyfield the winner.

Tyson's personal and professional journey to the bout with Holyfield was troubled in several respects. As a child he had numerous behavioral problems that led him to be placed in a residential facility in upstate New York. At the age of twelve, Tyson was taken into the home of Cus D'Amato and Camille Ewald. D'Amato became Tyson's mentor and trainer. Leaving school after the tenth grade, Tyson became a boxer. His professional career was initially very successful. In the early years of his boxing career, many people thought he was unbeatable. However, when Cus D'Amato died in 1985, Tyson experienced the death as one would experience the loss of a parent.

In 1992, Tyson's professional boxing career and personal life were both derailed after he was convicted of rape and sentenced to six years in an Indiana prison. His sentence was reduced for good behavior and he was released after serving three years. He resumed his boxing career, but his personal troubles outside the ring seemed to raise questions about his emotional stability.

After the bout with Holyfield, the Nevada State Athletic Commission revoked Tyson's license to box and fined him $3 million. They stated that Tyson would be eligible to apply for a new license after one year, provided that his behavior during the ensuing time showed that he could control himself. He would need to persuade the commission that he could box again without engaging in the outrageous behavior he displayed in the fight with Holyfield.

Once the year had passed, Tyson applied for a new boxing license. On July 17, 1998, Tyson announced that he would apply for a license to box in New Jersey instead of in Nevada.[2] His decision angered members of the Nevada State Athletic Commission, perhaps because his application in New Jersey was viewed as a way of avoiding having to answer to the commission's concerns about his behavior inside the boxing ring. Moreover, Tyson's application placed members of the New Jersey boxing commission under scrutiny, because the question was raised whether the state was "more concerned with making money from Tyson's fights than seeing the orderly regulation of boxing."[3]

Members of the Nevada State Athletic Commission expressed their expectation that the New Jersey commission would take note of the fact that Tyson's license had been revoked in Nevada. However, a loophole in the law might have allowed Tyson to get a license to box without having to answer to the Nevada commission. The state athletic commissions responsible for regulating the sport of boxing are administrative agencies, governmental bodies empowered by the executive branch of government to oversee certain activities. Federal laws pertaining to the regulation of boxing require that states recognize the rulings of other state commissions when they suspend a license to box. In Tyson's case, his license had been revoked, not suspended, and he apparently intended to take advantage of this loophole by getting the New Jersey commission to consider his application to box.

Although Tyson had obtained a license to box in New Jersey back in 1990, he had not renewed it and therefore was required to participate in a public hearing where he would need to demonstrate why he should be granted a license. The standard boxing application rules do not normally require a public hearing, but the New Jersey commission consulted with the state attorney general's office in light of Tyson's license revocation in Nevada. The New Jersey commission decided to hold a public hearing so that a public legal record could be established.[4]

In preparation for the hearing, Tyson was required to meet with a psychologist, Dr. Bert Rothman, who later testified that he found no signs of mental disturbance and that Tyson would not be prone to engage in the behavior he exhibited in the Holyfield fight that led to his disqualification and the suspension of his boxing license.[5] However, Dr. Rothman's examination of Tyson consisted of only a one-hour meeting.

At Tyson's hearing before the New Jersey Athletic Control Board, a number of people testified on his behalf, including his wife and Rothman. Tyson testified on his own behalf and admitted that he had bought property in New Jersey merely to increase the chances that he would be granted a boxing license. He expressed remorse for having bitten Holyfield's ear. The explanation he gave for his actions was that he "snapped."[6] In addition, when Tyson was asked about his conviction for rape in 1992, he said that the incident had provided him an opportunity to receive mental health treatment that he was continuing at the time of his appearance before the New Jersey Board.

However, a key moment came when Tyson's attorney began to make his closing argument as to why the boxer should be issued a license to box in New Jersey. While his attorney spoke to the board, Tyson became upset over having to repeatedly defend himself and blurted out: "How many fucking times do I have to say this?"[7] The impulsive nature of his outburst cast doubt on Tyson's claim, and Dr. Rothman's finding, that he was in control of himself. Before the board could return its decision, Tyson withdrew his application to box in New Jersey and announced that he would seek to have his license in Nevada reinstated. As part of the administrative hearing process, members of the Nevada Athletic Commission required Tyson to undergo a thorough mental health evaluation.

The forensic evaluation of Tyson's psychiatric status was conducted by a team of experts from the Law and Psychiatry Service at Massachusetts General Hospital. Two members of the team were psychiatrists, two were neurologists, one was a clinical psychologist, and the other was a neuropsychologist. The task assigned to this team of experts by the Nevada State Athletic Commission was to answer a series of questions about Tyson's mental health. Among the questions to be answered were the following: (1) What was Tyson's psychiatric diagnosis? (2) What treatment, if any, was needed or proposed? (3) What was Tyson's ability to handle stress in unpredictable situations? (4) What was the potential for Tyson to commit another major foul in the boxing ring? and (5) Did the team of experts believe Tyson was mentally fit to comply with the rules and regulations of boxing?[8]

What made the referral questions in this case so unusual was the fact that the Nevada State Athletic Commission was essentially requesting a forensic psychological evaluation in the course of a state administrative proceeding (the reinstatement of a license) to address the rather unusual question of whether or not a professional boxer was prone to violent or aggressive outbursts that constituted major rule violations in a sport where success is measured by whether or not one can knock out an opponent. In other words, the professionals who evaluated Tyson were being asked to predict if he might become "too violent" when he stepped into the boxing ring.

The two psychiatrists on the evaluation team, Dr. Ronald Schouten and Dr. David Henderson, interviewed Tyson and reviewed a number of records, including findings from hearings conducted by the New Jersey Athletic Commission and Nevada State Athletic Commission concerning Tyson's conduct. Schouten, who was the lead examiner, met with Tyson for a total of six hours, and Henderson interviewed the boxer for an hour and a half.[9] The evaluation also involved the examiners watching tapes of the Tyson-Holyfield match. Additionally, they also interviewed Tyson's wife and other professionals who had some involvement with him over the years.

The ten-page report written by Schouten summarized the entire evaluation and provided an overview of Tyson's personal history. Among the various experiences noted was the fact that Tyson was extremely close to Cus D'Amato and Camille Ewald, the couple who took Tyson into their home when the boxer was twelve years old. Tyson viewed these two people as parents. Interestingly, the history in Schouten's report noted that Tyson had spent his early years in Brooklyn before he was sent to a school in upstate New York because of behavioral problems. However, no details are provided about the early relationship he had with his biological parents other than to note that they were both deceased. In any case, when D'Amato died, Tyson experienced the death "as that of a child losing a parent."[10] The history also details Tyson's arrest and conviction for rape in 1992 before exploring the details of Tyson's mental state on the night of the fight with Holyfield.

The psychiatrists asked Tyson whether he had been experiencing symptoms of depression or other psychological problems at the time of the fight. Tyson told Schouten that he "was experiencing significant depression at the time, in the context of multiple financial and personal problems."[11] However, Tyson also said that he had "snapped" and bit Holyfield's ear because he felt he had been the victim of head butting in an earlier fight between the two boxers. Tyson had suffered a cut in their first bout and when he was cut in the second fight and got no response after protesting to the referee, he "felt that this was no longer a prize fight, but had become a street fight."[12]

During his interviews with the psychiatrists, Tyson displayed a sense of responsibility for his family as well as feelings of guilt over the success he had in his life. "I have no self-esteem but the biggest ego in the world," he told Schouten, and explained that he often used his egocentricity as a defense against underlying feelings of poor self-esteem.

The notion that an inflated ego really masks underlying feelings of inadequacy is commonly found in popular psychology. More recently, however, a number of researchers have questioned whether high self-esteem is really necessary for success or if it is even possible for low self-esteem to be masked by over-confidence or arrogance. Rather, it has been suggested that perhaps people become violent when the favorable views they have of themselves are threatened, instead of when underlying feelings of inadequacy break through. Psychologist Roy F. Baumeister has shown how the combination of high self-esteem and an unflattering evaluation by others are among the main causes of violent behavior.[13]

Tyson displayed his sensitivity to unflattering or negative evaluations by others in his psychiatric interview. He told Schouten about his "sense of humiliation at being asked to undergo an evaluation by mental health professionals" and that he was "deeply embarrassed" that people knew he was undergoing the examination given the highly publicized nature of his case and that everyone might think he was a "psycho."[14] As a result, Tyson would become angry with the evaluation process and had to take frequent breaks in order to continue. In fact, at one point during his examination with the psychologist on the evaluation team, Dr. David Medoff, Tyson voiced a desire to harm Medoff because of the humiliation he experienced over having to be evaluated. Medoff wrote in his report that "at no time did [he] feel physically threatened or endangered" by Tyson.[15] Instead, Medoff interpreted Tyson's statement as an expressed fantasy brought about by frustration rather than as a true statement of intent to harm the psychologist.

As part of the examination, Tyson also underwent a neurological evaluation by Drs. Jeremy Schmahmann and Barry Jordan to assess whether there were any underlying brain abnormalities that could account for Tyson's erratic behavior. The diagnostic testing included an electroencephalogram (EEG) to assess for abnormal electrical activity in the brain and a magnetic resonance image scan (MRI) to determine if there were structural problems in Tyson's brain. Results from both of these tests were normal.[16]

A thorough examination of Tyson's brain functions was important in his particular case because several details of the boxer's history raised questions about whether his violent outburst in the Holyfield fight may have been due to brain damage. Tyson admitted to Schmahmann that he had lost conscious-

[handwritten margin note: don't several concussions cause antisocial PD?]

ness several times in his life, although never in the boxing ring. Surprisingly, and perhaps because of his success as a boxer, Tyson had never been knocked unconscious at any time prior to his bout with Holyfield. As a youngster, however, Tyson had been knocked out after having been hit in the head with a baseball bat. On another occasion he was assaulted with a brick. One other time he was beaten up so badly that he collapsed. Still, Schmahmann found no abnormalities in Tyson's motor responses, reflexes, attention, memory, language skills, spatial reasoning, or judgment. It is important to note, however, that Schmahmann's neurological examination revealed no impairment in areas where neuropsychological testing by Dr. Thomas J. Deters showed Tyson to be impaired.

[handwritten margin note: conflicting reports]

One problem in Tyson's neurological functioning that Schmahmann identified was in the area of executive functioning, which is controlled by the frontal lobes of the brain. Executive functioning is broadly defined as the ability to initiate appropriate responses to the environment by planning behavior, shifting to new ways of responding when circumstances change, and the ability of monitor and recognize whether one's behavior is appropriate in various situations. Schmahmann's report noted that Tyson's difficulties with executive functioning were subtle and relatively mild. However, the neurologist said that in light of Tyson's history of impulsive behavior "the stressors in the past combined with the relative weakness in the executive control system make it imperative that Mr. Tyson have some outlet other than boxing to vent his frustrations and deal with the psychological issues that have caused him trouble in the past."[17] More important was Schmahmann's conclusion that it was "impossible from a clinical neurologic perspective to predict whether Mr. Tyson is likely to lose control of his actions in the future."[18]

[handwritten margin note: so used to winning, novel situation (being beat) don't know how to respond]

Neuropsychological testing by Deters involved nearly two dozen tests being administered to Tyson to evaluate his cognitive functions, including intelligence, memory, attention, complex problem solving, and motor skills. The findings from this portion of the evaluation revealed that Tyson's performance was average in several areas, including general intelligence, long-term memory, expressive and receptive language, and verbal reasoning and concept formation. However, like the neurologists who examined Tyson, the neuropsychologist found evidence of problems with impulse control and executive functioning. The neuropsychologist concluded that he was "unable to predict whether or not Mr. Tyson will lose control of his behavior in a future boxing match." Furthermore, Dr. Deters stated that "Mr. Tyson seems to have a clear understanding that he will have no future chance of returning to boxing if he commits the same, or a similar foul" such as the biting of Evander Holyfield's ear.

The psychologist who conducted personality testing as part of the comprehensive evaluation of Tyson, Dr. David Medoff, saw Tyson over a two-day period. Medoff's examination consisted of a brief clinical interview and three widely used psychological tests.[19] The Bender Gestalt Visual-Motor Integration test consists of a series of geometric shapes that a person is asked to copy; the test measures visual-perceptual functioning. Given the extensive neuropsychological testing that had been conducted by Deters, use of the Bender Gestalt as a screening in Tyson's case seemed to be unnecessary. The two other psychological tests administered to Tyson were the Rorschach Inkblot Test and the Minnesota Multiphasic Personality Inventory–2 (MMPI–2). These tests are used to identify personality dynamics and patterns that are helpful in understanding how a person interacts with others, functions in various settings, and deals with stress.

Medoff's testing revealed that Tyson's MMPI–2 results were similar to people "who are irritable, angry and argumentative, and with whom it may be difficult to interact due to these characteristics."[20] Moreover, the testing indicated that Tyson experienced depression, sadness, and pessimism. He tended to blame other people for the problems his anger caused, and he was suspicious of others. Results from the Rorschach indicated that Tyson experienced "instances of faulty judgment and errors in decision making," as well as a number of distracting thoughts that he was generally able to manage but which increased when he was under stress. Interestingly, Medoff noted in his report that Tyson's scores appeared to fall within the range of scores of nonpatients in a normative sample of Rorschach responses. However, the psychologist also noted that there were no norms available for professional boxers on the Rorschach and therefore it was "impossible to confidently determine the clinical implications" of Tyson's results.[21]

Overall, Medoff's evaluation concluded that Tyson did not appear to have any major mental illness or personality disorder. In addition, Tyson's ability to control and tolerate stress was considered to be similar to that of most people, but periods of poor judgment and impaired decision making were sometimes triggered by distracting thoughts when Tyson was under more stress. Medoff did not make any specific statements about Tyson's ability to return to the boxing ring or whether he might commit another major foul in the future. One other interesting note from Medoff's report was that Tyson appeared to have difficulty forming close relationships and that his values and beliefs seemed to be rigid and fixed, making it likely that change in therapy would be difficult.

With respect to the five specific questions the Nevada State Athletic Commission wanted Tyson's examiners to answer, Schouten summarized the findings of the evaluation team in his report. First, the diagnostic team concluded that Tyson suffered from a chronic form of depression called dysthymia, and a cognitive disorder (characterized by problems in short-term memory, fine-motor coordination, and verbal learning and memory—presumably as a result of several blows to the head that he experienced over the course of his boxing career).[22] Dysthymic disorder is characterized by a depressed mood that lasts most of the day and is present more days than it is absent for at least two years.[23] In addition, the disorder is accompanied by at least two other symptoms of depression such as a disturbance in appetite, hopelessness, poor concentration, difficulty making decisions, low self-esteem, low energy, or sleep disturbance. The evaluation revealed that in addition to his chronic depression, Tyson had low self-esteem and difficulty making decisions. He was also diagnosed with features of borderline personality disorder, which is characterized by unstable relationships, impulsive behavior, inappropriate or intense anger, and an unstable self-image.

Second, the team of evaluators had "the unanimous opinion . . . that Mr. Tyson should be engaged in a course of regular psychotherapy with the goal of building trusting relationships, understanding and managing his emotional responses to specific situations, and anger management skills."[24] Furthermore, the team recommended that even though Tyson had a depressive disorder and the most effective approach to treatment depression calls for antidepressant medications to be used in conjunction with psychotherapy, Tyson's treatment should consist primarily of psychotherapy without the use of medication. In light of Tyson's traveling schedule, lifestyle, and side effects of antidepressant medications, the team felt that medication was not necessary for Tyson to return to boxing and that if he was allowed to box again he would obtain relief from some of the stressors that were contributing to his depression.

The third question addressed by the evaluation team had to do with Tyson's ability to handle stress in unpredictable situations. To answer this question, the evaluators drew a distinction between their observations of Tyson responding to the stress of having to undergo the mental health evaluation and the stress of being in the boxing ring. Schouten wrote that the team felt Tyson's ability to handle the stress of unpredictable situations was "fair to good" because he was able to compose himself and respond appropriately even after he experienced humiliation and frustration over the course of the entire evaluation. On the other hand, the team "saw no definitive evidence that Mr. Tyson would be unable to handle unpredictable events in the [boxing] ring" and noted that his ability to deal with the stress of boxing was due to the mastery he had over his sport.

The last two questions addressed by the evaluation team were really what the Nevada State Athletic Commission wanted to know: Would Tyson commit another major foul if he returned to the boxing ring and was he mentally fit to compete without snapping? The prediction of violent behavior has been shown to be difficult in that mental health professionals have not developed specific tests for predicting future violence with a very high degree of accuracy. Professionals continue to debate the merits of clinical versus actuarial approaches to assessing dangerousness.[25] Clinical approaches typically involve detailed interviews and testing of the individual, with the professional then rendering a professional opinion about whether or not the person poses a risk for danger to others. Actuarial approaches to predicting violence are based on statistical methods using specific variables to yield a probability of the likelihood that a person will or will not become violent. Many factors influence the accuracy of predictions of violence, including situational variables that are often unpredictable or unforeseen, the time frame over which predictions are made, and the confidence that one can place in predictions. Even when mental health professionals are able to agree on specific variables that are useful in appraising a person's risk for violence, those professionals often differ in the importance given to different variables and the manner in which variables are combined to arrive at a determination of violence potential.

At the present time, many advocate a risk-assessment approach in which specific factors that raise or lower a person's potential for violence are identified and general estimates are offered as to a person's risk for violence under certain conditions (e.g., low, moderate, or high risk for violence). Professionals also tend to qualify their evaluations based on the time over which a person's risk is assessed and the reliability of the information that forms the basis of an expert opinion about violence potential.

The professionals who evaluated Tyson were presented with the extremely difficult task of making an assessment of dangerousness in a situation that was highly specific: whether or not a boxer would commit an act of violence or aggression in the ring that constitutes a major rule violation. Although there is research to show that certain factors raise a person's potential for violence (e.g., history of violent behavior, substance abuse, psychopathic personality features), no research exists to provide any inkling of the factors that would increase the risk that an accomplished heavyweight boxer like Mike Tyson would "snap" and commit a major foul in the boxing ring. Therefore, the experts who evaluated Tyson were in the position of having to use a combination of rational clinical judgment, an appraisal of the general research on prediction of violence, and an analysis of Tyson's history in the boxing ring.

The final report of the team of forensic experts acknowledged the difficulties of their task when they stated:

> It is not possible to predict the future behavior of any individual. Fouls are committed in boxing, as they are in other sports. There is thus some risk of a foul occurring by virtue of being a boxer or an athlete in general. While past behavior is the best predictor of future behavior, that fact argues both ways for Mr. Tyson. On the one hand, it could be said that his commission of a foul puts him at increased risk of committing another offense. On the other hand, Mr. Tyson's history of limited point deductions in 48 previous bouts suggests that he is at low risk of another foul, especially given the consequences to date of the June 28, 1997, incident.[26]

The team of experts concluded that Tyson was "mentally fit to return to boxing, to comply with the rules and regulations, and to do so without repetition of the" biting incident which led to revocation of his boxing license.[27] Dr. Schouten and his colleagues presented their findings before the Nevada State Athletic Commission. In addition, Tyson's request to be reinstated was supported by the testimony of two athletes who are legends in their respective sports. Basketball star Magic Johnson told the commission that he would provide support to Tyson by helping the boxer make good decisions. Boxing great Muhammad Ali, stricken with symptoms of Parkinson's disease, had his wife read a statement to the commission in which he said there was no more severe punishment than preventing someone from earning a living at their profession and that he would be there to provide Tyson with guidance.[28]

After a three-hour hearing the commission voted 4 to 1 to reinstate Tyson's license to box in Nevada; this ruling came over a year after the Tyson-Holyfield fight that led to the revocation of his license to box. Although Tyson went on to box in several bouts in subsequent years, he continued to experience difficulties both inside and outside of the ring. He went through a divorce and had other incidents where his emotional stability was questioned, including having his face permanently tattooed, becoming involved in a scuffle during a media appearance for his fight with Lennox Lewis, and making provocative comments during media appearances for some of his other bouts. For example, he attempted to intimidate an opponent by boasting he could "eat the children" of the other boxer.

Nevertheless, the forensic mental health evaluation that was undertaken by a team of experts during his application for reinstatement of his license remains noteworthy in several respects. The experts undertook a challenging evaluation that involved a highly specific and unusual question that most forensic mental health professionals never face during their careers—namely, whether or not a professional boxer poses a risk for aggression or violence that constitutes a major rule violation while engaging in a sport known for being aggressive and violent. In addition, the experts performed a comprehensive evaluation, worked together as a team, and presented their findings in a manner that demonstrated their commitment to answering a number of specific questions, while qualifying their findings appropriately. Finally, the issue of violence risk assessment in this particular case took place not during a criminal or civil commitment proceeding, but during the hearing of a state administrative hearing that had the authority only to grant or deny Tyson's request to engage in the sport of professional boxing in the state of Nevada. In short, this case involved an assessment of whether a person would become "a bit too violent" in a highly unusual and very public case.

▸18

DARYL ATKINS

Mental Retardation,

Decency, and the

Death Penalty

B y the time Daryl Atkins turned eighteen, his juvenile criminal record included over a dozen prior felonies, most of which involved larceny, burglary, and robbery without a firearm. His criminal career was all the more remarkable because it had not begun until he was fourteen years old and because by the age of nineteen, he was out of custody, living at home in Virginia with his parents, and still committing burglaries, robberies, and other serious crimes.

For example, on April 29, 1996, four young adults were robbed at gunpoint by three men on a street in Hampton, Virginia. Later all four would identify Daryl Atkins as one of the robbers, though not the gunman. About six weeks later, in June 1996, Atkins and an acquaintance, twenty-six-year-old William Jones, broke into a townhouse in Hampton, Virginia, and stole a television, a VCR, a leather coat, and jewelry. Three weeks after that burglary, a pizza deliveryman was robbed at gunpoint in Hampton by three masked men, one of whom was Daryl Atkins. The robbers made off with $26. About two months later, a Hampton woman was attacked and shot in the stomach in her yard while mowing the lawn. The shooter was later identified as Daryl Atkins.

Though none of these adult offenses had resulted in an arrest, Atkins's freedom finally came to an end a week later when he and William Jones committed a robbery that ended in the death of its victim. Later, Atkins and Jones each admitted their involvement in the crime but gave authorities conflicting versions of what happened.

According to Atkins, at around 11:00 A.M. on August 16, 1996, he and Jones had begun drinking whiskey and malt liquor and smoking marijuana laced with cocaine and had spent most of the day and evening consuming alcohol and drugs: approximately thirty to fifty dollars worth of marijuana, ten dollars worth of cocaine, fifty dollars worth of hard liquor, and five or six forty-ounce bottles of malt liquor. By Atkins's account, during the evening Jones borrowed a gun from one of their drinking buddies, and the duo decided to walk to a nearby 7-11 store, rob someone, and use the proceeds to purchase more alcohol. Atkins admitted coming up with a plan whereby Jones would wave to or holler at a potential victim to get him to stop; then, when the victim came close, Jones would produce the gun and rob him. Instead, Jones approached a pickup truck driven by Eric Nesbitt, an Air Force airman, who had pulled into the convenience store parking lot.

According to Atkins, Jones pulled the gun and forced his way into the driver's side of the truck while Atkins entered the vehicle from the passenger's side. At Jones's direction, Atkins demanded Nesbitt's wallet, which contained only $60. Jones and Atkins then drove Nesbitt to a nearby automatic teller machine, where a surveillance camera videotaped them forcing him to withdraw $200 in cash. At that point, Atkins admitted, he held the gun while Nesbitt reached across Jones to make the withdrawal. The pair then drove Nesbitt to a secluded location where Atkins said he returned the gun to Jones, who ordered Nesbitt out of the truck, shot him eight times in the arms, stomach and back, and, in so doing, also accidentally shot Atkins in the leg.

Though he initially invoked his right to remain silent, William Jones eventually agreed with much of what Atkins had to say. Jones, however, claimed that it was Atkins who first approached Nesbitt, and Atkins who shoved his way into the truck while pointing a gun at the twenty-one-year-old airman. Also, according to Jones, it was Atkins's idea to drive Nesbitt to a secluded area and tie him up. When the three men arrived at the scene, according to Jones, Atkins shot and killed Nesbitt and was accidentally shot in the leg when Jones struggled to take the gun away from him.

In the end, prosecutors chose to believe, or at least rely upon, Jones's account of the robbery and killing. In exchange for Jones's plea of guilty to murder and agreement to testify against Atkins, the prosecutor agreed not to seek the death penalty for Jones. It is not clear why the state chose Jones's account over that of Atkins, but it may have been because Atkins not only had a lengthy record of prior criminal offenses and substance abuse but was also a high school dropout who was obviously not very bright. Atkins had never been employed, had a history of learning disabilities, had achieved a grade point average of only 1.26, and was ranked 347 out of a senior class of 371 when he left school.

Jones testified against Atkins, who was convicted of capital murder, and the question of the death penalty was presented to the jury. At a sentencing hearing to determine whether Atkins should die for his crime, defense counsel argued that Atkins was mentally retarded and thus should be spared the ultimate punishment.

The debate over Atkins's intellectual capacity rather quickly developed into a "battle of the experts." Dr. Evan Nelson, a forensic psychologist, examined and psychologically tested Atkins, using the standard, widely accepted, and most up-to-date intelligence test, the Wechsler Adult Intelligence Scale, Third Edition (WAIS–III).

Nelson testified that Atkins's performance on the WAIS–III resulted in a full-scale IQ of 59, that only 1 percent of the population has IQ scores of 59 or lower, and that Atkins was "mildly mentally retarded."[1] Nelson based his diagnosis of mild mental retardation not only on the WAIS–III results but also on (1) interviews with Atkins, members of his family, and correctional officers at the jail where he had been for eighteen months; and (2) school and legal records, including the statements Atkins made to the police.[2]

Nelson also explained in his testimony that a diagnosis of mental retardation is not based solely upon an IQ score but also takes into account the person's ability to function independently as compared to other people the same age. For example, according to the American Association of Mental Retardation, "*Mental retardation* refers to substantial limitations in present functioning. It is characterized by significantly subaverage intellectual functioning, existing concurrently with related limitations in two or more of the following applicable adaptive skill areas: communication, self-care, home living, social skills, community use, self-direction, health and safety, functional academics, leisure, and work. Mental retardation manifests before age 18."[3] Similarly, the American Psychiatric Association's diagnostic standards indicate that "The essential feature of Mental Retardation is significantly subaverage general intellectual functioning . . . accompanied by significant limitations in adaptive functioning in at least two of the following skill areas: communication, self-care, home living, social/interpersonal skills, use of community resources, self-direction, functional academic skills, work, leisure, health, and safety."[4]

With regard to Atkins's functioning, Dr. Nelson testified that while the convicted killer had never before been diagnosed as mentally retarded, he had received poor grades in school, often failed tests and classes, and was placed in special remedial courses. Nelson also testified that Atkins's deficits had been manifest throughout his life and that, while he might have "scored a little higher" on the WAIS–III had he not been depressed at the time the test was administered, his IQ of 59 was not an "aberration, malingered result, or invalid test score."[5]

"The possibility that Mr. Atkins was malingering," Dr. Nelson reported, "was considered and ruled highly unlikely."[6] As the psychologist indicated in his written report of the evaluation, this conclusion was based upon a number of factors:

> From the available school records, it was evident that this defendant had always been of limited intellect. In 8th grade, he scored in the 15th percentile on standardized achievement tests; in 10th grade he scored at the 6th percentile; he failed driver's education twice; and he barely passed the Virginia Literacy Passport subtests on reading and math. Furthermore, although a presentence report from 5/1/97 reported that the defendant was never in "Special Education," that is incorrect. After consultation with a Bethel High School guidance counselor who reviewed the defendant's transcript, it turned out that Mr. Atkins was, indeed, placed in a lower level classes [sic] for slow learners and in classrooms with intensive instruction to reme-diate deficits. Furthermore, persons who are malingering IQ tests usually have an uneven pattern of scores on the multiple subtests because they do not know how many questions to answer accu-rately versus pretend not to know, and the results of Mr. Atkins' test was a fairly uniform pattern of scores.[7]

In his testimony, Dr. Nelson made it clear that Atkins's history of aca-demic failure had begun as early as the second grade. School records reviewed by Nelson indicated that Atkins failed that grade because "work of grade too difficult."[8] After repeating second grade, Atkins struggled through third grade and was "socially promoted" from fourth to fifth grade.[9] In junior high school, Atkins was referred for testing for special education but never received it. Instead he was placed in the lowest of three academic tracks and was eventu-ally promoted to the ninth grade, although the records indicated that he did not meet the requirements for promotion to high school. In ninth grade, he man-aged a D+ average, but in tenth grade, which he took twice, his average fell to D- on both attempts. Eventually placed in a specially structured class for slow learners, he succeeded briefly before leaving school without a diploma.

In rebuttal, the prosecution presented the testimony of another psychol-ogist, Dr. Stanton Samenow. Samenow also had interviewed Atkins, reviewed his school records, and interviewed correctional officers who had observed

Atkins in jail. Samenow did not interview anyone who had information regarding Atkins's functioning outside of custody. Nor did he perform any formal intelligence tests. Instead, he asked Atkins some questions taken from an outdated (1972) version of the Wechsler Memory Scale as well as some items from the WAIS–III. He also administered a projective test known as the Thematic Apperception Test (TAT), a personality test in which the subject is presented with drawings and asked to tell a story about each. The TAT is not and never has been recognized as a measure of intelligence.

Confronted on cross-examination about his reliance on portions of an outdated test instead of administering a full version of a current intelligence test, Samenow acknowledged that the ethical principles of the American Psychological Association, of which he was a member, required the use of up-to-date tests. But Samenow qualified his reply by claiming that this ethical principle applied only "When one is doing a full evaluation with testing, which I was not doing."[10]

The prosecution psychologist testified that, although he did not contest the way in which Dr. Nelson had computed Atkins's IQ scores, his own observations led to the conclusion that Atkins was not mentally retarded but rather of *at least* average intelligence. Samenow said he based this conclusion on his assessment of Atkins's vocabulary, knowledge of current affairs, and other responses. For example, Samenow reported that Atkins knew that John F. Kennedy had been president in 1961, knew the name of the state's current governor, and used "sophisticated words" including orchestra, decimal, and parable.[11] Samenow noted that Atkins was able to recall information he had been asked to remember and was able to understand cause and effect. Samenow testified that although Atkins's academic performance had been "by and large terrible," he said that was because Atkins "is a person who chose to pay attention sometimes, not to pay attention others, and did poorly because he did not want to do what he was required to do."[12]

Addressing the issue of Atkins's adaptive functioning, Dr. Samenow testified that:

> Well, Mr. Atkins never lived independently. In other words, he
> was not a self-supporting member of society. However, he told
> me he was able to wash his clothes, wash and dry his clothes, he
> used his parents' washing machine and dryer. He told me—when I
> asked him if he was able to cook, he gave me his recipe for cooking
> chicken.
>
> This Defendant . . . lived a life in which he didn't work, and I
> don't mean just didn't hold a job, that he didn't do, but then again

there are a lot of 18-year-olds who maybe haven't worked because they've been in school. But he didn't work in school either.

So the point is he chose . . . a certain way of life, and there was no lack of ability to adapt and to take care of basic needs, certainly.[13]

In addition to the testimony of the two psychologists, the jury also heard graphic testimony from some of the victims of Atkins's many prior violent felony convictions, people Atkins had abducted, shot, pistol-whipped, and beaten with a beer bottle. Weighing this evidence, the jury concluded that Atkins's crime had been "outrageously or wantonly vile, horrible or inhuman"[14] and thus sentenced Atkins to death. On appeal, the Virginia Supreme Court initially upheld the verdict but overturned the sentence because a legally defective jury sentencing form had failed to alert jurors to the possibility of imposing a sentence of life in prison. The case was remanded to the trial court for a new sentencing proceeding, at which the evidence offered the jurors, including the testimony of the psychologists, was largely the same as in the first sentencing hearing. Again Atkins was sentenced to die. This sentence also was appealed, and the Supreme Court of Virginia affirmed, holding that the death penalty had been properly imposed.

One justice, however, dissented, concluding that Dr. Samenow's testimony was simply not to be believed:

I simply place no credence whatsoever in Dr. Samenow's opinion that the defendant possesses at least average intelligence . . .

Dr. Samenow admitted that he does not contest the manner in which Dr. Nelson computed the defendant's IQ scores. Additionally, Dr. Samenow admitted that some of the questions he administered to the defendant were based upon a test developed in 1939. Dr. Samenow described this test as "an old standard," yet, he used this obsolete test even though he acknowledged that the Ethical Principles of Psychologists and Code of Conduct, Ethical Standards 2.07 (1992) of the American Psychological Association, prohibits the use of obsolete tests and outdated test results and specifically states that "psychologists do not base such decisions or recommendations on tests and measures that are obsolete and not useful for the current purpose."[15]

When Atkins's appeal reached the U.S. Supreme Court in 2002, many expected the death sentence to be affirmed there as well. After all, in 1989, the Supreme Court held in *Penry v. Lynaugh* that imposing the death penalty on a mentally retarded criminal defendant did not violate the Eighth Amendment's ban on cruel and unusual punishment.[16] Moreover, the facts in *Penry* were much more sympathetic to the defendant than those in *Atkins*.

Johnny Penry, then twenty-two, also had committed a brutal murder and been sentenced to die. However, Penry, whose IQ was 54, was not only mentally retarded but diagnosed with organic brain damage, most likely caused by birth trauma and/or beatings he received at an early age. Expert testimony indicated that Penry "had the mental age of a 6 1/2-year-old [and] social maturity, or ability to function in the world . . . of a 9- or 10-year-old."[17] Evidence further established that Penry was essentially unable to learn, had never even finished first grade, had been severely beaten in the head, abused and neglected as a child, and had been in and out of state institutions for the retarded and mentally ill until he was twelve years old. His aunt testified that, even then, it had taken her over a year to teach Penry to print his name. Even the doctors who testified for the prosecution "acknowledged that Penry was a person of extremely limited mental ability, and that he seemed unable to learn from his mistakes."[18]

In rejecting Penry's claim that executing the mentally retarded constituted cruel and unusual punishment of the sort barred by the Eighth Amendment to the Constitution, the U.S. Supreme Court concluded that:

> In sum, mental retardation is a factor that may well lessen a defendant's culpability for a capital offense. But we cannot conclude today that the Eighth Amendment precludes the execution of any mentally retarded person of Penry's ability convicted of a capital offense simply by virtue of his or her mental retardation alone. So long as sentencers can consider and give effect to mitigating evidence of mental retardation in imposing sentence, an individualized determination whether "death is the appropriate punishment" can be made in each particular case. While a national consensus against execution of the mentally retarded may someday emerge reflecting the "evolving standards of decency that mark the progress of a maturing society," there is insufficient evidence of such a consensus today.[19]

That consensus, found lacking in 1989, had apparently "emerged" some thirteen years later when the U.S. Supreme Court considered Atkins's appeal. In 2002, reversing their earlier holding in *Penry*, the Court held in *Atkins* that executing a mentally retarded criminal offender does violate the Eighth Amendment. As the Court's landmark decision explained:

> Much has changed since *Penry*'s conclusion that the two state statutes then existing that prohibited such executions, even when added

to the 14 States that had rejected capital punishment completely, did not provide sufficient evidence of a consensus. Subsequently, a significant number of States have concluded that death is not a suitable punishment for a mentally retarded criminal, and similar bills have passed at least one house in other States . . .

An independent evaluation of the issue reveals no reason for the Court to disagree with the legislative consensus. Clinical definitions of mental retardation require not only subaverage intellectual functioning, but also significant limitations in adaptive skills. Mentally retarded persons frequently know the difference between right and wrong and are competent to stand trial, but, by definition, they have diminished capacities to understand and process information, to communicate, to abstract from mistakes and learn from experience, to engage in logical reasoning, to control impulses, and to understand others' reactions. Their deficiencies do not warrant an exemption from criminal sanctions, but diminish their personal culpability. In light of these deficiencies, the Court's death penalty jurisprudence provides two reasons to agree with the legislative consensus.

First, there is a serious question whether either justification underpinning the death penalty—retribution and deterrence of capital crimes—applies to mentally retarded offenders. As to retribution, the severity of the appropriate punishment necessarily depends on the offender's culpability. If the culpability of the average murderer is insufficient to justify imposition of death, the lesser culpability of the mentally retarded offender surely does not merit that form of retribution. As to deterrence, the same cognitive and behavioral impairments that make mentally retarded defendants less morally culpable also make it less likely that they can process the information of the possibility of execution as a penalty and, as a result, control their conduct based upon that information. Nor will exempting the mentally retarded from execution lessen the death penalty's deterrent effect with respect to offenders who are not mentally retarded.

Second, mentally retarded defendants in the aggregate face a special risk of wrongful execution because of the possibility that they will unwittingly confess to crimes they did not commit, their lesser ability to give their counsel meaningful assistance, and the facts that they are typically poor witnesses and that their demeanor may create an unwarranted impression of lack of remorse for their crimes.[20]

The U.S. Supreme Court's decision in *Atkins* has already been the subject of much debate, with some critics expressing the fear that many capital murder defendants will now pretend to be mentally retarded in order to avoid a sentence of death. Indeed, Justice Antonin Scalia raised this concern in his dissenting opinion in *Atkins*:

> One need only read the definitions of mental retardation adopted by the American Association of Mental Retardation and the American Psychiatric Association to realize that the symptoms of this condition can readily be feigned. And whereas the capital defendant who feigns insanity risks commitment to a mental institution until he can be cured (and then tried and executed), the capital defendant who feigns mental retardation risks nothing at all. The mere pendency of the present case has brought us petitions by death row inmates claiming for the first time, after multiple *habeas* petitions, that they are retarded.[21]

This concern about the malingering of mental retardation, however, seems misplaced. Contrary to Justice Scalia's unsubstantiated assertion, mental retardation is difficult to fake. As the American Psychological Association, American Psychiatric Association, and American Academy of Psychiatry and the Law informed the Supreme Court in their amicus (friend-of-the-court) brief filed in *Atkins*,

> False positive diagnoses of mental retardation due to malingering (i.e., the opportunistic feigning of symptoms) are essentially unknown. . . . Indeed, to the extent feigning is an issue relating to diagnoses of mental retardation, it arises because individuals with retardation try to cover up their disability due to the lifelong stigma that often attaches to it.[22]

Successfully faking or malingering mental retardation in order to avoid a death sentence is almost impossible to conceive of for several reasons. First, diagnosis of mental retardation must be based upon, among other things, the individual's score on one or more objective and standardized tests used to measure intellectual functioning. As Dr. Nelson explained to the jury in his testimony at Atkins's sentencing hearings, "It would be pretty hard to malinger. . . . You'd have to have extraordinary knowledge of the test, have decided in advance which questions you're going to get, do the equivalent of card counting in your head, keep track of how many questions you've said right or wrong."[23] To put it more bluntly, a person capable of faking mental retardation on an objective, standardized intellectual test would almost certainly be too obviously bright to carry off the deception, even if he or she were some-how capable of fooling the psychological tests.

Second, mental retardation is a developmental disorder, the diagnosis of which requires evidence of significant limitations in adaptive functioning, beginning in childhood. Thus, to successfully feign retardation in order to avoid execution for a capital crime, would-be defendants would have to begin laying the groundwork for their malingered defenses in early childhood, years before they would even be age-eligible for the death penalty.

Other critics of the *Atkins* decision have complained that making mental retardation an automatic barrier to the death penalty will lead to difficult line drawing (if not hair splitting) and turn many capital sentencing proceedings into "battles of the experts" such as occurred in *Atkins* itself.

This complaint, however, also seems without merit. As for drawing the line between who is and who is not mentally retarded, as already noted this is a reasonably objective process. Not only is intelligence measured by standard-ized, objective, and well-established instruments, but so is adaptive function-ing. As the amicus brief in *Atkins* informed the Court:

> Clinicians have at their disposal objective rating scales and assess-ment methods for the comprehensive evaluation of adaptive func-tioning skills. Such instruments were largely developed for the express purpose of testing adaptive functioning as it relates to mental retardation, and the tests accordingly have a high degree of validity in connection with this use. . . . In addition to validity, the reliability of particular adaptive functioning tests has been deter-mined through extensive and intensive analyses.[24]

One concern that may have some arguable validity with regard to this line-drawing criticism relates to the inherent possibility of error in the mea-surement of intelligence or IQ. But while this issue may result in a small increase in the number of people diagnosed as mentally retarded, it has little practical effect on the validity and reliability of IQ scores.

By commonly accepted clinical and legal definition, a diagnosis of mental retardation requires an IQ of no greater than 70. Where an individual's IQ is substantially lower or higher than 70, there is little if any problem in deter-mining whether or not the person meets the IQ criterion for a diagnosis of mental retardation. IQs close to 70 are not quite so easy to characterize one way or the other because standardized intelligence tests are subject to mea-surement error, which varies among instruments but is generally in the range of no more than plus or minus five points. As one authority put it: "The best a psychometrician can do is state the odds that the true IQ will be included within some range above and below the obtained score. Averaging across all the age ranges, a person's true IQ will be within [plus or minus] 5 points of his/her measured IQ more than 95 percent of the time."[25]

As a practical matter, this problem is dealt with by expanding the range of IQs considered to meet the intellectual criterion for retardation to include those as high as 75. While this correction means that some rather small percentage of capital murder defendants who do not in fact have IQs in the retarded range may appear to, they would not be diagnosed as mentally retarded unless they also met the other diagnostic criteria, such as significant limitations in adaptive functioning and pre-adult onset.

As for the specter of many capital sentencing hearings being turned into battles of the experts, to begin with, most such proceedings already involve expert, often conflicting, testimony. It has long been clear that convicted capital defendants have a constitutional right to present any and all potentially mitigating evidence to the jury charged with sentencing them. Given the nature of many of these offenders and their crimes, not surprisingly, many if not most opt to present psychological and/or psychiatric testimony regarding mental illness, mental retardation, addiction, family dysfunction, and so forth. And, when they do, the prosecution is ordinarily allowed to present evidence and/or other expert testimony to rebut the defendant's experts. This, of course, is exactly what happened in Atkins's sentencing hearings.

But, as is clear from the Atkins case, such a battle of the experts need not occur if defendants are fully, carefully, and competently evaluated—as, of course, they ought to be in this literally "life and death" context. As the U.S. Supreme Court heard from psychological and psychiatric professionals in their amicus brief in Atkins:

> Qualified professionals who conduct a complete mental retardation examination of an individual will be able to make an objective determination whether the individual has mental retardation, in the sense that independent professionals undertaking separate assessments should reach the same conclusion.
>
> To achieve objectivity, however, certain safeguards must be followed. The assessment must be performed by qualified professionals with experience relating to mental retardation and to administration of IQ and adaptive functioning tests. The evaluation must also be complete, i.e., it must include a thorough assessment of each of the three necessary criteria indicating mental retardation. Compliance with these safeguards should curtail unnecessary legal wrangling, conflicting "diagnoses," and both false positive and false

negative determinations concerning whether the individual has mental retardation.[26]

Atkins was evaluated by two psychologists, one of whom did a complete evaluation and concluded that he was mentally retarded. The other conducted what could be characterized at best as an incomplete evaluation. Not only did he rely upon outdated and inadequate methods of psychological testing but, as one of the dissenting judges wrote in Atkins's state appeal, "an assessment of mental retardation is predicated upon the subject's IQ score and the subject's adaptive behavior. Dr. Samenow, however, could not validly opine about the defendant's adaptive behavior because he had not interviewed anyone who had observed the defendant prior to his incarceration."[27]

In fairness to Dr. Samenow, it should be recalled that he testified that he was not "doing a full evaluation" in this case.[28] Had he done such an evaluation, he too might have concluded that Atkins was mentally retarded, and there would have been no "battle of the experts."

The true test of that proposition in this case, however, may be yet to come. When the U.S. Supreme Court ruled that the Eighth Amendment barred sentencing the mentally retarded to death, the justices remanded Daryl Atkins's case to the Virginia courts "for further proceedings not inconsistent with this opinion."[29] The state court responded by ruling that still another hearing will be held to determine whether Atkins is mentally retarded—a proceeding in which the judge has ruled that Atkins must prove that he is retarded by a preponderance of the evidence (i.e., that it is more likely than not that he is retarded).

The prosecutor in the case responded, predicting that Atkins will be unable to prove that he is mentally retarded no matter what standard of evidence the court uses. In her words, "He's no Rhodes scholar. But he is not mentally retarded, either."[30]

⌐ 19

ANDREA YATES

An American Tragedy

∎

On the evening of June 19, 2001, thirty-six-year-old Andrea Yates of Clear Lake, Texas, sat in her home and watched cartoons. After some time had passed, she went outside to play basketball with her husband, Russell, and their seven-year-old son, Noah, who was the oldest of their five children. Without uttering a word, Yates suddenly went inside and got into bed while still in her clothes and slept until the next day.[1] In the morning, her husband made sure Yates took antidepressant medications prescribed by her psychiatrist. For nearly two years, Yates had been suffering from severe postpartum depression and psychosis. When Russell Yates left home for his engineering job at the Space Shuttle Program at NASA's Johnson Space Center,[2] the last image he would take in of his wife as a free person was of her eating cereal out of a box.

Shortly after her husband's departure at around 9:00 A.M., Yates drew bath water to within three inches of the top of the tub.[3] Beginning with her three-year-old son, Paul, Yates pushed him face down into the tub, held him underneath the water until he drowned, placed him on the bed, and covered him with a sheet. She proceeded to do the same with two-year-old Luke and five-year-old John. Each child was put face down in the tub, drowned, and laid on the bed next to the bodies of the other children.

After Yates drowned her six-month-old daughter, Mary, she called her son Noah into the bathroom. When the boy saw his sister face down in the tub, he asked his mother "What happened to Mary?"[4] When his mother did not answer, Noah became frightened and tried to run away, but Yates grabbed him and held the boy face down under the water. Noah struggled with his mother and managed to get his face out of the water a couple of times to gasp for air. Each time, Yates forced her son back down into the water and after a three-minute struggle the boy was dead.

After making sure that Noah was indeed dead, Yates took Mary's body out of the tub and placed her daughter's lifeless body on the bed and covered it as she had done with the other children. However, Noah was left in the tub because his body was too heavy for his mother to lift. Yates then called 911 and asked for a police officer. Once she got off the phone with the 911 dispatcher, she called her husband. Just before 10:00 A.M., Russell Yates received a call from his wife.

"You need to come home," Yates said to her husband. As Russell Yates inquired as to why, he asked "Is anyone hurt?" "Yes," replied his wife, "the children."[5] When Rusty Yates arrived home, he found the police there and learned that his wife had drowned their five children.

The case soon became national news and attention focused immediately on a search for the reason why a mother would kill all of her children. There were several inconsistencies in Yates's history that made it all the more puzzling that she would commit such a horrific crime. How did the life of this former high school valedictorian, swimming champion, college graduate, and professional nurse spiral down to such a point that she would kill each of her children? Several issues piqued the public's interest in the case. The fact that Yates and her husband had five children in a period of seven years raised questions of whether the young mother was acting out against her children as a means of getting back at her husband.

However, the most relevant details of the Yates case emerged when it was revealed that since at least 1999—approximately two years before killing her children—Yates had begun a marked decline into severe mental illness. After her attorneys made it known they would defend her by raising the insanity defense and the prosecutor decided to seek the death penalty for Yates, the case polarized opinions about personality responsibility, mental illness, the responsiveness of the mental health system, and the culpability of people close to Andrea Yates.

A nurse by education and training, Yates married her husband in 1989 and worked until 1994 when her first child, Noah, was born. Shortly after the birth of her son, Yates had a vision in which she saw an image of a knife that transformed into a vision of someone being stabbed.[6] Although Yates never told anyone of this incident until after her arrest, the event was the first indication that she might suffer from a postpartum mental disorder.

According to the American Psychiatric Association's formal diagnostic classification system, the *Diagnostic and Statistical Manual for Mental Disorders* (4th ed.), postpartum mental disorders can include severe mood changes or psychosis and occur within four weeks following the birth of a child. According to the diagnostic manual:

> Symptoms that are common in postpartum-onset episodes, though
> not specific to postpartum onset, include fluctuations in mood,
> mood lability, and preoccupation with infant well-being, the inten-
> sity of which may range from overconcern to frank delusions. The
> presence of severe ruminations or delusional thoughts about the
> infant is associated with a significantly increased risk of harm to the
> infant.[7]

Subsequent events revealed that Yates's disturbing vision following the birth of Noah was not an isolated incident and foreshadowed a continuing decline into mental illness.

In the middle of 1996, the Yates family moved to Florida so that Russell Yates could work on a project for NASA. Around this time, Andrea Yates wrote a letter to Rachel Woroniecki, the wife of a traveling evangelist, in which she expressed feelings of loneliness. As a result of this contact, Yates was directed to read passages from the Bible that told how women should love their husbands and children and subject themselves to their husbands.[8] The move to Florida also brought about a change in lifestyle for the Yates family. Russell Yates decided that he wanted to see what it would be like to live on the road, so they leased their home in Texas, sold many of their possessions, and moved into a trailer.

Once Russell Yates had completed his work in Florida, the family moved back to their trailer park in Texas. However, Russell and Andrea maintained their contact with the Woronieckis. When the evangelist and his wife decided to sell their three-hundred-square-foot mobile home—a 1978 GMC bus that was converted into a mobile home for the preacher and his family—Russell Yates decided it was an ideal time to make further changes in the family's lifestyle. In May of 1998, he bought the Woronieckis' mobile home and in October of the same year he sold the family house. For the next year, the Yates family lived in the mobile home.[9] As Russell and Andrea Yates continued to have children and live in the unconventional surroundings of a converted bus, Andrea Yates became more isolated, lonely, and severely depressed.

To many people who knew Andrea Yates, she appeared to be a "model of efficiency" in the home,[10] and the family was described as loving and happy. Moreover, she was captivated by the fire-and-brimstone preaching of Woroniecki, although her husband was more skeptical about organized religion.[11] Andrea Yates became more religiously preoccupied and the effect Woroniecki had on her began to concern both her husband and her family.

In June 1999, after the birth of the couple's fourth child and while also caring for her father who was suffering from Alzheimer's disease, Yates tried to commit suicide by taking an overdose of her father's prescription medication. She was hospitalized and diagnosed with severe depression. The psychiatrist who took care of Yates during this first hospitalization would later testify that she was "severely mentally ill. . . . left to her own devices, she would not have survived. She was not eating or taking in fluids."[12]

A few months later, she was hospitalized a second time after her husband had to wrestle away a knife that she was holding to her throat. Yates was diagnosed as having severe depression with psychotic features; she was hearing voices and had concerns that she might "hurt somebody."[13] Doctors also questioned whether she might have schizophrenia.

Over the next year or so, Yates apparently functioned fairly well as she continued to see her psychiatrist and was given various antidepressant medications in a search to find the most effective treatment. Although one of her physicians recommended that she and her husband not have any more children, the couple's fifth child was born in November of 2000. In addition to the birth of her daughter, Yates was experiencing several other stressors at the same time, including continuing to care for her father with Alzheimer's disease and having to deal with his subsequent death in March 2001.[14] A conclusion drawn by many people following the case was that these stressors, all experienced within a relatively short period of time, and her history of severe mental illness, triggered the horrific acts that resulted in the death of her children.

But other questions were also raised about Yates's motives for killing her children. Was she angry at her husband over the fact that he wanted so many children, sold the family home, and had her living in a remodeled bus? Was she suffering from severe postpartum mental illness that caused her to take the lives of her children?

Her criminal trial became one of the most closely watched in recent history. An interesting subplot emerged when the role of her husband in the children's deaths was scrutinized. Russell Yates was seen by some observers—fairly or not—as equally, if not more, responsible for the deaths of the couple's five children. There were highly publicized media accounts of his controlling nature, desire for more children, rigid religious beliefs, and perceived indifference to his wife's depression.[15] For example, television commentator Bill O'Reilly made his own public observations: "Russell Yates knew his wife was having psychological problems, yet he continued to get her pregnant, even after she attempted suicide. Mr. Yates himself admitted the house was in deplorable condition yet felt he could leave his wife unsupervised with the children. That is on Mr. Yates."[16]

Within days of her arrest, Yates was evaluated by a clinical psychologist, Dr. Gerald Harris, to evaluate her competence to stand trial. Harris found Yates to be psychotic; she was experiencing hallucinations where she saw Satan on the walls of her jail cell and would take up to two minutes to respond to questions Harris posed to her during their interviews.[17] A psychologist appointed by the prosecution, Dr. Steven Rubenzer, also evaluated Yates and found that she had some difficulty with attention and concentration, took a long time to respond to questions, and did not show any evidence of faking her illness.[18]

By the time Yates appeared at her competency hearing to determine if she could understand the court proceedings and assist in her defense, she had been treated in the Harris County jail's psychiatric unit for her psychosis for three months.[19] In the state of Texas, pretrial competency hearings may be argued before a jury and, in Yates's case, a jury of eleven women and one man were to determine if she was competent to stand trial. Presiding over the case was State District Court Judge Belinda Hill, who had been rated by the Houston Bar Association as one of the top criminal judges in the city. Judge Hill instructed the jurors that they were to determine only the issue of whether Yates was able at the present time to understand the court proceedings and to assist in her defense. After hearing conflicting opinions from Dr. Harris (who was of the opinion that Yates was not competent because of her religious delusions) and Dr. Rubenzer (who was of the opinion that Yates was competent to stand trial despite her mental illness), the jury deliberated on the issue.

Yates believed that by being convicted and receiving the death penalty she would be able to kill Satan. Consequently, her attorneys and Harris believed she was unable to assist rationally in mounting a defense. The jury initially voted 8–4 in favor of finding Yates incompetent. However, over the course of several more hours of deliberation, opinions shifted and Yates was found competent to stand trial.[20]

Of course, the key issue in Yates's trial was whether she was insane at the time she drowned her five children. The legal standard for insanity in Texas has been characterized as extremely narrow and nearly impossible to meet.[21] Following the acquittal of John Hinckley, Jr., for the attempted assassination of Ronald Reagan, Texas moved from a fairly liberal test of insanity to a much more restrictive standard. The standard in place at the time of Yates's trial was a revised M'Naughten test. Most states that have a M'Naughten insanity test require that for a person to be held insane at the time of a crime, he or she must have been unable to either (1) know the nature or consequences of an act or (2) know that the act was right or wrong. In Texas, only the second of these two standards was adopted. Therefore, in order for Yates to be found insane at the time of she drowned her children, it would be of no significance whether she knew the nature or consequences of what she did. Rather, the only determination was whether she knew drowning her children was wrong.

The expert testimony presented by both the defense and prosecution focused on the issue of whether she knew the wrongfulness of her actions. Both the prosecution and defense agreed that Andrea Yates was mentally ill. Her history of serious psychiatric difficulties was well documented prior to her arrest.

Yates was admitted twice in 1999 to inpatient psychiatric facilities after failed suicide attempts. At various times, her condition was noted to be severely depressed. She was often unresponsive or responded minimally to questions, showed severe pessimism and hopelessness in her thinking, appeared withdrawn, and was treated with various antidepressant and antipsychotic medications. There was a one-month inpatient admission in March 2001 soon after her father died because she was depressed and refusing to drink liquids. Her husband and brother had to assist Yates to the hospital because she was resistant to any help. Her treating psychiatrist prescribed various medications, but she showed minimal improvement. Following her discharge, she was placed in a partial hospitalization program that allowed her to go home in the evening while she attended intensive outpatient programming during the day. In May 2001, Yates was once again readmitted to the hospital and the use of electroconvulsive therapy was discussed with her husband because she was not eating or drinking and had not responded well to previous treatments. Russell Yates refused to consider shock treatments even though his wife continued to show marginal changes in her condition. She disclosed little to her therapists, claiming to have no major issues to discuss. Following her discharge, and just two days before Yates drowned her children, her husband had a discussion with her psychiatrist about the most appropriate medication. Concerns were raised that she was not doing well on her current medications and was having nightmares.

This history of psychiatric illness emerged in detail during Yates's trial. However, the major difference of opinion among the experts who evaluated her was whether she knew that the actions of drowning her children were wrong, as defined under Texas insanity law. The principal expert for the defense was Dr. Phillip Resnick, a nationally renown forensic psychiatrist who had testified in a number of high-profile insanity cases and who had extensive experience studying woman who kill their children. According to Resnick, Yates did not kill her children out of feelings of revenge against her husband and there was no evidence that the deaths of the children were the result of a pattern of abuse or neglect.[22] Rather, the evidence indicated that there was no rational motive for the drownings—suggesting acute psychosis—and that Yates believed by killing her children she was serving their best interests, indicating an altruistic motive.

Resnick was of the opinion that Yates laid her children on the bed and covered them out of respect, rather than trying to conceal the bodies. Furthermore, Yates suffered from religious delusions and Resnick testified that he believed she was saving her children from Satan by killing them. The psychiatrist testified that, "Mrs. Yates had a choice to make: to allow her children to end up burning in hell for eternity or to take their lives in earth. . . . She would give up her life on earth . . . and her afterlife for the purpose of eliminating Satan and protecting her children from the fate of eternal damnation."[23]

That is, Yates's delusions caused her to believe that the only way to save her children from Satan was to kill them. The implication of Resnick's testimony was that even though Yates knew killing her children was *legally* wrong, she believed it was *morally* right because of her religious delusions.

The prosecution's principal expert was Dr. Park Dietz, a forensic psychiatrist who was a nationally recognized expert witness at the time who had testified in many high-profile insanity trials like the Hinckley case. Dietz testified that he did not typically offer opinions on the ultimate issue of sanity, but added that he provided opinions on a criminal defendant's knowledge of wrongfulness at the time of a criminal offense,[24] a subtle distinction that has minimal significance and seemed to create the appearance that Dietz was unwilling to address the ultimate legal issue of Yates's sanity. With respect to the issue of Yates's understanding of the wrongfulness of her actions, Dietz testified:

> My opinion with reasonable medical certainty is that at the time of the drowning of each of the children, Mrs. Yates knew that her actions were wrong in the eyes of the law . . . in the eyes of society . . . in the eyes of God. . . . Mrs. Yates may have believed the killings were in the best interest of the children and that the ends—saving the children—justified the means, which was to wrongly and illegally kill them.[25]

Dietz, whose testimony and methods of forensic evaluation are noted for their detail and thoroughness, provided several examples of Yates' thinking and behavior that supported the opinion that she knew her actions were wrong. The fact that Yates attributed her actions to Satan was one indication that she knew her actions were wrong. Dietz testified:

> Mrs. Yates indicates that at that time before the homicide she had the idea of killing her children and she attributed the origin of that idea to Satan. So, of course, the idea comes from her mind, but she's mistakenly thinking Satan put it there. The fact that she regards it as coming from Satan is the first indication of her knowing that this is wrong. Because she recognizes even the idea of killing your children is an evil idea that comes from Satan. She doesn't think this is a good idea that comes from God.[26]

Other aspects of Yates's thinking and behavior that were used to support Dietz's opinion included the fact that she concealed her thoughts of harming the children from others because she knew they were wrong and that other people would try to stop her.[27]

The most controversial portion of Dietz's testimony came when Yates's attorney cross-examined the prosecution expert. A point raised by defense attorney George Parnham was Dietz's lack of clinical experience with postpartum depression. During cross-examination, Parnham asked Dietz about his various consulting experiences and the forensic psychiatrist stated that he was a consultant to the television show *Law and Order*. When Parnham asked if any of the shows dealt with postpartum depression, Dietz stated, "As a matter of fact, there was a show of a woman with postpartum depression who drowned her children in the bathtub and was found insane, and it was aired shortly before this crime occurred."[28]

The defense recalled one of its expert witnesses, forensic psychiatrist Dr. Lucy Puryear, to rebut Dietz's testimony. During cross-examination of Puryear, prosecutor Joseph Owmby pressed the defense expert on the notion that Yates may have gotten the idea to drown her children and claim insanity from the episode of *Law and Order* that Dietz had mentioned during his testimony. There was a problem, however. The episode of which Dietz spoke had never aired.[29]

After Puryear had concluded her rebuttal testimony, the defense rested its case. Closing statements were made and the jury was charged with the law governing the case. Although the jury had heard over three weeks worth of testimony, it rendered its verdict after less than three-and-a-half hours of deliberation. Yates was found guilty of capital murder and faced a sentencing hearing to determine if she would receive life in prison or the death penalty.

On the evening the guilty verdict was rendered, Yates's defense attorney, George Parnham, discovered that *Law and Order* had never aired an episode in which a mother had drowned her children and claimed insanity. When the show's creative director was contacted, he confirmed that a show like the one Dietz described had never been written, produced, or televised.[30] Dietz had consulted with writers on plots for hundreds of shows. When the erroneous testimony was brought to Dietz's attention, he wrote to prosecutors and told them that he had been mistaken and confused the episode he described with infanticide cases and other episodes for *Law and Order*.[31]

The erroneous testimony became an issue that Parnham raised on Yates's behalf in asking for a mistrial. Parnham claimed that the erroneous testimony misled jurors into thinking that Yates had planned the murders of her children by watching a television show. However, the judge denied the motion. During the penalty phase of her trial, however, jurors were informed of the incorrect testimony. Yates avoided the death penalty and was sentenced instead to life in prison.

Subsequent interviewing of the jurors revealed that they were persuaded by Dietz's account of Yates's crimes. Jurors found that a number of defense experts all agreed Yates did not know that her actions were wrong but had differing accounts of how her mental illness affected her thinking at the time she drowned her children. Instead, jurors found Dietz's coherent and detailed account of Yates's motives more convincing. Given the apparent persuasiveness and influence of Dietz's testimony, along with the erroneous mention of the *Law and Order* episode that never aired, the defense has appealed the verdict in the Yates case.

An investigative journalist covering the Yates case had been a producer and consultant for NBC, the network on which *Law and Order* appeared. Following announcement of the verdict, Yates wrote a letter to the journalist expressing her distress over the fact that people may have mistakenly thought she got the idea to drown her children from a television show. She wrote, "I guess it bothered me the jury didn't think I was mentally ill and I was offended they thought there was a 'hidden motive.' But it was a . . . terrible case and I am grateful the jury didn't give me the death penalty."[32] Parnham, Yates's attorney, was even more direct. After the jury gave its recommendation against the death penalty in favor of life in prison without the possibility of parole, Parnham told the journalist that helping to uncover the error in Dietz's testimony had saved Yates's life.

But the controversy over Dietz's testimony did not end with Yates's sentence of life in prison. Her attorneys appealed to the Court of Appeals for the First District in Texas. Among the many errors that Yates's attorneys claimed in the appeal were the trial judge's failure to sustain the defense's motion for a mistrial and a violation of Yates's due process rights because the prosecution had relied on "false or perjured testimony."[33] Yates's attorneys argued in her appeal that Dietz's false testimony about the *Law and Order* episode that never aired constituted a major error because it provided critical support for the prosecution's theory that Yates knew her actions were wrong, that her crime was premeditated, and that she deceptively used a television show to create an explanation for her actions that would provide her with an excuse, namely insanity.

On January 6, 2005, the Court of Appeals for the First District of Texas brought the Yates case into the spotlight once again when it ruled in favor of her appeal. The court found that even though there was no evidence on the record that Dietz "intentionally lied in his testimony," his reference to the *Law and Order* episode was "false" and a material piece of evidence dealing with Yates's insanity defense.[34] Moreover, the appellate court found that the prosecution made use of the evidence when it cross-examined the defense's rebuttal witness, Puryear, and in its closing statement. The prosecutor argued to the jury that Yates "gets very depressed and goes to Devereux [the hospital]. And at times she says these thoughts came to her during that month. These thoughts came to her, and she watches *Law and Order* regularly, she sees this program. There is a way out. She tells that to Dr. Dietz. A way out."[35]

Because the testimony was false, went directly to the material issue of Yates's sanity, and was used by the prosecution in its cross-examination of a defense expert and in closing arguments before the jury, the trial judge's failure to grant the defense's motion for a mistrial was an error. The result of the appellate court decision could mean that Yates will be granted a new trial and the entire case will once again hinge on her sanity at the time of the killing. Prosecutors have requested that the Court of Appeals for the First District of Texas re-hear the appeal. If their attempt to have the conviction upheld fails, they have vowed to appeal to the Texas Court of Criminal Appeals. It seems clear that the tragedy of Andrea Yates and her children will continue to linger in the media, as well as the Texas criminal courts, until it can be legally resolved.

A number of issues have made the Yates case one of the most interesting, yet controversial, trials in recent history. Among the factors contributing to debates about the case include the narrow definition of insanity under Texas law, the varying theories offered by experts about why Yates drowned her

children, and, of course, the horrific deaths of the five Yates children and varying opinions about the most appropriate punishment for Yates. However, an
equally interesting issue was the scrutiny given to the actions of both Andrea
and Russell Yates that pointed to a gender bias that exists when people try to
explain the causes of criminal behavior for men and women.

There is a tendency for people to attribute the cause of a woman's violent
behavior to biological or psychological factors that are outside of her control,
while the violent actions of a man are often attributed to situational factors
that are within his control.[36] Moreover, social science research indicates that
people tend to view the insanity defense as more acceptable for females than
males.[37] As a result, one might expect there to be greater public sympathy for
Andrea Yates in her plea of insanity than for Russell Yates in his role as the
innocent father whose children were murdered.

Because Andrea Yates's depression appeared to have been postpartum,
in that it was triggered following the birth of her fourth child, there was
a tendency to attribute the cause of her mental illness to biological factors
that were beyond her control. While the public was no doubt horrified by her
actions, there was considerable support for her among women, particularly
those who could understand the stressors she faced, including having to raise
five young children, suffering from severe depression, and having to deal with
a dying father.[38]

Her husband, on the other hand, did not fare well in the view of some as
the grieving father whose five children were murdered by their mother. As
noted earlier, some observers of the case suggested that the "wrong parent
was being prosecuted," and that Russell Yates was the more culpable parent
because he did not heed warning signs that his wife might be dangerous.[39]
However, Russell Yates claimed that he was never informed that his wife had
violent fantasies and assumed that because she had responded to antipsychotic medication in the past that she would respond again in the future if she
became ill.[40] Nevertheless, there were some calls from the public to have Russell Yates prosecuted as an accessory in the death of his children.

One of the most intriguing aspects of the Yates case, however, remains
the way in which gender roles and expectations in society influenced some of
the public commentary that was made on the case. Social science research has
dispelled several myths about the insanity defense. Contrary to widely held
beliefs, the insanity defense is not raised very often in criminal cases. When
the defense is raised, it is more likely to be unsuccessful than successful and
individuals acquitted by reason of insanity spend more time confined to a psychiatric hospital than an individual convicted of a comparable crime spends
in prison. In short, there are risks to the defendant who raises an insanity

defense and successfully makes his or her case. Gender biases, and the differing ways violent criminal behavior is explained for males and females, compound the distorted views that many people have of the insanity defense.

The circumstances surrounding Andrea Yates's crime prompted strong ambivalent feelings. While her actions generated horror and outrage, there were many who could sympathize with the fact that she was mentally ill, faced serious stressors and demands, and was in a situation where it was easy to be overwhelmed and "snap." The final disposition in her case remains an open question. Perhaps one day her behavior will be explained to the satisfaction of all. Yet, the case of Andrea Yates and her husband continues to be an interesting study in how expectations of men and women behaving in accordance with their gender roles can compound the controversies that surround the insanity defense in criminal cases.

► 20

MICHAEL
KANTARAS

What Makes

a Man a Man?

◢

As a very young child, Margot Kantaras felt more like a boy than a girl and came to consider herself a male despite her female body. Her parents even referred to her as their "son."[1] Growing up she engaged in typically male pursuits such as football, baseball, basketball, wrestling, and fishing. It was not until she was twenty-six years old, however, that Margot became aware of the possibility of physically becoming a male.

In 1985, after watching "What Sex Am I?"—an HBO television program on the treatment of gender disorders—Margot contacted a clinic mentioned in the show and was soon diagnosed with gender identity disorder.[2] According to the American Psychiatric Association's *Diagnostic and Statistical Manual of Mental Disorders* (4th ed.), gender identity disorder is manifested in "a strong and persistent cross-gender identification," "the desire to be, or insistence that one is, of the other sex" and "persistent discomfort about one's assigned sex" resulting in "clinically significant distress or impairment in social, occupational or other important areas of functioning."[3]

Doctors told Margot that, in essence, she was a man with a woman's body. Shortly thereafter, she underwent a variety of treatments including hormone therapy and sex-reassignment surgery (including hysterectomy, ovariectomy, and reconstructive mastectomy), which left her with a deepened voice, facial hair, a more masculine body, male pattern baldness and an elongated clitoris that doctors described as a "small phallus."[4] Given the cost (anywhere from

$25,000 to $100,000) and significant medical risks involved, Margot did not undergo phalloplasty, which is the surgical construction of a penis.

A year later, Margot legally changed her name to Michael Kantaras. Then, at her request and based upon medical evidence, an Ohio court amended Margot's birth certificate to reflect her new name and gender.

In 1989, thirty-year-old Michael Kantaras met Linda Forsythe and they became sexually intimate. At the time, Michael had a girlfriend, and Linda had been living with a boyfriend for about four years. Michael explained his gender history to Linda, who was initially incredulous but shortly came to understand and accept Michael's status as a woman who had become a man. Soon Linda learned that she was pregnant; her boyfriend, the putative father, moved away. Three weeks after Linda's son Matthew was born, she began living with Michael Kantaras. On July 18, 1989, when Matthew was six weeks old, Michael and Linda were married in a civil ceremony in Florida. Shortly thereafter, Michael legally adopted Matthew. In both the marriage and the adoption, Michael represented to authorities that he was a man.

Not satisfied with an only child, Michael and Linda began discussing how they might conceive another offspring. Michael told Linda that years earlier he had discussed this possibility with his brother, Tom, who had agreed that if Michael (then Margot) ever married, he would donate his sperm so that Michael's wife could be artificially inseminated. In fact, that is exactly what happened. In 1991, Michael and Linda went to a fertility clinic and, on the second attempt at artificial insemination, Linda was successfully impregnated with Tom's sperm. In 1992, Linda gave birth via cesarean section to a daughter, Irina.

Seven years later, Michael and Linda separated. Michael left Linda to begin a relationship with her best friend, Sherry Noodwang. Michael brought a divorce action against Linda, she countersued seeking an annulment, and the two became embroiled in a contentious legal battle over the custody of Matthew and Irina. Fighting to exclude Michael from the children's lives, Linda claimed that her ex-husband was not a man and thus could not legally have been a husband or a father. She testified that "Michael Kantaras is a woman who thinks that he is a man"[5] and cited Florida laws banning same-sex marriages and adoptions by homosexuals.

When Michael Kantaras sued for divorce and custody, the legal odds were clearly against him. The question of whether a transgendered person could be legally recognized as having a gender other than that with which he or she was born had never before come to the attention of a court in Florida but had been litigated in other states. Courts in Kansas, New York, Ohio, and Texas had all refused to recognize the marriages of postoperative transsexuals. Only one U.S. court, in New Jersey, had recognized the marriage of a transsexual.

In the New York case, the court rejected a female-to-male transsexual's claim for divorce, holding that there had never been a marriage because he could not carry out the sexual and procreative functions of marriage. As that court explained its ruling:

> Assuming, as urged, that defendant was a male entrapped in the body of a female, the record does not show that the entrapped male successfully escaped to enable defendant to perform male functions in a marriage. Attempted sex reassignment by mastectomy, hysterectomy, and androgenous hormonal therapy, has not achieved that result. The comment by Dr. George Burou, specialist in male-to-female surgery, who over the past 15 years has performed more than 700 such operations in Casablanca, applies with equal pertinency to this defendant: "I don't change men into women. I transform male genitals into genitals that have a female aspect. All the rest is in the patient's mind."[6]

In the New Jersey case, which involved a male-to-female transsexual, the court based its acceptance of the marriage at least in part on the testimony of several medical experts, including two psychologists. One psychologist "expressed the opinion that if a person had a female psychic gender and underwent a sex reassignment operation, that person would be considered female although no person is 'absolutely' male or female."[7] The other psychologist testified that, having undergone sex reassignment surgery, the transsexual's body was "now in line with the psyche."[8]

Michael Kantaras also relied on the testimony of numerous medical experts, including three psychologists. The first psychologist to testify was Dr. Walter Bockting, who specialized in the treatment of transsexualism and gender identity disorders. In his expert testimony, Dr. Bockting, who had not examined or treated Michael Kantaras, defined these terms for the court:

> Well, transsexualism is—the term that we use today is gender identity disorder. And gender identity disorder is defined as having an intense discomfort with one's sex and gender assignment at birth, and an intense discomfort with one's primary and secondary sex characteristics. At the same time, there is a preoccupation with obtaining the sex characteristics of the opposite sex. So they're in intense conflict between the basic conviction and psychological

sense of who a person is. And their anatomy, their body, they have conflict. Patients who have an intense conflict in that area meet criteria for gender identity disorder. An intense conflict means that they report clinically significant distress as a result of this mismatch between their body and their sense of identity. Gender identity disorder is a conflict between the anatomy and your gender identity. Gender identity is a basic conviction of being a man or a woman. And I think most of us take this for granted because it is so consistent with our body and our anatomical sex. But what we have learned from transsexuals is that's not the case for everyone and that their sense of being a man or a woman is [in] conflict with their body.[9]

Dr. Bockting further testified as to the prevalence of transsexualism: "Based on studies in the Netherlands they found that one in 11,900 persons is male to female (M to F) transsexual. And one in every 30,400 is female to male. The male to female are more common. They are three times as common as female to males."[10]

Michael also presented the expert testimony of Dr. Collier Cole, a clinical psychologist who specialized in the assessment and treatment of sexual disorders and had treated more than two hundred female-to-male transsexuals. Transsexualism, he told the court, cannot be "cured" but can be effectively treated with surgery, hormones, and counseling: "There have been a number of studies in the last 20 years to indicate that people can be very well adjusted, can go on to lead very productive lives having followed this type of procedure that is currently espoused in modern medical literature of dealing with individuals of this concern."[11] In his vast experience, he testified, "There was not a single individual who regretted their decision to go through this process at all."[12]

Dr. Cole testified that in 1985 he evaluated Michael Kantaras, diagnosed him as a transsexual, and ruled out any underlying psychopathology. He also told the court that he had examined Michael four times since the surgery. Michael, the doctor testified, was "a very typical case."[13]

Dr. Cole also refuted Linda's allegation that Michael was a homosexual. Asked whether when "a transsexual man has intimate sexual relations with a woman [he is] engaging in a lesbian relationship," Cole replied, "Absolutely not."[14] "In this particular case," he further testified, "we have an individual who has an identity of male and like most men he's turned on by women. So we would have a heterosexual."[15]

Dr. Cole also told the court that in his experience a significant number of female-to-male transsexuals, such as Michael, had successful marriages, raised children, and were good fathers and good male role models. He added that in a study of over four hundred transsexuals, he and his colleagues had found that these individuals had no greater incidence of psychopathology, depression, or suicide attempts than "normal" Americans.[16]

Asked by the trial judge what effect it would have on Michael to be legally ruled a female, Dr. Cole replied "I think it would be absolutely devastating. . . . In my mind it's much like a sexual assault victim having to be dragged through the courts and the background and history smeared in the courts."[17]

The court also received expert input in the form of an affidavit from Dr. James Boone, a psychologist appointed by the court to treat Michael, Linda, and the children. Dr. Boone informed the court that:

> Michael is more emotionally stable but may have a history of being emotionally controlling of Linda . . . Linda is a chronically depressed and dependent-manipulative woman who is intensely angry with Michael for his perceived abandonment of her. . . . I suspect that her anger is to the level that she is willing to circumvent court orders to sabotage his visitation and relationship with the children.[18]

Dr. Boone also suggested that Linda might suffer from borderline personality disorder. As Dr. Cole explained in his testimony to the court, borderline personality disorder is a "serious" mental condition:

> Generally this is an individual who has a lot of instability in his or her life in terms of inter-personal relationships, work relationships and the like. Often these relationships can be very intense. If a person loves you or loves the job and then suddenly feels wronged in some fashion they can become very angry, very vindictive. In many cases there is evidence of individuals engaging in suicidal gestures or attempts, self-mutilating behavior. These are often the most difficult patients for any therapist to treat.[19]

Finally, the court heard the testimony of a fourth psychologist, Dr. Robert R. Dies, who had been appointed to conduct a custody evaluation. After evaluating Michael, Linda, and the children, Dr. Dies observed that Linda had "repeatedly and consistently undermined the quality of the relationship that the children had with their father . . . interfered with visits, in many ways downgraded Michael, blamed him, faulted him, and essentially made him look bad in the children's eyes."[20] For example, Dr. Dies reported that "the children have often heard Linda, and they report this in numerous occasions, hearing Michael described as a woman, an it, a he-she and given the name Markel which is a contamination of Margo and Michael."[21] Moreover, he noted that when Matthew was ten and Irina eight years old, Linda had disclosed to them not only that Michael was not their father as they had always believed but that he was born a woman, not a man. Linda reportedly also told the children that Michael was "living a lie" and "cannot be regarded as a man."[22] Dr. Dies also told the court that Linda "is much more inclined to distort the truth and to engage in behaviors that are quite inappropriate to suit her needs."[23]

Dr. Dies concluded that Michael was not only the "better parent" but also in a better position to meet the children's material needs and "more likely to allow frequent and continuing contact with the visiting parent."[24] Dies acknowledged that "Matthew and Irina have routinely stated that they would favor custody on behalf of their mother" but concluded that "it appears quite clear that the youngsters have been poisoned against their father and prevented from having a meaningful and constructive relationship with him due, in large part, to their mother's insidious and alienating tactics."[25]

Dr. Dies also reported that he conducted psychological testing with both parents. The test results indicated that while Michael "answered . . . in an honest fashion with little effort to conceal problems," Linda's results were marked by "extreme defensiveness and/or denial of psychological problems."[26]

Michael's test results, the psychologist reported, "suggested that he tends to be overly concerned with behaving in socially acceptable ways and that he strives to convince others that he is reasonable and logical."[27] The results in his case were similar to those of individuals who are "often insecure and have a strong need for attention, affection and sympathy [and are] frequently very dependent, but uncomfortable with the dependency and experience conflict because of it."[28]

Linda's psychological test results, on the other hand, suggested "that she may be inclined to disregard social standards and values due to an underdeveloped sense of conscience."[29] According to Dr. Dies's report, "Individuals with her pattern of scores are often unwilling to accept responsibility for their own behavior, rationalizing shortcomings and failures and blaming difficulties on other people."[30] Her results, the psychologist told the court, also "were consistent with those of people who harbor intense feelings of anger and hostility . . . expressed in occasional emotional outbursts."[31]

Comparing the test results of Michael and Linda, Dr. Dies concluded that:

> On the basis of the test results it would be difficult to argue
> strongly in behalf of either party as the preferred custodial parent.
> They are both angry, likely to behave in ways that will sometimes
> be self-serving and insensitive to others, but neither could be judged

to be a "bad parent" due to their test results. Nevertheless, Michael comes across as somewhat less inclined to engage in behaviors that are deliberately or openly deceptive.[32]

What appeared to influence Dr. Dies more than the test results was the way in which Linda seemed to systematically alienate the children from Michael:

> Linda and her family have given the children powerful and insidious messages that undermine Matthew's and Irina's relationship and respect for their father, as well as the woman with whom he plans his future (Sherry). The pervasive pattern of name-calling, blaming, manipulating have [sic] been harmful and destructive.[33]

Asked to make a custody recommendation, Dr. Dies said: "Based on the considerable volume of evidence from multiple sources which I independently confirmed, and using the major criteria from the Florida Statutes, my considered opinion is that Michael Kantaras would be the more appropriate parent for these children using the criterion of the best interest of the children."[34] Dr. Dies added, however, that he felt that the parents should have shared parental responsibility and thus Linda should have liberal visitation with Matthew and Irina.

In response to Michael's proof, including the testimony of the three psychologists, Linda presented little evidence but argued that a ruling that Michael was a man would so blur the lines of gender as to create a legally chaotic situation in which people could switch virtually at will. As her attorney told the court:

> If you open the door this much it's going to be like the barnyard door coming open. If Michael can be a male because Michael thinks he is a male, and because of some surgery, your honor, then we're headed for big trouble. . . . It will create utter chaos. I believe the floodgates will be opened. . . . He would like us to believe that his clitoris has somehow been magically transformed into a penis, but no one but Michael Kantaras can tell you that.[35]

The attorney added, questioning the motives of Michael's expert witnesses: "They are all part of this transsexual wave. They all have something to gain by the testimony in this case."[36]

Countering these arguments, Michael's attorney argued that Michael had already long been recognized as a man: "His family knows it, the community knows it, and the medical community knows it. And now, your honor, you've been asked to decide whether the legal community knows that Michael Kantaras is a man."[37]

Leaning heavily upon the testimony of the physicians and psychologists as well as that of the many other witnesses called by both parties, in February 2003, Judge Gerald O'Brien issued a groundbreaking 802-page decision holding that:

> Michael at the date of marriage was a male based on the persuasive weight of all the medical evidence and the testimony of lay witnesses in this case, including the following:
>
> (a) As a child, while born female, Michael's parents and siblings observed his male characteristics and agreed he should have been born a "boy."
>
> (b) Michael always has perceived himself as a male and assumed the male role doing house chores growing up, played male sports, refused to wear female clothing at home or in school and had his high school picture taken in male clothing.
>
> (c) Prior to marriage he successfully completed the full process of transsexual reassignment, involving hormone treatment, irreversible medical surgery that removed all of his female organs inside of his body, including having a male reconstructed chest, a male voice, a male configured body and hair with beard and mustache, and a naturally developed penis.
>
> (d) At the time of the marriage his bride, Linda was fully informed about his sex reassignment status, she accepted along with his friends, family and work colleagues that Michael in his appearance, characteristics and behavior was perceived as a man. At the time of the marriage he could not assume the role of a woman.
>
> (e) Before and after the marriage he has been accepted as a man in a variety of social and legal ways, such as having a male driving license; male passport; male name change; male modification of his birth certificate by legal ruling; male participation in legal adoption proceedings in court; and as a male in an artificial insemination program, and participating for years in school activities with the children of this marriage as their father.
>
> All of this was no different than what Michael presented himself as at the date of marriage.[38]

The judge also indicated that he had been influenced in his decision by Michael's typical male appearance:

The court had the opportunity to directly observe Michael Kantaras both inside the courtroom and in the hallways of the courthouse. Michael is visibly male. He has a deep, masculine voice, a chin beard and a mustache, a thinning hair line and some balding, wide shoulders, muscular arms and the apparent shifting of fat away from the hips toward the stomach. He has a pronounced maleness that prompts one to automatically refer to Michael with the pronoun he or him.[39]

Having held that Michael was legally a man despite having been born a woman, the judge further held that his marriage to Linda was thus legal and proper, that the adoption of Matthew was valid, and that, by virtue of his marriage to Linda, Michael was legally the father of Irina, who was conceived through artificial insemination.

Significantly, the judge also awarded Michael Kantaras primary physical custody of both children. Had the judge merely held that Michael was a man and thus legally capable of having married Linda and adopting Matthew, that might have been the end of this case. But since Linda had been denied custody and relegated to "liberal visitation" with the children, she appealed the trial court's judgment, reasserting her claims that Michael was not a man and thus legally incapable of marrying her or adopting her son.

In July 2004, in the midst of a growing national debate over same-sex marriage, the Court of Appeal of Florida reversed the trial judge's decisions regarding Michael's gender and marriage.[40] With regard to Michael's gender, the appellate court held "the common meaning of male and female, as those terms are used statutorily, refer to immutable traits determined at birth"[41] and deferred to the Florida legislature to determine if and when transgendered individuals such as Michael may claim a gender other than that with which they were born. This ruling, according to the court, also determined the question of marriage and adoption in the Kantaras case.

As regards the marriage between Michael and Linda, the appeals court observed that:

The Florida Legislature has expressly banned same-sex marriage. As amended in 1977 by chapter 77-139, Laws of Florida, the statute governing the issuance of a marriage license, at the time one was issued in this case, provided that no license shall be issued unless one party is a male and the other a female: "No county court judge or clerk of the circuit court in this state shall issue a license for the marriage of any person unless . . . one party is a male and the other party is a female."[42]

The appeals court further noted the Florida Defense of Marriage Act, enacted by the state legislature in 1997 prohibiting marriage between persons of the same sex and prohibiting the state of Florida from recognizing any such marriage, whether entered into within or outside of Florida.

By this court's reasoning, since Michael Kantaras was born a female, nothing (including surgery, gender reassignment, hormonal treatments, etc.) thereafter could legally be said to have made Michael a man. Thus, under the 1977 statute, Michael was never legally married to Linda. But even if he had been, that marriage would not be recognized by the state after 1997. As a result, the court voided Michael's divorce and granted Linda's petition for an annulment.

The Court of Appeal decision did not reach the issue of the validity of Michael's adoption of Matthew. If allowed to stand, that court's ruling that Michael is not a man would, however, appear to void the adoption as well as the marriage. Since the appeals court has held that Michael is and always has been a woman, and Florida law bars same-sex couples from adopting a child, it follows that Michael never legally adopted Matthew. Moreover, since Michael never adopted, and under current law cannot adopt, Irina, he is not legally her father either.

The appeals court stated explicitly that its decision did not reverse the trial judge's decision on custody but also made it clear that it was remanding the case to the trial court for a new determination on that issue:

> Our holding that the marriage is void . . . does not take into consid-
> eration the best interests of the children involved in this case. While
> we recognize that the trial judge went to great lengths to determine
> the best interests of the children, the issue of deciding primary
> residential custody was dependent on the trial court's conclusion
> that the marriage was valid. We do not attempt to undertake a
> determination of the legal status of the children resulting from our
> conclusion that the marriage is void. The legal status of the children
> and the parties' property rights will be issues for the trial court to
> examine in the first instance on remand.[43]

In early 2005, the Florida Supreme Court declined (without written opinion) to accept Michael's petition for review, thus leaving intact the appeals court's judgment.[44] The bad news for Michael Kantaras and perhaps the children as well is that when the trial court re-confronts the issue of custody and visitation, as directed by the appeals court, Michael will in all likelihood have no legal standing to seek custody. Since legally he was and still is a woman, he was never married to the children's mother and was never legally their father, biological or adoptive. Having no direct blood relationship or legal tie to the children, he would seem to have no legal claim whatsoever to custody of—or even visitation with—the children he has been a father to throughout their lives.

Ironically, under current Florida laws, including the Defense of Marriage Act, if Michael ever wants to "remarry" in that state, he will have to marry a man, thus committing himself to the very kind of relationship (same-sex marriage) the Defense of Marriage Act was designed to prevent.

EPILOGUE

It is impossible to generalize from a mere twenty cases to the way psychological issues are handled by the legal system as a whole. That problem is compounded when so many cases, including many of those in this book, involve high-profile trials with famous or infamous litigants, leading attorneys, renowned expert witnesses, and intense media scrutiny. Still, despite certain extraordinary aspects that made these cases fascinating, in many ways they are not unlike countless others in which the legal system is informed (or sometimes misinformed) by psychology and related behavioral sciences.

What, if any, broader lessons can we learn from these great cases in law and psychology? The first, it would seem, is that over the past half-century psychology has become an essential and ever-expanding fixture in our system of justice. Whereas psychologists and psychiatrists were once involved primarily, if not exclusively, in traditional areas of the law (e.g., criminal responsibility, competence to stand trial, and the assessment of psychological harm), these twenty cases illustrate that the involvement of mental health professionals in the legal system now spans many other areas. Among the more recent legal arenas in which psychologists and psychiatrists have brought their skills to bear are cases involving profiling unknown criminal suspects, predicting dangerousness, assessing the best interests of the child, and psychological autopsies. Many of these applications were unheard of fifty years ago.

Perhaps a second point to be taken from the cases in this book is that psychology remains a "soft" science, the inexact nature of which is subject to controversy if not exploitation in an intensely adversarial system of justice. As a number of the cases examined here make clear, expert psychological opinions are often in conflict. Sometimes it appears that such conflict is the result of attorneys using "hired guns," experts paid to give testimony that supports one side of the case. In other instances, it appears that such conflicts are more likely the result of genuine differences of opinion within the relevant professions, differences that are not unreasonable given the often subjective nature of psychology and the other behavioral sciences. In our view, the cases we have discussed generally demonstrate that, despite the relatively "soft" nature of the science, expert psychological testimony can be, and usually is, reasonably objective and that "hired guns" or experts who sell their testimony to whomever wants to pay are the rare exception, rather than the rule.

A theme that emerges in many of these cases is how the courtroom setting often becomes an arena where competing psychological theories and opinions are scrutinized under the close eye of judges, juries, and the public. Some cases involve one psychological expert offering an opinion about the validity of a particular method of research or evaluation, followed by another expert who offers a critique of the expert's methods or a completely different theory or perspective. Is this form of scientific debating merely the soft sciences airing their dirty laundry about unresolved principles or theories? We do not think so. Rather, judges and juries, and even the laws of evidence governing expert testimony, appear to recognize that reasonable experts from the same field can have different opinions. The challenge, of course, is for the process of direct testimony and cross-examination to bring out the prevailing opinion that will influence the final outcome.

The third lesson is that the relationship of psychology to the legal system is not always a harmonious one. As these cases illustrate, the modern legal system would be hard pressed to ignore input from psychology and psychological experts. Indeed, as the law has evolved in many of the areas covered in this book (as well as in even more areas not covered here), such input is now virtually if not literally required. Still, as can be seen in a number of these cases, even where psychological input comes from honest and well-intentioned experts, there is sometimes serious question as to whether such input has actually helped or hindered the justice system. Our conclusion in that regard is that, on the whole, these cases vividly and sometimes powerfully illustrate the salutary influence psychology has on the way the law resolves complicated issues dealing with the human mind and behavior.

Perhaps the final lesson worth noting here is that while most of the cases we examined in this book have been fully resolved, most of the psychological issues they raised so dramatically remain unresolved and will continue to command the attention of psychologists, the courts, the public, and the media in the decades ahead. Indeed if the history of law and psychology in the last fifty years recounted in these cases is an indicator of the future—and we believe it is—we expect to see a continued and rapid growth in the role played by psychology in the legal system. Issues such as criminal profiling; mental illness and retardation; prediction of dangerousness; psychological autopsy; child custody; or the reliability of eyewitness, confession, and repressed memory evidence are raised in countless civil and criminal cases that make their way through the courts on a daily basis. Most of these cases are ordinary in the sense that they do not draw the kind of public fascination associated with the cases chronicled in this book. However, given the seemingly endless and generally appropriate creativity of lawyers and the courts in fashioning new claims and defenses and the steady and growing stream of psychological research into these and other legal issues, there can be little doubt that there are many more great cases in law and psychology to come.

NOTES

INTRODUCTION

1. Elizabeth Frost-Knappman and David S. Shrager, *A Concise Encyclopedia of Legal Quotations* (New York: Barnes & Noble Books, 1998), 80.
2. See, e.g., Charles Patrick Ewing, "Yes: Good Lawyering Can Weed Out Unscientific Testimony," *American Bar Association Journal*, 83, 76; Margaret A. Hagen, *Whores of the Court: The Fraud of Psychiatric Testimony and the Rape of American Justice* (New York: Regan Books), 199.

CHAPTER 1
GEORGE METESKY *Profiling the "Mad Bomber"*

1. See, e.g., "Profilers Say Sniper Feasts on Attention; Police Statements Could Provoke Killer," *Washington Post* (October 13, 2002): A22.
2. Brent Turvey, *Criminal Profiling* (San Diego, Calif.: Academic Press, 1999); Paul Britton, *The Jigsaw Man* (London: Corgi Books, 1997).
3. J. R. Cochran, "Fair Play George Metesky," *New York Daily News* (October 27, 1999): 13; James A. Brussel, *Casebook of a Crime Psychiatrist* (New York: Grove Press: 1968), 14.
4. Ibid., 15–16.
5. Ibid., 17.
6. Ibid., 18.

7. Troy Lennon, "Profile of a Bomber," *Daily Telegraph* (Sydney, Australia), January 7, 2002.

8. Brussel, *Casebook of a Crime Psychiatrist*, 21–22.

9. Charles Delafuente, "Recalling the Mad Bomber, Whose Rampage Shook New York," *New York Times* (September 10, 2004): B1.

10. Lynn Bixby, " 'Mad Bomber' of Waterbury Terrorized New York for 17 Years," *The Hartford Currant* (July 2, 1995): A6.

11. Delafuente, "Recalling the Mad Bomber."

12. Jennifer Warren and Richard C. Paddock, "Blackmail Can Lead to a Terrorist's Downfall," *Los Angeles Times* (September 24, 1995): A3.

13. Lennon, "Profile of a Bomber."

14. V. A. Musetto, "The Man Who Hated Con Ed," *New York Post* (November 16, 2001): 15A.

15. Brussel, *Casebook of a Crime Psychiatrist*, 48–52, 59.

16. Ibid., 13–14.

17. Ibid., 36.

18. Ibid.

19. Ibid., 37.

20. Ibid., 38–39.

21. Ibid., 47–48.

22. Ibid., 49.

23. Ibid., 55–60.

24. Ibid., 60.

25. Turvey, *Criminal Profiling*.

CHAPTER 2

LEE HARVEY OSWALD *The Formative Years of an Assassin*

1. *The Warren Commission Report: Report of the President's Commission on the Assassination of President John F. Kennedy* (New York: St Martin's Press, 1964).

2. *Final Report of the Select Committee on Assassinations* (Washington: Government Printing Office, 1979).

3. *Warren Commission Report*.

4. *Final Report of the Select Committee on Assassinations*.

5. Gerald Posner, *Case Closed: Lee Harvey Oswald and the Assassination of JFK* (New York: Random House, 1993).

6. *Warren Commission Report*.

7. Laurence Steinberg and Robert G. Schwartz, "Developmental Psychology Goes to Court," in *Youth on Trial: A Developmental Perspective on Juvenile Justice*, ed. Thomas Grisso and Robert G. Schwartz (Chicago: University of Chicago Press, 2000), 9–31.

8. Ibid.

9. Thomas Grisso, *Forensic Evaluation of Juveniles* (Sarasota, Fla.: Professional Resource Press, 1998).

10. *Kent v. United States*, 383 U.S. 541 (1966); *In re Gault*, 387 U.S. 1 (1967).

11. Diane Holloway, *The Mind of Oswald: Accused Assassin of President John F. Kennedy* (Victoria, B.C.: Trafford, 2000), 2.

12. *Warren Commission Report.*

13. Ibid.

14. Ibid.

15. Ibid., 380.

16. *Warren Commission Report.*

17. Posner, *Case Closed.*

18. Stephen J. Lally, "Should Human Figure Drawings Be Admitted into Court?" *Journal of Personality Assessment* 76 (2001): 135–149; Joseph T. McCann, "Projective Assessment of Personality in Forensic Settings," in *Comprehensive Handbook of Psychological Assessment: Vol. 2: Personality Assessment,* ed. Michel Herson (New York: John Wiley, 2004), 562–572.

19. *Warren Commission Report,* 381.

20. Posner, *Case Closed.*

21. From the testimony of Dr. Renatus Hartogs as cited in Posner, *Case Closed,* 12.

22. Donald W. Hastings, "The Psychiatry of Presidential Assassination: Part IV: Truman and Kennedy," *Lancet* (July 1965): 294–301.

23. Ibid., 296. Although Hastings does not list Hartogs by name, it can be readily assumed that he was talking about Hartogs since no other "New York psychiatrist" is known to have evaluated Oswald.

24. David A. Rothstein, "Presidential Assassination Syndrome," *Archives of General Psychiatry* 11 (1964): 245–254.

25. Robert A. Fein and Bryan Vossekuil, "Assassination in America: A Study of Assassins and Near Lethal Approachers," *Journal of Forensic Sciences* 44 (March 1999): 321–333.

26. Holloway, *Mind of Oswald,* 97–98.

27. David A. Rothstein, "Presidential Assassination Syndrome II: Application to Lee Harvey Oswald," *Archives of General Psychiatry* 15 (1966): 260–266.

28. Ibid., 265.

29. *Warren Commission Report,* 382.

30. Ibid.

CHAPTER 3

PATRICIA HEARST *Uncommon Victim or Common Criminal?*

1. William Carlsen, "The Kidnapping That Gripped the Nation," *San Francisco Chronicle* (February 4, 1999): A1.

2. Ibid.

3. Patricia Campbell Hearst, *Every Secret Thing* (New York: Doubleday, 1982), 42.

4. Ibid., 63.

5. Ibid., 118–120.

6. Ibid., 147.

7. Ibid.

8. Ibid., 148.

9. Marilyn Baker, *Exclusive: The Inside Story of Patricia Hearst and the SLA* (New York: Macmillan, 1974), 169.

10. Hearst, *Every Secret Thing*, 156.

11. Shana Alexander, *Anyone's Daughter* (New York: Viking Press, 1979), 127.

12. Ibid.

13. Ibid.

14. Ibid., 365.

15. "Trial Ends," *Facts on File World News Digest* (March 20, 1976): 201, B1.

16. Michael Taylor, "Haunted by Past; She Still Faces Legal Troubles, Decades after Her Terrorist Days," *San Francisco Chronicle* (October 7, 1999): A3.

17. Hearst, *Every Secret Thing*, 85.

18. Ibid.

19. Ibid., 86–87.

20. Ibid., 96.

21. Ibid., 97.

22. Ibid., 158.

23. Alexander, *Anyone's Daughter*, 70.

24. Hearst, *Every Secret Thing*, 377.

25. Ibid., 378.

26. Ibid.

27. *United States v. Patricia Hearst*, trial transcript, reproduced in *The Trial of Patty Hearst* (San Francisco: The Great Fidelity Press, 1976), 257.

28. Ibid., 257–258.

29. Ibid., 258.

30. Alexander, *Anyone's Daughter*, 70.

31. Ibid.

32. Trial transcript, *Trial of Patty Hearst*, 263.

33. Ibid., 294.

34. Ibid.

35. Ibid.

36. Ibid.

37. Ibid., 301.

38. Ibid., 302.

39. Ibid., 301.

40. Ibid., 324–325.

41. Ibid., 437.

42. Ibid., 438.

43. Ibid., 591.

44. Ibid., 488.

45. Ibid., 520.
46. Ibid., 519.
47. Ibid., 527.
48. Ibid., 556.
49. Hearst, *Every Secret Thing*, 443.
50. Ibid., 401.

CHAPTER 4
THE GUILDFORD FOUR *"You Did It, So Why Not Confess?"*

1. Alan M. Dershowitz, *Why Terrorism Works: Understanding the Threat, Responding to the Challenge* (New Haven, Conn.: Yale University Press, 2002).
2. See, for example, Seth F. Kreimer, "Too Close to the Rack and the Screw: Constitutional Constraints on Torture in the War on Terror," *University of Pennsylvania Journal of Constitutional Law* 6 (2002): 278–325; Sanford Levinson, "'Precommitment' and 'Postcommitment': The Ban on Torture in the Wake of September 11," *Texas Law Review* 81 (2003): 2013–2053; and John T. Parry, "What Is Torture, Are We Doing It, and What If We Are?" *University of Pittsburgh Law Review* 64 (2003): 237–262.
3. Tim Pat Coogan, *The IRA*, rev. ed. (New York: Palgrave, 2000).
4. Bob Woffinden, *Miscarriages of Justice* (London: Hodder & Stoughten, 1987).
5. Ibid.
6. Ibid.
7. Ibid., 1.
8. Ibid.
9. Gisli H. Gudjonsson and James A. C. MacKeith, "The Guildford Four and the Birmingham Six," in *The Psychology of Interrogations, Confessions, and Testimony*, ed. Gisli Gudjonsson (Chichester, England: John Wiley, 1992), 260–273.
10. Woffinden, *Miscarriages of Justice*.
11. Ibid.
12. Gudjonsson and MacKeith, "Guildford Four and the Birmingham Six."
13. Ibid.
14. Ibid.
15. Ibid.
16. Ibid.
17. Woffinden, *Miscarriages of Justice*.
18. Ibid.
19. Gudjonsson and MacKeith, "Guildford Four and the Birmingham Six."
20. Ibid.
21. Ibid.
22. Ibid., 265.
23. Ibid.
24. Ibid.

25. Ibid.
26. Glenn Frankel, "British Court Overturns Convictions in IRA Case," *Washington Post* (October 20, 1989): 36A.
27. Ibid.
28. "Blair Apologises to Guildford Four," *BBC News*, June 6, 2000, http://news.bbc.co.uk/1/hi/northern_ireland/778940.stm (accessed March 10, 2003).
29. "Guildford Four Members Demand Settlement," *BBC News*, October 19, 1999, http://news.bbc.co.uk/1/hi/northern_ireland/478929.stm (accessed March 10, 2003).
30. "Blair Apologises to Guildford Four."
31. Woffinden, *Miscarriages of Justice*.

CHAPTER 5

PROSENJIT PODDAR AND TATIANA TARASOFF
Where the Public Peril Begins

1. *Tarasoff v. Regents of the University of California*, 17 Cal. 3d 425; 551 P. 2d 334; 131 Cal. Rptr. 14 (Sup. Ct. Cal., 1976).
2. *People v. Poddar*, 10 Cal. 3d 750 (Sup. Ct. Cal., 1974).
3. Ibid.
4. Leon VandeCreek and Samuel Knapp, *Tarasoff and Beyond: Legal and Clinical Considerations in the Treatment of Life-Endangering Patients* (Sarasota, Fla.: Professional Resource Press, 1993).
5. Ibid.
6. Ibid.
7. *Tarasoff v. Regents of the University of California*.
8. Alan A. Stone, "The Tarasoff Decisions: Suing Psychotherapists to Safeguard Society," *Harvard Law Review* 90 (1976): 358–378.
9. VandeCreek and Knapp, *Tarasoff and Beyond*.
10. *People v. Poddar*.
11. Fillmore Buckner and Marvin Firestone, " 'Where the Public Peril Begins': Twenty-five Years After Tarasoff," *Journal of Legal Medicine* 21 (2000): 187–222.
12. Ibid.
13. Buckner and Firestone, " 'Where the Public Peril Begins.' "
14. Ibid., 195.
15. Ibid.
16. Ibid.
17. *Tarasoff v. Regents of the University of California*.
18. John G. Fleming and Bruce Maximov, "The Patient or His Victim: The Therapist's Dilemma," *California Law Review* 62 (1974): 1025–1068.
19. Stone, "Tarasoff Decisions."
20. Fleming and Maximov, "The Patient or His Victim," 1032.

21. Ibid., 1051–1052.
22. Stone, "Tarasoff Decisions," 377.
23. *Tarasoff v. Regents of the University of California*, 345.
24. Ibid., 347.
25. VandeCreek and Knapp, *Tarasoff and Beyond*.
26. *Peck v. Counseling Service of Addision County*, 499 A. 2d 422 (Vt. 1985).
27. *Brady v. Hopper*, 570 F. Supp. 1333 (D. Colo. 1983).
28. VandeCreek and Knapp, *Tarasoff and Beyond*.
29. Buckner and Firestone, " 'Where the Public Peril Begins.' "
30. Ibid.
31. Stone, "Tarasoff Decisions."

CHAPTER 6

DAN WHITE *The Myth of the Twinkie Defense*

1. Associated Press, "Assault Defense: Tea Made Me Do It," *St. Petersburg Times,*
   July 12, 2003, http://www.sptimes.com/2003/07/12/State/Assault_defense_Tea_
   .shtml (accessed September 5, 2005).
2. Alan M. Dershowitz, *The Abuse Excuse and Other Cop-Outs, Sob Stories, and
   Evasions of Responsibility* (Boston: Little, Brown, 1994), 339.
3. Mike Weiss, *Double Play: The San Francisco City Hall Killings* (Reading, Mass.:
   Addison-Wesley, 1984), 209.
4. Ibid., 215.
5. Ibid., 218.
6. Trial transcript, *People v. Daniel James White* (Superior Court of San Francisco)
   No. 98663 (1979).
7. Ibid., statement of Daniel White to San Francisco Police Inspector Frank Falzon.
8. Ibid.
9. *People v. Gorshen*, 336 P.2d 492 (Cal. 1959); *People v. Wells*, 202 P.2d 53 (Cal.
   1969); *People v. Wolff*, 394 P.2d 959 (Cal. 1964); *People v. Conley*, 411 P.2d 911
   (Cal. 1966).
10. Cal. Penal Code 187 (as enacted in 1872).
11. *People v. Wells.*
12. *People v. Conley.*
13. Trial transcript, *People v. Daniel James White.*
14. Ibid.
15. "Twinkie Shrink Stabbed," *ABC News*, July 12, 2003, http://www.abcnews.
    go.com (accessed July 1, 2004).
16. *People v. Daniel James White.*
17. The Straight Dope Science Advisory Board, "Did a Murderer Escape Punish-
    ment Using the 'Twinkie Defense'?" November 15, 2000, http://www
    .straightdope.com/mailbag/mdimcapacity.html (accessed November 9, 2004).
18. Trial transcript, *People v. Daniel James White.*

19. Ibid.
20. Ibid.
21. Ibid.
22. "The Case That Shocked the City," *The Recorder* (January 31, 1996): 1.
23. Ibid.
24. *People v. White*, 117 Cal. App. 3d 270 (Cal. Ct. of Appeal, 1981): 278.
25. Ibid.
26. Cynthia Gorney, "The Legacy of Dan White; A Stronger Gay Community Looks Back on the Tumult," *Washington Post* (January 4, 1984): D1.
27. Chris Carlsson, "White Night Riot," http://www.shapingsf.org/ezine/gay/files/whitengt.htm (accessed November 10, 2004).
28. Carol Pogash, "Myth of the 'Twinkie Defense': The Verdict in the Dan White Case Wasn't Based on His Ingestion of Junk Food," *San Francisco Chronicle*, November 23, 2003, http://www.sfgate.com (accessed November 10, 2004).
29. Ibid.
30. *People v. White*, 281.
31. Ibid., 282.
32. Ibid.
33. Act of September 19, 1981, ch. 404, sec. 1, 1981 Cal. Stat. 1591, 1592, codified at Cal. Penal Code sec. 28 (West 2002).
34. Mike Weiss, "Mayhem Shadowed Therapist's Life; Expert on Relationships Examines Why Many of His Have Ended Badly," *San Francisco Chronicle* (May 22, 2001): A1.
35. "Twinkie Shrink Stabbed."
36. Andrew Gumbel, "Twinkie, a Chocolate Cake that Leaves Murder and Mayhem in its Wake," *The Independent of London* (October 11, 2000): 16.
37. Pervaiz Shallwani, "Ex-Wife of 'Twinkie Defense' Doctor Found Dead; Woman Was Suspected of Stabbing Psychiatrist," *San Francisco Chronicle* (October 9, 2000): A19.
38. Pogash, "Myth of the 'Twinkie Defense.'"

CHAPTER 7
CAMERON HOOKER *Judging the Experts?*

1. "Elizabeth Smart Found Alive," CNN.com, http://www.cnn.com/2003/US/West/03/12/smart.kidnapping/ (accessed November 11, 2004).
2. Ibid.
3. Katherine Ramsland, "The Initial Revelation," in *The Case of the Seven-Year Sex Slave*, http://www.crimelibrary.com/criminal_mind/psychology/sex_slave/index.html?sect=19 (accessed November 11, 2004).
4. Christine McGuire and Carla Norton, *Perfect Victim* (New York: Dell, 1988).
5. Ibid.
6. Ibid.

7. Katherine Ramsland, "Over the Border into Trouble," in *The Case of the Seven-Year Sex Slave*, http://www.crimelibrary.com/criminal_mind/psychology/sex_slave/2.html?sect=19 (accessed November 11, 2004).
8. *People v. Hooker*, 198 Cal. App. 3d 1365; 244 Cal. Rptr. 337; 1988 Cal App. LEXIS 146 (Ct. App. Cal., 1st Dist., Div. 4, 1988). The subsequent history of this case reveals that on June 9, 1999, the Reporter of Decisions was directed not to publish the opinion. Available at http://www.courtinfo.ca.gov/opinions/.
9. McGuire and Norton, *Perfect Victim*.
10. Ibid.
11. Ibid., 78.
12. Katherine Ramsland, "Time to Leave," in *The Case of the Seven-Year Sex Slave*, http://www.crimelibrary.com/criminal_mind/psychology/sex_slave/9.html?sect=19 (accessed November 11, 2004).
13. *People v. Hooker*.
14. Ibid., 5.
15. McGuire and Norton, *Perfect Victim*, 290.
16. Ibid., 291.
17. Ibid., 331.
18. Ibid.
19. *People v. Hooker*, 11.
20. McGuire and Norton, *Perfect Victim*, 358.
21. Ibid., 362.
22. *People v. Hooker*.
23. Ibid., 8.
24. Ibid.
25. Katherine Ramsland, "Hooker's Defense," in *The Case of the Seven-Year Sex Slave*, http://www.crimelibrary.com/criminal_mind/psychology/sex_slave/12.html?sect=19 (accessed November 11, 2004).

CHAPTER 8
JOHN W. HINCKLEY, JR. *Shooting for the Stars*

1. Douglas Linder, "The Hinckley Trial," http://www.law.umkc.edu/faculty/projects/ftrials/hinckley/hinckleymono.HTM (accessed September 26, 2005).
2. Peter W. Low, John Calvin Jeffries, and Richard J. Bonnie, *The Trial of John W. Hinckley, Jr.* (Mineola, N.Y.: Foundation Press, 1986), 94.
3. Lincoln Kaplan, *The Insanity Defense and the Trial of John W. Hinckley, Jr.* (Boston: Godine, 1984), 14.
4. Ibid., 11–12.
5. *M'Naughten's Case*, 8 Eng. Rep. 718 (1843).
6. American Law Institute, *Model Penal Code* (New York: American Law Institute, 1955), Section 4.01.
7. Kaplan, *Insanity Defense*, 59.

8. Ibid.

9. Low, Jeffries, and Bonnie, *Trial of John W. Hinckley, Jr.*, 28.

10. Kaplan, *Insanity Defense*, 85–86.

11. Low, Jeffries, and Bonnie, *Trial of John W. Hinckley, Jr.*, 53–54.

12. Ibid., 61, 80–81.

13. Douglas Linder, "Use of the Insanity Defense in the Aftermath of the Hinckley Trial," http://www.law.umkc.edu/faculty/projects/ftrials/hinckley/backlash.htm (accessed September 5, 2005).

14. Ibid.

15. George F. Will, "Insanity and Success," *Washington Post* (June 23, 1982): A27.

16. "Hinckley Verdict," *The MacNeil Lehrer Report* (June 22, 1982): Transcript no. 1757.

17. 18 USCS § 17 (Added Oct. 12, 1984, P.L. 98-473).

18. Federal Rules of Evidence, Rule 704(b), as amended 12 Oct. 1984, P.L. 98-473.

19. See, e.g., Insanity Defense FAQs, http://www.pbs.org/wgbh/pages/frontline/shows/crime/trial/faqs.html (accessed September 5, 2005).

20. Douglas Linder, "John Hinckley at St. Elizabeth's Hospital: Still Seeking His Freedom," http://www.law.umkc.edu/faculty/projects/ftrials/hinckley/hinckleyeliz.HTM (accessed September 5, 2005).

CHAPTER 9
JUDAS PRIEST *A Message in the Music*

1. Cy Ryan, "Mother Says She Never Knew Her Son Listened to Judas Priest," *United Press International, BC Cycle* (July 18, 1990).

2. *Vance v. Judas Priest*, 1990 WL 130920 (Nev. Dist. Ct., 1990), 17.

3. Chuck Philips, "Trial to Focus on Issue of Subliminal Messages in Rock," *Los Angeles Times* (July 16, 1990): F1.

4. Ryan, "Mother Says She Never Knew."

5. Ibid.

6. Philips, "Trial to Focus."

7. Ibid.

8. Ibid.

9. Matt Neufeld, "Judas Priest Rocks Out After Its Exoneration," *Washington Times* (October 23, 1990): E1.

10. Richard Harrington, "In Defense of Heavy Metal: The Trials of Rob Halford, Soft-spoken Lead Screamer of Judas Priest," *Washington Post* (January 6, 1991): G1.

11. Pamela Marsden Capps, "Rock on Trial: Subliminal Message Liability," *Columbia Business Law Review* (1991): 27–50.

12. Berta Blen, "To Hear or Not to Hear: A Legal Analysis of Subliminal Communication Technology in the Arts," *Rutgers Law Review* 44 (1992): 871–922.

13. Ibid.

14. *Vance v. Judas Priest*, 8.

15. Ibid., 11.
16. Ibid.
17. Ibid., 12.
18. Timothy Moore, "Scientific Consensus and Expert Testimony: Lessons from the Judas Priest Trial," *Skeptical Inquirer* 20 (June 1996): 32.
19. Ibid.
20. *Vance v. Judas Priest*, 12.
21. Ibid.
22. Moore, "Scientific Consensus and Expert Testimony."
23. *Vance v. Judas Priest*, 14.
24. Ibid.
25. *Vance v. Judas Priest*, 1990 WL 130921 (Nev. Dist. Ct., 1990).
26. Moore, "Scientific Consensus and Expert Testimony."
27. Capps, "Rock on Trial."
28. Ibid., 48.
29. Ibid.
30. Ibid., 49.
31. Neufeld, "Judas Priest Rocks Out After Its Exoneration."

CHAPTER 10
JOHN DEMJANJUK *Is He "Ivan the Terrible"?*

1. Gail S. Goodman, Allison D. Redlich, Jianjian Qin, Simora Ghetti, Kimberly S. Tyda, Jennifer M. Schaaf, and Annette Hahn, "Evaluating Eyewitness Testimony in Adults and Children," in *The Handbook of Forensic Psychology*, 2nd ed., ed. Alan K. Hess and Irving B. Weiner (New York: John Wiley, 1999), 218–272.
2. Eric Lichtblau, "Death Camp Suspect Loses His Citizenship," *Los Angeles Times* (February 22, 2002): 16A.
3. George D. Moffett, "Israeli Judges Convict Former Auto Worker of Being 'Ivan the Terrible,'" *Christian Science Monitor* (April 19, 1988): 7.
4. Debbie Nathan and Jan Haaken, "From Incest to Ivan the Terrible: Science and the Trials of Memory," *Tikkun* 11 (1996): 29.
5. Ibid.
6. Ethan Bronner, "Israel to Review Demjanjuk Verdict: Files May Reveal Mistaken Identity," *The Boston Globe* (December 20, 1991): 36.
7. "Demjanjuk's Alleged Nazi Past to be on Trial Again," *Los Angeles Times* (May 27, 2001): 20A.
8. Elizabeth Loftus and Katherine Ketcham, *Witness for the Defense: The Accused, the Eyewitness, and the Expert Who Puts Memory on Trial* (New York: St. Martin's Press, 1991).
9. Ken Myers, "'Ivan'—or Just Plain John?" *National Law Journal* (April 6, 1987): 6A.

10. Ibid.
11. Willem A. Wagenaar, *Identifying Ivan: A Case Study in Legal Psychology* (New York: Harvester, 1988): 96.
12. Goodman et al., "Evaluating Eyewitness Testimony," 241.
13. Loftus and Ketcham, *Witness for the Defense*, 218.
14. Ibid.
15. Ibid.
16. Nathan and Haaken, "From Incest to Ivan the Terrible."
17. Goodman et al., "Evaluating Eyewitness Testimony."
18. Nathan and Haaken, "From Incest to Ivan the Terrible."
19. Loftus and Ketcham, *Witness for the Defense*, 211.
20. Peter Tague, "How Often Do Witnesses Make False Identifications in Criminal Trials?" *Chicago Daily Law Bulletin* (July 10, 1991): 2.
21. Loftus and Ketcham, *Witness for the Defense*, 212.
22. Ibid.
23. Aldert Vrij, "Psychological Factors in Eyewitness Testimony," in *Psychology and Law: Truthfulness, Accuracy, and Credibility*, ed. Amina Memon, Aldert Vrij, and Ray Bull (London: McGraw-Hill, 1998), 105–123.
24. Nathan and Haaken, "From Incest to Ivan the Terrible."
25. Tom Teicholz, *The Trial of Ivan the Terrible: State of Israel vs. John Demjanjuk* (New York: St. Martin's Press, 1990).
26. Ibid.
27. Ibid.
28. Ibid.
29. Ibid., 258.
30. Ibid.
31. Ibid.
32. Ibid., 260.
33. Ibid., 262.
34. Wagenaar, *Identifying Ivan*, 151.
35. Ibid.
36. Ibid., 171.
37. Bronner, "Israel to Review Demjanjuk Verdict."
38. Teicholz, *Trial of Ivan the Terrible*.
39. Ibid.
40. Joshua Muravchik, "Demjanjuk: A Summing-up; Reevaluation of Alleged War Criminal John Demjanjuk," *Commentary* 103 (April 1997): 46.

CHAPTER 11

THE USS IOWA *Equivocating on Death*

1. Kevin Helliker, "How an Autopsy Could Save Your Life," *The Wall Street Journal* (June 3, 2003): D1.

2. Charles C. Thompson, *A Glimpse of Hell: The Explosion on the USS Iowa and Its Cover-up* (New York: W. W. Norton, 1999).

3. Molly Moore, "Navy's USS *Iowa* Probe Called Flawed; Accusation Against Hartwig Unsupported, Hill Panel Concludes," *The Washington Post* (March 3, 1990): A14.

4. Thompson, *Glimpse of Hell*, 16.

5. Ibid., 57.

6. Ibid., 74.

7. Ibid., 84–88.

8. Ibid., 101.

9. Ibid., 110, 124.

10. Ibid., 135.

11. Ibid., 292–294.

12. John Lancaster, "*Iowa* Sailor Exonerated in Blast; Navy Repudiates Investigation Results," *The Washington Post* (October 18, 1991): A1.

13. Thompson, *Glimpse of Hell*, 245.

14. Stephen G. Michaud and Roy Hazelwood, *The Evil That Men Do* (New York: St. Martin's Press, 1998).

15. Lancaster, "*Iowa* Sailor Exonerated in Blast."

16. Thompson, *Glimpse of Hell*, 76.

17. Dave Moniz, "'I've Known in My Heart All Along': Navy Apology Vindicates Survivor of USS *Iowa* Explosion," *The Houston Chronicle* (October 18, 1991): A16.

18. Thompson, *Glimpse of Hell*, 252.

19. Ibid., 92.

20. Ibid.

21. Ibid.

22. Michaud and Hazelwood, *Evil That Men Do*, 155–156.

23. Ibid., 156.

24. *Hearing of the House Armed Services Subcommittee on Investigations of the House Armed Services Committee.* Transcript of proceedings, December 21, 1989.

25. Thompson, *Glimpse of Hell*, 358–360.

26. *Hearing of the House Armed Services Subcommittee.*

27. Ibid.

28. Ibid.

29. Ibid.

30. Ibid.

31. Norman Poythress, Randy K. Otto, Jack Darkes, and Laura Starr, "APA's Expert Panel in the Congressional Review of the USS *Iowa* Incident," *American Psychologist* 48 (1993): 8–15.

32. Thompson, *Glimpse of Hell*, 333.

33. Michaud and Hazelwood, *Evil That Men Do*.

34. Ibid.

35. Ibid., 157.
36. Randy K. Otto, Norman Poythress, Laura Starr, and Jack Darkes, "An Empirical Study of the Reports of APA's Peer Review Panel in the Congressional Review of the U.S.S. *Iowa* Incident," *Journal of Personality Assessment* 61 (1993): 425–442.
37. Poythress, Otto, Darkes, and Starr, "APA's Expert Panel."
38. Ibid.
39. Moore, "Navy's USS *Iowa* Probe Called Flawed."
40. Moniz, "'I've Known in My Heart All Along.'"
41. Thompson, *Glimpse of Hell*, 394.
42. Ibid.
43. Michaud and Hazelwood, *Evil That Men Do*, 159.
44. Ibid. Although it does not appear to be noted by whom the blast was intentionally caused.
45. Susanne M. Schafer, "Navy Apologizes to Sailor's Family, Admits *Iowa* Blast Cause Unknown," *The Commercial Appeal* (October 18, 1991): A2.

CHAPTER 12
JEFFREY DAHMER *Serial Murder, Necrophilia, and Cannibalism*

1. Anne E. Schwartz, *The Man Who Could Not Kill Enough* (New York: Birch Lane Press, 1992), 65–66.
2. American Psychiatric Association, *Diagnostic and Statistical Manual of Mental Disorders*, 4th ed. (Washington, D.C.: American Psychiatric Association, 1994), 638.
3. Schwartz, *Man Who Could Not Kill Enough*, 64.
4. Ibid., 66.
5. Ibid.
6. Robert J. Dvorchak and Lisa Holewa, *Milwaukee Massacre* (New York: Dell, 1991), 92.
7. Schwartz, *Man Who Could Not Kill Enough*, 69.
8. Richard W. Jaeger and M. William Balousek, *Massacre in Milwaukee* (Oregon, Wisc.: Waubesa Press, 1991), 59.
9. Ed Bauman, *Step into My Parlor* (Chicago: Bonus Books, 1991), 31.
10. Schwartz, *Man Who Could Not Kill Enough*, 91.
11. Bauman, *Step into My Parlor*, 31.
12. Dvorchak and Holewa, *Milwaukee Massacre*, 117.
13. Ibid., 118.
14. Jaeger and Balousek, *Massacre in Milwaukee*, 23.
15. John Lloyd, "Humanity Takes Just One Small Step to Another Golgotha," *Scotland on Sunday* (March 17, 1996): 16.
16. Brian Masters, *The Shrine of Jeffrey Dahmer* (London: Coronet Books, 1993), 247.
17. Ibid., 246–247.
18. Ibid., 227.

19. Rogers Worthington, "Dahmer Judge to Call Own Experts; Court Forensic Specialists Could Be Pivotal to Jury Decision," *Chicago Tribune* (February 6, 1992): 6C.

20. Jerry C. Smith, "Dahmer Personality," *United Press International, BC Cycle* (February 15, 1992).

21. Associated Press, "Question of Self-Control May Decide Dahmer Case," *New York Times* (February 9, 1992): 23.

22. Masters, *Shrine of Jeffrey Dahmer*, 246–247.

23. Maureen O'Donnell, "Four Experts Call Dahmer Sane; Three Disagree," *Chicago Sun-Times* (February 14, 1992): 10.

24. Smith, "Dahmer Personality."

25. Jerry C. Smith, "Psychologist: Dahmer Illness Began in Childhood," *United Press International, BC Cycle* (February 5, 1992).

26. Richard W. Jaeger, "Prosecutor Challenges Psychiatrist's Claims," *Wisconsin State Journal* (February 6, 1992): 1B.

27. Associated Press, "Witness Disputes Dahmer Lobotomies," *Madison Capital Times* (February 6, 1992): 5A.

28. Richard W. Jaeger, "Dahmer Wanted Zombies; Killer's Experiments Explained," *Wisconsin State Journal* (January 19, 1992): 1A.

29. Masters, *Shrine of Jeffrey Dahmer*, 257.

30. Rogers Worthington, "Dahmer Jury Nears Decision Time; Conflicting Testimony about Sanity Complicates Task," *Chicago Tribune* (February 14, 1992): 6C.

31. Ibid.

32. Masters, *Shrine of Jeffrey Dahmer*, 262.

33. Rogers Worthington, "Doctor: Desire, Not Disease, Pushed Dahmer," *Chicago Tribune* (February 13, 1992): 10C.

34. Associated Press, "Dahmer Able to Control Sexual Urges, Psychiatrist Says," *Kitchener-Waterloo Record* (February 14, 1992): A8.

35. Associated Press, "Question of Self-Control," 23.

36. Smith, "Dahmer Personality"; Associated Press, "Witness Disputes."

37. Ibid.

38. Masters, *Shrine of Jeffrey Dahmer*, 252.

39. Ibid.

40. "Dahmer: 'Your Honor. It Is Now Over,'" *Chicago Sun-Times* (February 17, 1992).

41. Michael C. Buelow, "Inmate Charged in Dahmer Slaying," *Chicago Sun-Times* (December 15, 1994): 1.

CHAPTER 13
WOODY ALLEN AND MIA FARROW *A Swing of King Solomon's Sword*

1. Katherine Kuehnle, *Assessing Allegations of Child Sexual Abuse* (Sarasota, Fla: Professional Resource Press, 1996).

2. "Judge Denounces Woody, Mia Keeps Kids, Allen Pays Legal Fees," *The Record* (June 8, 1993): A1.

3. Richard Perez-Pena, "Woody Allen Tells of Affair as Custody Battle Begins," *New York Times* (March 20, 1993): 25.

4. Debra A. Poole and Michael E. Lamb, *Investigative Interviews of Children: A Guide for Helping Professionals* (Washington, D.C.: American Psychological Association, 1998).

5. Tracey L. Miller, "Nanny Says Mia Selective in Taping Abuse Allegation," *United Press International, BC Cycle* (April 5, 1993).

6. Samuel Maull, "Therapist Feared Farrow Wanted to Injure Allen," *Chicago Sun-Times* (March 30, 1993): 2.

7. "Doubting Therapist Fired by Mia Farrow," *The Toronto Star* (March 27, 1993): A20.

8. David Kocieniewski, "Shrink Raps: Doc Knocks Woody and Mia as Parents," *Newsday* (March 31, 1993): 7.

9. Ibid.

10. Ibid.

11. Ibid.

12. Tracey L. Miller, "Psychiatrist: Woody Was Committed to Being a Good Father," *United Press International, BC Cycle* (March 30, 1993).

13. Kocieniewski, "Shrink Raps."

14. Peter Marks, "Yale Study About Allen Flawed, Expert Testifies," *New York Times* (April 28, 1993): B4.

15. Ibid.

16. Ibid.

17. Ibid.

18. Ibid.

19. Ibid.

20. Ibid.

21. Peter Marks, "Allen Loses to Farrow in Bitter Custody Battle," June 8, 1993, http://partners.nytimes.com/books/97/02/23/reviews/farrow-verdict.html (accessed October 5, 2004).

22. Ibid.

23. John J. Goldman, "Farrow Wins Custody of Three Children She, Allen Share," *Los Angeles Times* (June 8, 1993): A1.

24. Peter Marks, "N.Y. Judge, in Scathing Ruling, Rejects Allen's Custody Attempt," *The Houston Chronicle* (June 8, 1993): A7.

25. Ibid.

26. Goldman, "Farrow Wins Custody of Three Children."

CHAPTER 14

GARY AND HOLLY RAMONA *Recovered Memories or False Allegations?*

1. Moira Johnson, *Spectral Evidence* (Boulder, Colo.: Westview Press, 1997), 77.

2. Jane Meredith Adams, "Father Sues Therapists in Abuse Memory Case," *Chi-*

cago Tribune (March 25, 1994): 2N; Cynthia Grant Brown and Elizabeth Mertz, "A Dangerous Direction: Legal Intervention in Sexual Abuse Survivor Therapy," *Harvard Law Review* (January 1996): 556.

3. Johnson, *Spectral Evidence*, 148–149, 163.

4. Ibid., 84.

5. Ibid., 83.

6. Ibid., 98.

7. Ibid.

8. Ibid., 101.

9. Ibid., 102.

10. See Gary M. Ernsdorff and Elizabeth Loftus, "Let Sleeping Memories Lie? Words of Caution about Tolling the Statute of Limitations in Cases of Memory Repression," *Journal of Criminal Law and Criminology* (Spring 1993): 129.

11. *Molien v. Kaiser Foundation Hospitals*, 616 P.2d 813.

12. Ibid., 817.

13. Victoria Slind-Flor, "He Says 'Recovered' Memories Ruined Him," *National Law Journal* (April 18, 1994): A10.

14. *Ramona v. Ramona*, 66 Cal. Rptr. 2d 766, 773.

15. Johnson, *Spectral Evidence*, 257.

16. Katy Butler, "Memory on Trial," *San Francisco Chronicle* (July 24, 1994): 5/Z1.

17. Johnson, *Spectral Evidence*, 259.

18. Ibid.

19. Ibid., 261–262.

20. Ibid., 266.

21. Ibid., 267.

22. Ibid., 269.

23. Ibid., 274.

24. Elizabeth F. Loftus and Jacqueline E. Pickrell, "The Formation of False Memories," *Psychiatric Annals* (1995): 720–725.

25. Johnson, *Spectral Evidence*, 276.

26. Ibid., 278.

27. Ibid.

28. Ibid., 279.

29. Ibid., 281.

30. Ibid.

31. Ibid., 282.

32. Ibid., 284.

33. Ibid., 285.

34. Ibid., 319.

35. Ibid.

36. Ibid., 320.

37. See Lenore Terr, "Childhood Traumas: An Outline and Overview," *American Journal of Psychiatry* (1991): 10–20; Lenore Terr, *Unchained Memories:*

True Stories of Traumatic Memories, Lost and Found (New York: Basic Books, 1994).

38. See Harry N. MacLean, *Once Upon a Time: A True Story of Memory, Murder, and the Law* (New York: HarperCollins, 1993); Mary Curtius, "Man Won't Be Retried in Repressed Murder Case; Prosecutor Says There Is Not Enough Evidence to Reconvict Him of Crime Daughter Recalled Years Later," *Los Angeles Times* (July 3, 1996): A1.

39. Johnson, *Spectral Evidence*, 340.

40. Ibid., 341.

41. Ibid.

42. Ibid.

43. Ibid.

44. Ibid., 342.

45. Ibid., 343.

46. Ibid., 344.

CHAPTER 15
COLIN FERGUSON *A Fool for a Client?*

1. This right is currently codified at 28 USC § 1654 (1994).

2. 422 U.S. 806 (1975) at 819.

3. Ibid., 834.

4. Ibid., 838–839, quoting *Powell v. Alabama*, 287 U.S. 45 (1932).

5. 509 U.S. 389 (1993) at 399–400.

6. Ibid., 412–413.

7. Kevin McCoy, "Clues to the Fury Within Him; Ferguson Was 'Bomb Waiting to Explode,'" *Newsday* (December 9, 1993): 5.

8. "Train Killings Called Bias Crime; Hate Notes Found on Suspect," *Chicago Tribune* (December 9, 1993): N3.

9. Ibid.

10. "Death on the L.I.R.R.," *New York Times* (December 9, 1993): B8.

11. John G. D'Alessandro, Examination Report, *People v. Colin A. Ferguson* (Docket No. 27126, Nassau County Court, December 28, 1993): 6.

12. Robin Topping, "Weighing Competence vs. Sanity," *Newsday* (February 5, 1995): A6.

13. Brief for the Respondent, *People v. Colin A. Ferguson*, 248 A.D.2d 725; 670 N.Y.S.2d 327 (1998): 40.

14. Richard G. Dudley, Jr., M.D., Psychiatric evaluation, *In the Matter of Colin Ferguson* (November 27, 1994): 13.

15. Brief for the Appellant, *People v. Colin A. Ferguson*, 248 A.D.2d 725; 670 N.Y.S.2d 327 (1998): 6.

16. Ibid., 8.

17. Maureen Fan, "Ferguson Lawyers Seek New Test," *Newsday* (August 12, 1994): A23.

18. Ibid.

19. Ibid.

20. Sylvia Adcock. " 'Black Rage' Strategy; New Insanity Defense in LIRR Massacre," *Newsday* (March 15, 1994): 7.

21. Brief for the Respondent, *People v. Colin A. Ferguson*, 248 A.D.2d 725; 670 N.Y.S.2d 327 (1998): 41.

22. Peter Marks, "L.I.R.R. Murderer Argues for Reversal," *New York Times* (March 21, 1995): B5.

23. Brief for the Appellant, *People v. Colin A. Ferguson*, 248 A.D.2d 725; 670 N.Y.S.2d 327 (1998): 37.

24. "Colin Ferguson Defends Himself in Court," *Larry King Live* (February 14, 1995): Transcript 1357-1.

25. Ibid.

26. Richard G. Dudley, Jr., M.D., Psychiatric evaluation, *In the Matter of Colin Ferguson* (November 27, 1994): 14.

27. "Train Massacre Trial Scene of Surreal Drama," *Charleston Gazette* (January 30, 1995): P2A.

28. Brief for the Appellant, *People v. Colin A. Ferguson*, 248 A.D.2d 725; 670 N.Y.S.2d 327 (1998): 63–64.

29. Ibid., 65.

30. "Surreal Trial on Par with Unusual Shooting," *St. Petersburg Times* (January 30, 1995): 4A.

31. "Colin Ferguson's Long Island Rail Road Shooting Case," *CNBC News Transcripts* (January 8, 1998).

32. "The Abrams Report," *MSNBC* (October 20, 2003): Transcript No. 102000cb464; "Train Massacre Trial."

33. Maureen Fan, "It's Up to the Jury; Ferguson's Fate Weighed Today," *Newsday* (February 17, 1995): A4.

34. "Defendants Who Serve as Their Own Attorneys During Trials," *Weekend Edition Sunday*, National Public Radio (February 24, 2002).

35. Bruce Frankel, "Conspiracy Theories Close Shooting Trial," *USA TODAY* (February 17, 1995): 10A.

36. John T. McQuiston, "Rail Gunman to Spend Life Behind Bars," *New York Times* (March 23, 1995): B1.

37. Fan, "It's Up to the Jury."

38. "The Verdict in the Colin Ferguson Trial," *CNBC News Transcripts* (February 7, 1995).

39. Ibid.

40. Douglas Mossman and Neal Dunseith, " 'A Fool for a Client': Print Portrayals of 49 *Pro Se* Criminal Defendants," *Journal of the American Academy of Psychiatry and Law* (2001): 408.

CHAPTER 16

RALPH TORTORICI *A Question of Competence*

1. Trial transcript, testimony of Patricia Ford, *People v. Ralph Tortorici*, Albany County Court, 374–375.
2. "Progress Notes" (Capital District Psychiatric Center) regarding Ralph Tortorici (August 31, 1991).
3. "A Well Documented History of Mental Illness," *PBS Frontline*, http://www.pbs .org/wgbh/pages/frontline/shows/crime/ralph/incidents.html (accessed September 5, 2005).
4. Ibid.
5. James Dao, "Gunman Terrorizes Students in Campus Siege," *New York Times* (December 15, 1994): B1.
6. "Clinical Summary" (Mid-Hudson Psychiatric Center) regarding Ralph Tortorici (March 3, 1995).
7. Ibid.
8. Ibid.
9. *People v. Tortorici*, 92 N.Y.2d 757 (1999), 761.
10. Ibid.
11. Ibid., 763.
12. Report of Lawrence A. Siegel, M.D., regarding Ralph Tortorici (January 7, 1996), 1. Available at http://www.pbs.org/wgbh/pages/frontline/shows/crime/ralph/ siegel.html (accessed September 5, 2005).
13. Ibid., 8.
14. Ibid.
15. Ibid., 1, 8.
16. Ibid., 8.
17. Ibid.
18. Trial transcript, statement of Peter Lynch, *People v. Ralph Tortorici*, Albany County Court, 134–135.
19. Ibid., statement of Cheryl Coleman, 133.
20. "Interview: Cheryl Coleman," *PBS Frontline*, http://www.pbs.org/wgbh/pages/ frontline/shows/crime/interviews/coleman.html (accessed September 5, 2005).
21. Trial transcript, statement of Hon. Larry Rosen, *People v. Ralph Tortorici*, Albany County Court, 135–136.
22. "The Prosecution's Summation," *PBS Frontline*, http://www.pbs.org/wgbh/ pages/frontline/shows/crime/ralph/psummation.html (accessed September 5, 2005).
23. "Interview: Peter Lynch," *PBS Frontline*, http://www.pbs.org/wgbh/pages/ frontline/shows/crime/interviews/lynch.html (accessed September 5, 2005).
24. "Interview: Larry Rosen," *PBS Frontline*, http://www.pbs.org/wgbh/pages/ frontline/shows/crime/interviews/rosen.html (accessed September 5, 2005).
25. *Pate v. Robinson*, 383 U.S. 375 (1966), 385.
26. *People v. Smyth*, 3 N.Y.2d 184 (1957), 187.

27. *People v. Tortorici*, 671 N.Y.S.2d 162 (1998).

28. *People v. Tortorici*, 92 N.Y.2d 757 (1999).

29. *Tortorici v. New York*, 528 U.S. 834 (1999) (Petition for writ of *certiorari* unanimously denied).

30. Cheryl Coleman, " 'Guilty but Mentally Ill' Verdict Needed?: Yes," *New York Law Journal* (September 23, 1999): 2.

31. *Dusky v. United States*, 362 U.S. 402 (1960), 402.

32. Ibid.

33. "Interview: Cheryl Coleman."

34. Coleman, "'Guilty but Mentally Ill' Verdict Needed?" 35; "Interview: Peter Lynch."

36. Ibid.

37. Ibid.

38. Ibid.

39. Ibid.

40. Report of Lawrence A. Siegel, M.D., 8.

41. Ibid., 8–9.

42. *People v. Tortorici*, 92 N.Y.2d 757 (1999), 766–767.

43. Ibid., 773.

CHAPTER 17

MIKE TYSON *Predicting the Violence of a Professional Fighter*

1. Bryan Robinson, *The Mike Tyson Boxing License Hearing*, http://www.courttv.com/trials/tyson/ (accessed December 12, 2002).

2. Ibid.

3. Ibid.

4. Ibid.

5. Ibid.

6. Ibid.

7. Ibid., paragraph 11.

8. Ronald Schouten, *Independent Medical Evaluation of Michael Gerard Tyson for the Nevada State Athletic Commission*, September 30, 1998, http://www.lvrj.com.

9. Ibid.

10. Ibid., 3.

11. Ibid.

12. Ibid.

13. Roy F. Baumeister, *Evil: Inside Human Violence and Cruelty* (New York: W. H. Freeman, 1999).

14. Schouten, *Independent Medical Evaluation*, 6.

15. David Medoff, *Report of Psychological Testing*, September 30, 1998, http://www.lvrj.com.

16. Jeremy D. Schmahmann, *Neurological Evaluation*, September 30, 1998, http://www.lvrj.com.
17. Ibid., 6.
18. Ibid.
19. Medoff, *Report of Psychological Testing.*
20. Ibid., 8.
21. Ibid.
22. Schouten, *Independent Medical Evaluation.*
23. American Psychiatric Association, *Diagnostic and Statistical Manual of Mental Disorders,* 4th ed. (Washington, D.C.: American Psychiatric Association, 1994).
24. Schouten, *Independent Medical Evaluation*, 8.
25. John Monahan, Henry J. Steadman, Eric Silver, Paul S. Appelbaum, Pamela C. Robins, Edward P. Mulvey, Loren H. Roth, Thomas Grisso, and Stephen Banks, *Rethinking Risk Assessment: The MacArthur Study of Mental Disorder and Violence* (New York: Oxford University Press, 2001).
26. Schouten, *Independent Medical Evaluation*, 9.
27. Ibid., 10.
28. Kathryn Rubenstein, "Tyson Allowed to Go Another Round," http://www.courttv.com/trials/tyson/101998.html (accessed December 12, 2002).

CHAPTER 18

DARYL ATKINS *Mental Retardation, Decency, and the Death Penalty*

1. *Atkins v. Virginia*, 536 U.S. 304 (2002), 309.
2. Ibid.
3. American Association of Mental Retardation, *Mental Retardation: Definition, Classification, and Systems of Supports,* 9th ed. (Washington, D.C.: 1992), 5.
4. American Psychiatric Association, *Diagnostic and Statistical Manual of Mental Disorders,* 4th ed. (Washington D.C.: American Psychiatric Association, 2000), 41.
5. *Atkins v. Virginia*, 309.
6. Evan Nelson, "Capital Sentencing Evaluation" of Daryl Atkins, April 15, 1998.
7. Ibid.
8. Respondent's Motion to Dismiss Writ of Certiorari as Improvidently Granted, *Atkins v. Virginia*, 277.
9. Ibid.
10. Ibid., 529.
11. Ibid., 479.
12. Ibid., 480–481.
13. Ibid., 483–484.
14. *Atkins v. Commonwealth*, 260 Va. 375 (2000), 379.
15. Ibid., 394–395.

16. *Penry v. Lynaugh*, 492 U.S. 302 (1989).

17. Ibid., 346.

18. Ibid., 310.

19. Ibid., 340.

20. *Atkins v. Virginia*, 304.

21. Ibid., 353–354.

22. American Psychological Association, American Psychiatric Association, and American Academy of Psychiatry and the Law, Brief Amicus Curiae, *McCarver v. North Carolina*, 2000 U.S. Briefs 8727 (June 8, 2001), 18 (also filed in *Atkins v. Virginia*).

23. Respondent's Motion to Dismiss Writ of Certiorari as Improvidently Granted, *Atkins v. Virginia*, 440.

24. American Psychological Association, American Psychiatric Association, and American Academy of Psychiatry and the Law, Brief Amicus Curiae, *McCarver v. North Carolina*, 2000 U.S. Briefs 8727 (June 8, 2001), 16 (also filed in *Atkins v. Virginia*).

25. Robert J. Gregory, *Foundations of Intellectual Assessment* (Boston: Allyn and Bacon, 1999), 100.

26. American Psychological Association, American Psychiatric Association, and American Academy of Psychiatry and the Law, Brief Amicus Curiae, *McCarver v. North Carolina*, 2000 U.S. Briefs 8727 (June 8, 2001), 3–4 (also filed in *Atkins v. Virginia*).

27. *Atkins v. Commonwealth*, 260 Va. 375 (2000), 395.

28. Respondent's Motion to Dismiss Writ of Certiorari as Improvidently Granted, *Atkins v. Virginia*, 529.

29. *Atkins v. Virginia*, 321.

30. Adam Liptak, "New Challenge for Courts: How to Define Retardation," *New York Times* (March 14, 2004): 20.

CHAPTER 19

ANDREA YATES *An American Tragedy*

1. Debrah W. Denno, "Time Line of Andrea Yates's Life and Trial: April 1993–April 2002," *Duke Journal of Gender Law and Policy* 10 (2003): 61–84.

2. "Two Tragedies: Dad Says He Loves Wife Accused of Killing Kids," June 23, 2001, http://abcnews.go.com (accessed August 22, 2001).

3. "Transcript of Andrea Yates Confession," *Houston Chronicle*, February 21, 2002, http://www.chron.com/cs/CDA/story.hts/special/drownings/1266294 (accessed September 5, 2005).

4. Ibid.

5. "Two Tragedies."

6. Denno, "Time Line," 61.

7. American Psychiatric Association, *Diagnostic and Statistical Manual of Mental Disorders*, 4th ed. (Washington D.C.: American Psychiatric Association, 2000), 422.

8. Denno, "Time Line," 61.

9. Ibid.

10. Scott Commerson, "Villain or Victim? Myths, Gender, and the Insanity Defense," *Developments in Mental Health Law* 22 (Feb. 2003): 1–17.

11. Debrah W. Denno, "Who Is Andrea Yates? A Short Story about Insanity," *Duke Journal of Gender Law and Policy* 10 (2003): 1–60.

12. Carol Christian, "Doctor: Yates Illness Severe," *Houston Chronicle*, March 6, 2002, http://www.chron.com/archives (accessed July 11, 2003), 2.

13. Commerson, "Villain or Victim?" 3.

14. Ibid.

15. Mike Snyder, "Russell Yates on Trial, Too, with Public's Commentary," *Houston Chronicle*, March 13, 2002, http://www.chron.com/archives (accessed July 11, 2003).

16. Bill O'Reilly, "Talking Points: First, Do No Harm," *Fox News*, June 29, 2001, http://www.foxnews.com/printer_friendly_story/0,3566,28430,00.html (accessed November 16, 2004).

17. Denno, "Time Line," 70.

18. Ibid., 71.

19. Suzanne O'Malley, *"Are You There Alone?": The Unspeakable Crime of Andrea Yates* (New York: Simon & Schuster, 2004).

20. Ibid.

21. Denno, "Who Is Andrea Yates?" 16.

22. O'Malley, *"Are You There Alone?"*

23. Ibid., 157.

24. Ibid.

25. Ibid., 201.

26. "Portions of Prosecuting Psychiatrist Park Dietz's Testimony in the Andrea Yates Trial, March 7, 2002," *Duke Journal of Gender Law and Policy* 10 (2003): 97–139, 109.

27. Denno, "Who Is Andrea Yates?" 20.

28. O'Malley, *"Are You There Alone?"* 201.

29. Ibid.

30. Ibid.

31. Denno, "Who Is Andrea Yates?" 23.

32. O'Malley, *"Are You There Alone?"* 218.

33. *Yates v. Texas*, Nos. 01-02-00462-CR and 01-02-00463-CR. [Online.] January 6, 2005, http://www.1stcoa.courts.tx.us/opinions/html (accessed January 6, 2005), 2.

34. Ibid., 11.

35. Ibid., 7.

36. Commerson, "Villain or Victim?" 1.

37. Ibid.

38. Ibid.

39. Snyder, "Russell Yates on Trial Too."

40. Lisa Teachey, "Jurors Say They Believed Yates Knew Right from Wrong," *Houston Chronicle*, March 18, 2002, http://www.chron.com/archives (accessed July 11, 2003).

CHAPTER 20

MICHAEL KANTARAS *What Makes a Man a Man?*

1. Opinion, *In re the Marriage of Michael J. Kantaras v. Linda Kantaras*, Circuit Court of the Sixth Judicial Circuit in and for Pasco County, Florida, Case No. 98-5375, February 2003, 62.

2. Ibid., 47.

3. American Psychiatric Association, *Diagnostic and Statistical Manual of Mental Disorders*, 4th ed. (Washington, D.C.: American Psychiatric Association, 1994), 532–533.

4. Opinion, *In re the Marriage of Michael J. Kantaras v. Linda Kantaras*, 359.

5. Ibid., 180.

6. *Frances B. v. Mark B., Formerly Known as Marsha B.*, 355 N.Y.S.2d 712 (1974), 717.

7. *M.T. v. J.T.*, 140 N.J. Super. 77 (1976), 81.

8. Ibid., 82.

9. Opinion, *In re the Marriage of Michael J. Kantaras v. Linda Kantaras*, 268.

10. Ibid., 270.

11. Ibid., 376.

12. Ibid.

13. Ibid., 357.

14. Ibid., 350.

15. Ibid.

16. Ibid., 371.

17. Ibid., 381.

18. Ibid., 783–784.

19. Ibid., 774.

20. Ibid., 423.

21. Ibid., 428–429.

22. Ibid., 529.

23. Ibid., 786.

24. Ibid., 206.

25. Ibid., 201.

26. Ibid., 787.

27. Ibid.

28. Ibid.

29. Robert R. Dies, Ph.D., Custody evaluation, *Kantaras v. Kantaras*, April 28, 2001, 17.
30. Ibid.
31. Ibid.
32. Ibid., 18.
33. Opinion, *In re the Marriage of Michael J. Kantaras v. Linda Kantaras*, 789.
34. Ibid., 510.
35. Matt Bean, "Lawyers Have Last Words in Transsexual Custody Battle," *Court TV*, February 8, 2002, http://www.courttv.com/trials/kantaras/020802_ctv.html (accessed November 6, 2004).
36. Ibid.
37. Ibid.
38. Opinion, *In re the Marriage of Michael J. Kantaras v. Linda Kantaras*, 795–796.
39. Ibid., 761.
40. *Kantaras v. Kantaras*, 884 So. 2d 155 (2004).
41. Ibid., 161.
42. Ibid., 157.
43. Ibid., 161.
44. *Kantaras v. Kantaras*, 2005 Fla. LEXIS 373 (2005).

INDEX

Printed in the USA/Agawam, MA
February 28, 2017

648792.030